COMBINES & HARVESTERS

Jeff Creighton

Motorbooks International
Publishers & Wholesalers

First published in 1996 by Motorbooks International Publishers & Wholesalers, 729 Prospect Avenue, PO Box 1, Osceola, WI 54020 USA

Library of Congress Cataloging-in-Publication Data
Creighton, J. J.
Combines & harvesters: photographic history/
J.J. Creighton.
p. cm.
Includes index.
ISBN 0-7603-0125-5 (pbk.: alk. paper)
1. Combines (Agricultural machinery) —History. 2. Harvesting machinery—History. 3. Agricultural machinery industry—United States—History. I. Title.
TJ1485.C74 1996
681'. 7631—dc20 96-719

On the front cover: A John Deere GP tractor pulls a John Deere Model 5A combine. The Model 5A was built from 1934 to 1951, and most were equipped with four-cylinder auxiliary engines that ran the thresher/separator units.

On the back cover: (Top) This photo of a Harris machine from the 1930s demonstrates how horses continued to play a role on the farm even into the 1930s, when tractors became common on the farm. (Bottom) Gleaner's Model GH hillside came out in 1969 and was produced until 1972. This machine is harvesting wheat near Walla Walla, Washington

Printed in the United States of America

CONTENTS

Acknowledgments

Putting this project together required hours of researching through various archives, personal contacts with those who make a living preserving such resources, and interviews with those who still have a passion for agricultural history, past and present. I would like to acknowledge those who made my task a lot easier.

Special thanks to Sandra Fitch, Coordinator, Ritzville City Library, for allowing me to search through the Kendrick Collection practically any time I wanted and for permitting me to take dozens of negatives and photos out for reproduction; to Stan Dammel for doing the reproduction work on nearly 100 of the photos contained in this book. Also to Gene Webb of St. John, Washington, and Harold Wegner of Reardan, Washington, for their personal photos and first hand knowledge of early grain harvesting equipment.

For the work on Chapter Two, I would like to thank John Skarstad and his staff from the Special Collections Dept., Shields Library, University of California at Davis, for access to the F. Hal Higgins Collection of literally thousands of documents and photos relating to the early California combine era. This particular chapter was composed almost entirely from primary resource material gained from the archives and without their help it would have been a futile undertaking; to Joycelyn A. Luster, Corporate Archivist of Caterpillar Inc., Peoria, Illinois, for the magnificent photos of early Holt harvesters and steam traction machines. How good is a chapter on Holt without the famous "Cat."

Thanks also to Marciel Cronrath, Lincoln County, Washington, historian for the use of the Harrington combine photos; to the University of Idaho at Moscow, Special Collections Dept., for their generosity and the Idaho National and Rhodes Harvester photos and information. Lastly, this chapter would have lacked the human touch without the help of contemporaries of this early period. Special thanks to Joe Jantz of Ritzville, Washington, for his first hand knowledge about the Houser-Haines and Holt combines; to Walt Nissen , also from Ritzville, for the early Harris machine information.

For the Gleaner chapter I am greatly indebted to Ross Yonn of the Allis-Gleaner Company (AGCO), Independence, Missouri, for sending me several pounds of company literature and for providing me archival photos. Without this first hand information this chapter would have been impossible.

As usual, Les Stegh from the Deere Archives, East Moline, Illinois, was more than accommodating in providing me with much needed archival photos for Chapter Five. For this I am very grateful. Other individuals involved with furnishing information on this chapter include: Rob Dewald for pertinent sales brochure information on the Deere model 36; Harold Wegner for operating manuals and sales material for the JD grain binder; Bill Hartz and Rudy Plager from Wheatland Equipment (Deere sales and service) Ritzville, Washington; Darrel Evans, an old Deere aficionado who loaned me everything but the kitchen sink; and to all those who didn't even know that I was climbing through their boneyards, I thank you.

For the Massey-Harris chapter , I am indebted to Sue Bennett of the Ontario Agricultural Museum, Brandt, Ontario, Canada. With numerous phone calls and a great deal of patience, she was most accommodating and aided greatly in funneling information to me on this chapter.

I must also express my thanks to my editor, Lee Klancher of Motorbooks International, for sticking with this project and for always being available to hear my seemingly never-ending questions and concerns regarding this book.

Introduction

I often wonder what the mid-19th century combine inventor Hiram Moore would have to say about the modern machine that developed from his tinkering in Kalamazoo County, Michigan, in 1836. Moore believed that cutting grain in one operation was as natural as the sun rising in the East. Binding, heading, and threshing was an excessively labor-intensive process he felt could be done with fewer people and pieces of equipment. His crude contraption would be the impetus for the combine that is so prevalent in today's grain fields.

The development of the combined harvester spans over 150 years and begins in the Golden State of California. Reaping and binding were the harvesting methods of choice in the Heartland and points east, while the massive fields of the Sacramento and San Joaquin Valley welcomed the new single-operation method with open arms. Development came early in that part of the country. Machines bearing the names Horner, Shippee, Minges, Dunning and Erich, Best, Holt, and Harris were found wherever large fields could be harvested.

As in any business, there wasn't room enough for everyone, and only those that took the idea of the combine one step further would survive. The name Holt is legend in combine development. Benjamin Holt was the Henry Ford of mechanized agriculture, probably doing more for the spread of the combine than Cyrus McCormick did for the reaper!

The combine would inevitably wind up in the Midwest, establishing its own regional reputation through such firms as John Deere, Gleaner, and Massey-Harris, just to name a few. Its worth would be tested from coast to coast, be dissected by a number of government agencies, and be scrutinized by just about every farmer east of the Rocky Mountains before being accepted in the late 1920s. This is the story of how a machine was developed for one particular region and then modified for another.

Obviously there was a great deal of harvesting methods before the arrival of the combine. Chapter 1 is dedicated to reaping, binding, heading, threshing, and the use of steam traction machines for harvesting small grains. Beyond this chapter, the rest of the story deals with the invention, development, commercial viability, and eventual success of the combined harvester and a discussion about the companies that brought so many innovations into the manufacture of their own machines. From the horse-drawn wooden framed machines to the tractor-pull models and on to the self-propelled combines, the story is not unlike the development of the automobile, or anything else for that matter, that makes life easier and more profitable at the same time.

This book is also about the people who built and operated these machines. From the rice farmer of central California to the bean farmer in Michigan, these are the people that have lived this history. Their experiences with machines, combines or otherwise, lend a great deal of knowledge to those of us who want to tell their story.

Chapter One

Early Harvesters

It is often argued whether Obed Hussey or Cyrus Hall McCormick invented the reaper. Looking back, one could say they were both responsible as each machine complimented the other. And both machines helped to launch over a century of agricultural development and achievement. The reaper would eventually evolve into the harvester, then the binder, and finally, the self-propelled combine. From this relatively "simple" machine came the Deerings, the Osbornes, and the Woods; the Holts, the Housers, and the Harris-

The Champion No. 1 Combined Reaper and Mower from a wood cut that appeared in the *Pacific Rural Press* circa 1880. With the three-rake assembly, grain or hay could be cut and windrowed for later shocking. The Champion line was absorbed by the newly formed International Harvester Company in 1902 and was dropped from the new line in 1917.

es; machines that would eventually define American harvesting.

Inventors like Hussey and McCormick usually build on ideas conceived by others. The reaper is a perfect example of this building process. According to Thomas Isern's *Bull Threshers an Bindlestiffs*, it was Pliny the Elder, a first century Roman who first used a "reaper" machine for the purpose of stripping grain on the "great estates in Gaul." This reaper was a two-wheeled cart powered by oxen; the front of the cart held a comb-like device that grabbed the stalks and then stripped the grain heads into the cart as it traveled though the field. Isern further explains that, "a man walked behind the oxen and pushed up and down on a bar that regulated the height of the comb." Other inventions that used the same general principles of operation soon followed. It wasn't until the late 18th century that improvements started to appear.

In 1780, William Pitt of Pendleford, England, devised the first tooth-cutting cylindrical device for harvesting grain. This device replaced the stationary comb, or fixed tooth mechanism,with a rotating cutter powered by a ground wheel. Besides the rotary style of stripping, others were experimenting with the rectilinear method (cutting blades that moved back and forth). Some of these early methods included horizontal blades that rotated close to the ground; the serrated type mounted on turning plates; and the garden shear style that became popular in the early 1800s.

The famous McCormick twine binder, one that even today can be found on numerous abandoned homesteads from Wisconsin to Washington state. This cut is representative of the thousands of ads that appeared throughout farm country during the notorious "Harvester War" of the 1880s and 1890s. A standard machine for harvesting the Midwest and the humid regions, the binder could also be found in the dryer Far West mainly for cutting 40 to 60 acres of "beardless" grain for animal feed.

Probably the greatest advance in cutting mechanisms was Brown and Ogle's invention of the reciprocating sickle. This particular cutter bar operated much as the modern day electric kitchen knife or reciprocating power saw. Upper and lower teeth moved opposite each other; the ground wheel and a pitman (connecting rod) supplied the cutting motion. These designs were all step-

The little known "Dennett Harvester" was a California product, shown here from another issue of the *Pacific Rural Press* circa 1883. This machine had the distinction of being able to operate in the hill country of California. The manufacturer even threw in a second set of knives for the standard six-foot cut machine. The "Dennett" also came with the Appleby knotting device and a simplified mechanism for threading the twine needle. The "Dennett" could be had for a mere $350.

Light Running New
JOHN DEERE
GRAIN BINDER
Here Are a Few of the Features That Have Made It Popular
1 Lighter-Running. Eleven sets of roller and ball bearings, self-aligning bearings, better lubrication and easiest possible handling of grain reduce draft.
2 Better Oiling Facilities. It is easy to get to every operating part with plenty of oil—thus reducing draft and wear.
3 Variable-Capacity Elevators. Handle smallest to largest volume of grain in the easiest way without waste and without clogging. Simple in design.
4 Improved Guard and Sickle. Knife operates in neck of guards and on hardened wearing plates like a mower knife. Cutter bar makes continuous guide for knife. Sections replaced with round-headed rivets—no filing flush of rivet ends to maintain shear cut—easy to repair.
5 Improved Reel. Lifts and shifts unusually easy. Gear-controlled at both ends—reel cannot sag or whip—insures better cutting, elevating and binding.
6 Easily-Operated Bundle Carrier. A boy can easily raise and lower it. Simple; great capacity; does not scatter bundles. Automatically swings back if it hits an obstruction.
7 All-Steel, Quick-Turn Tongue Truck. Wheels hold to the ground and take side draft and neck weight from horses. Keeps binder running straight. Flexible axle permits both wheels to conform to uneven ground.
Built in 6-, 7- and 8-Foot Sizes
Furnished with Any Standard Equipment Including Tractor Hitch.
Printed in U. S. A.

ping stones to Hussey and McCormick's invention of the commercially successful reaper.

The Hussey Reaper

Obed Hussey was born in Maine in 1792. He showed an interest early in life in just about anything mechanical. Described as a theorist and a genius, Hussey could also be moody, impatient, and sometimes just plain lazy. These traits, however, didn't deter his interest in mechanical invention.

Before his work on the reaper, Hussey had moved from his boyhood home in Maine to Nantucket, Massachusetts, and then on to Cincinnati, Ohio, where he devised a corn grinding machine, a sugar cane crusher, as well as a machine for grinding hook and eyes. While working on an improved candle mold in 1830, he became interested in a grain cutting machine. By 1831, Hussey was in Baltimore, Maryland, busy working in the loft of Richard B. Chenowith's implement factory, tinker-

Left
This photo comes from a Deere Brochure dated 1930. The "New Light Running" grain binder could be pulled by either horse or tractor. The binder is set up for horse power; the machine able to cut a six, seven, or eight-foot swath. Like other makes of binders, the Deere machines can still be found throughout farm country, usually without seats and windboards. *Deere Archives*

Possibly the most successful twine binder ever made and chief rival to the McCormick machine was the Deering grain binder. The Deering machine pioneered the use of roller bearings and used the Appleby knotting mechanism that was to be adopted by all other competitors. Though the binder could be a complicated machine, those who actually remember using them said that if you "greased it twice a day and had a good beveled grinding stone for sharpening the sickle," problems were few. The main complaint was the knotting mechanism. Now that could be a real bear!

Deere operating manuals were enormously helpful to the anxious farmer who was about to receive his first binder. From the 1930 manual: 1) the ground wheel; 2) the platform or grain wheel; 3) main frame; 4) the platform; 5) the reel pipe; 6) crated binder mechanism; and 7) the front elevator. Deere claimed that their binder was the most completely assembled binder on the market, and with the exception of the bolts for the reel arms and slats, all other bolts were in their proper places.

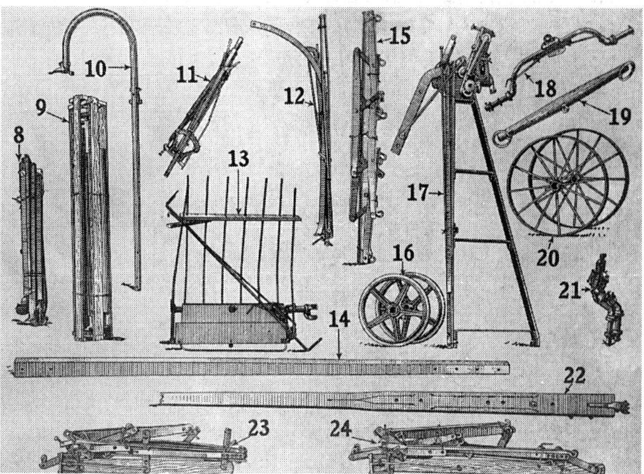

The following parts for the John Deere Light Running binder are: 8) rear elevator; 9) rollers; 10) seat pipe; 11) bundle levers; 12) bundle reel supports and rods; 13) bundle carriers; 14) lead tongue; 15) bundle eveners; 16) truck wheels; 17) stub tongue; 18) axle; 19) neck yoke; 20) transport wheels; 21) transport axles; 22) pole; 23) and 24) bundle eveners for three and four horses. Connection for the Fordson tractor could also be purchased as well as steering controls for any Deere tractor.

A testament to times gone by, this John Deere Light Running grain binder stands alone on the Don and Doug Wellsandt farm in Adams County, Washington. Probably a 1930s model, this machine was used for cutting small amounts of grain for horse and mule feed. The Deere machine entered the binder market relatively late (1911) but proved to be a popular machine and was produced up until the 1950s.

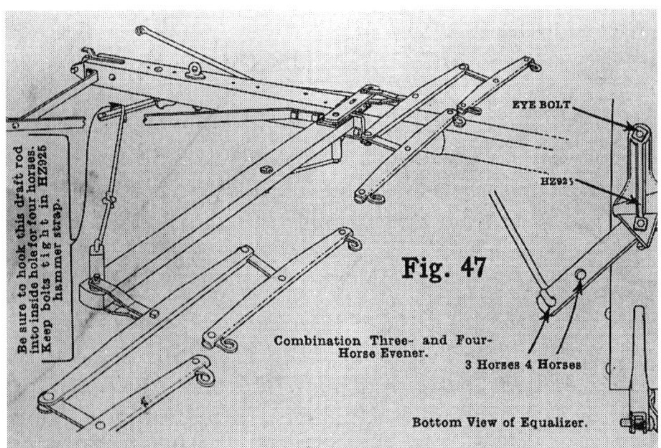

The above photo illustrates the three- and four-horse eveners for the John Deere binder, with a bottom view of the equalizer on the right. Eveners were essential for the distribution of weight between horses and also aided in keeping the horses in place.

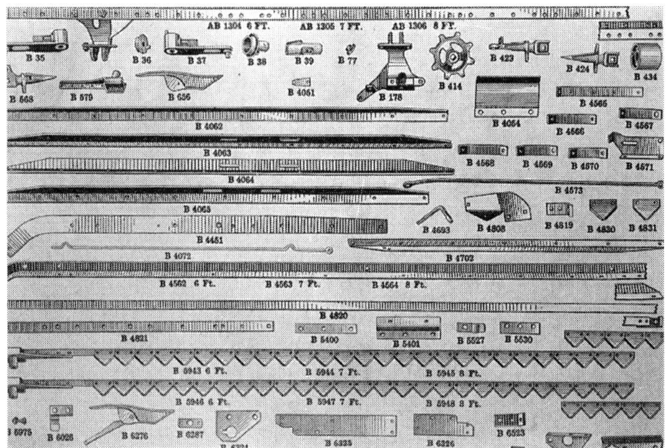

More attachments and parts for the John Deere binder, including various cutter bars and platform equipment.

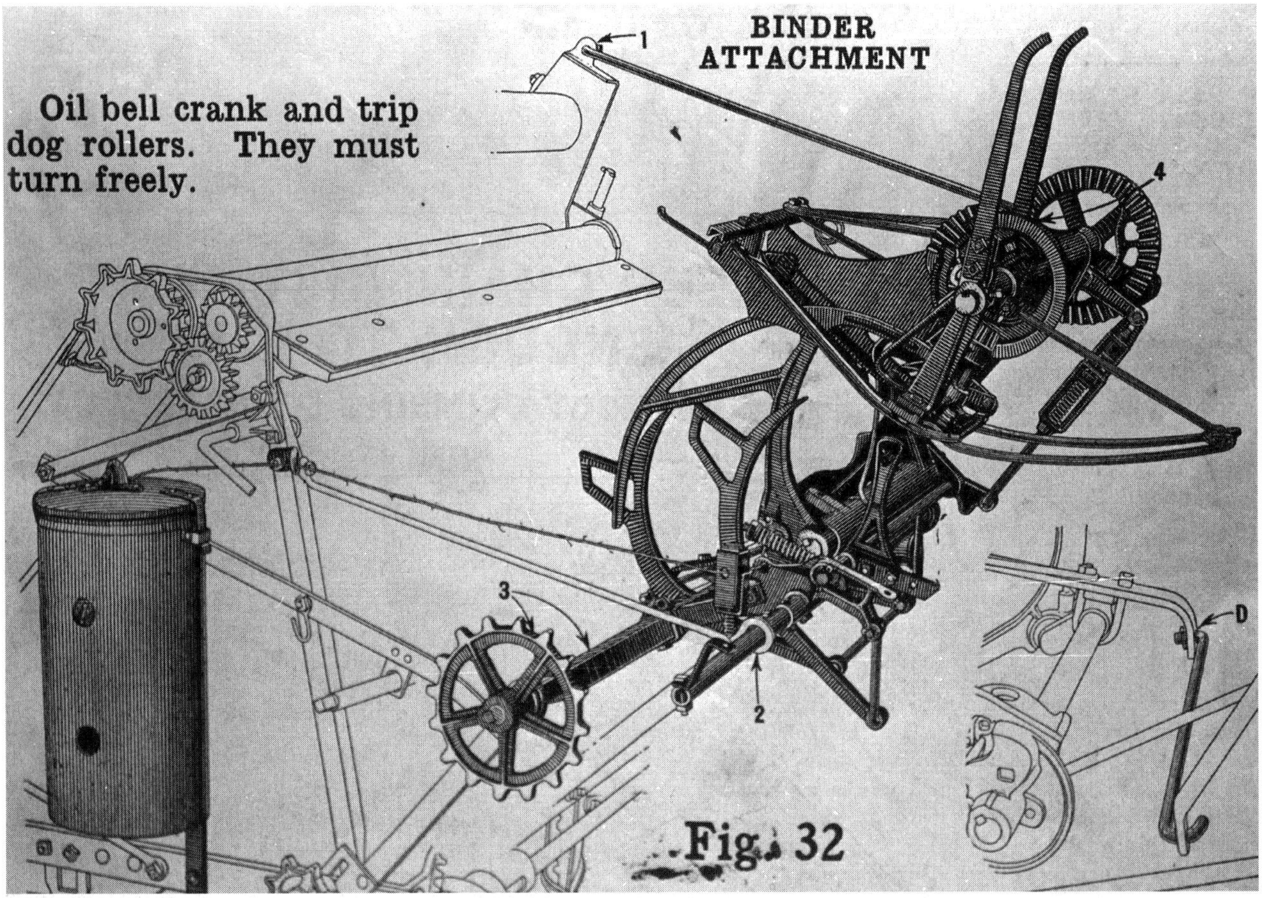

BINDER ATTACHMENT

Oil bell crank and trip dog rollers. They must turn freely.

1 2 3 4 D

Fig. 32

In the center, the binder attachment and knotting mechanism is shown. On the left are rollers from elevator to binder. At below is the twine can with brackets and on the lower right, the shift lever is shown. Probably the biggest hassle experienced with the binder was trying to get the exact setting for the knotter. If the knotter wasn't right, you could blow an entire day of cutting.

ing away at what became, by 1833, a full-sized reaper. His first public trial was before the Hamilton County Agricultural Society near Carthage, Ohio, where nine onlookers attested to the reaper's success. The machine was patented the same year.

Hussey's reaper was equipped with beveled triangular steel blades instead of a straight blade, the cutting action being supplied first by a two wheel design, then later by the addition of a the ground wheel attached to the left side of the platform. The cutting action was converted from circular motion to horizontal movement using a pitman arm. The problem with the Hussey machine was that a reel was never added to aid in bringing the cut grain on to the platform. This meant that the horse had to travel at a faster pace in order to cut the grain properly. The Hussey reaper remained essentially the same until the time of the inventors death in 1860.

Despite the Hussey machine's initial innovation, it did not fare well in field trials in the 1840s. It has been said that Hussey's refusal to incorporate improvements on his machine eventually led to a dramatic drop in sales. Whether it was competition or Hussey's obstinacy, Hussey sold the reaper business in 1858 and went to work on yet another invention, this time a steam plow. While in England, the inventor fell under the wheels of an oncoming train and was killed. The tragedy ended what surely would have been a long and prosperous career for Obed Hussey, a man who at the least shares the responsibility for inventing the reaper with his fierce rival, Cyrus Hall McCormick.

The McCormick Reaper

Cyrus Hall McCormick, born in Virginia in 1809, took out his first patent in 1834 but only manufactured 87 reaping machines at the farm in Rockbridge County by 1844. As Rogin explains, "Realizing the difficulty of trying to introduce harvesting machinery in a section of the country where farms were...small and labor cheap and plentiful," McCormick quickly took to the road demonstrating his reaper in western New York, Ohio, Illinois, and parts of Wisconsin. The road trip was a success, and orders for his machine rapidly increased.

The McCormick reaper at the outset was inferior to the Hussey when it came to the cutting mechanism, an

Taking a break for the photographer. The above shows the crew of a single binder powered by three horses; a driver and the five other folks standing around could be the shocking crew. The dog's job is unknown. This is an example of a very small outfit, probably one that was used for cutting animal feed. The location is somewhere in Idaho, 1912. *Ritzville Library Archives*

imperfection that wasn't remedied until McCormick took out a second patent in 1845. Another problem was that there was no room on the platform for the raker; both push and pull model reapers required the raker to walk along the left side of the machine while another person rode the horse. Mechanically, however, the McCormick reaper featured seven modes of operation that would be standard on all reapers made in the future. These included a side draft to keep horses in the stubble and not in the uncut grain; a horizontal cutting blade; a reel that guided the cut grain on to the platform; a ground wheel (bull wheel) to power the cutter and reel; the use of stationary fingers to vertically stand the grain for a better cut (helping somewhat in lodged grains); a vertical divider, and the open platform from which to rake off the cut grain. The later improvements discussed gave the McCormick a seat for the driver and self-raking devices for more efficiency in the field.

Various manufacturers began to build McCormick's reaper; the Globe Works of Seymour and Morgan (Brockport, New York), and Gray/Warner of Chicago just to name a few. The Globe Works has the distinction of being the first reaper factory in the United States. McCormick made the move to Chicago in 1847, and in partnership with Gray, erected the first reaper factory in the West. By the end of the harvest of 1850, McCormick claimed distribution of about 4,500 reapers in the United States.

Though the McCormick reaper was a far better machine in 1850 than it was in 1840, it didn't exactly sell itself. Inasmuch as the early "road shows" helped, McCormick realized that a system of salesmanship, advertisement, and one-on-one contact throughout rural areas was a must. Beginning in the 1840s, McCormick commissioned agents to handle sales in the small communities, first in the hinterlands around Chicago, then

A 10-foot ground-driven tractor binder in the early 1930s. The machine is powered by four horses and is working somewhere in the Midwest. Note the windboard at the rear of the platform. These gems are almost non-existent and like header "seats" command a high price from collectors. The windboard functioned just as it suggests; defraying air flow to keep the grain in its proper position on the platform. *Deere Archives*

Where it all started. Just as McCormick and Hussey succeeded, so to did the blacksmith of yesterday, serving much like the modern automotive garages of today. Whether shodding horses, repairing axles, or even inventing such outlandish contraptions like reapers and binders, the "Smithy" was essential in keeping mechanized farming going. This photo was taken around the turn of the century in the wheat belt of East Washington. The name of the gentleman in the picture is unknown. *Ritzville Library Archives*

H. E. Wagner showing his Grand Champion "Kamiac Chief," Spokane, Washingtion, in 1919. Wagner's Shires were used primarily for header work near the Palouse Country of Washington state, though his horses were well known as far away as Chicago. These draft horses easily consumed 40 pounds of hay per day. Gene Webb, the grandson-in-law of the man in the picture, continues on with the breeding of draft horses in Whitman County, Washington. Webb also saves a little bit of wheat after each season to be harvested by his team and a restored McCormick-Deering header. *Courtesy of Gene Webb*

Webb poses atop his McCormick-Deering header in 1986. According to Webb, the header was purchased by his father in the early 1930s. Gene raises Belgians on his spread outside of St. John, Washington. The horsepower on this particular day is furnished by "Wendy," "Wanda," "Bunny," "Blondie"' "Katie," and "Lindy." *Courtesy of Gene Webb*

later encompassing the entire West. Agents often received benefits such as protected territories and advanced payments for advertising costs. They even setup showrooms, often displaying their machines next to the competition. But most important, as historian William Cronon has written about the McCormick agents, "they were in effect the front guard of a carefully planned campaign to introduce mechanization to American farming." It was this kind of business sense that made McCormick the largest and best-known maker of harvest machinery in the nation.

The McCormick "reaper revolution," however, had a two-edged sword; not only did other similar inventions begin to appear like locusts on the horizon, McCormick also lost the exclusive patent rights to his reaper in 1848 . It was felt that McCormick's invention was far to important to the agricultural world to let one man control the output of such a machine, hence, scores of companies began reaper production. Be that as it may, McCormick used the company's central location, network of salesmen and dealerships, and aggressive participation in reaper field demonstrations to dominate the reaper market. Chicago, considered the "Gateway to the West," was in easy striking distance to the frontier, a growing region where fertile soils were most suitable for small grains. As celebrated Plains historian Walter Prescott Webb once reiterated, "Hussey located at Boston, the center of where the wheat fields were; McCormick located at Chicago, the center of where the wheat fields were to be."

The reaper was limited by poor operation on uneven ground. Stumps and rocks were often a problem in the eastern states, often making it impossible for reaper use. A

Three-quarter view of Webb's machine. The cutter bar is about 12 inches above ground. By the looks of the stubble it appears to be a short, stiff stand, ideal for header work. The horses are "pushing" the machine, three abreast on each side of the header pole. The rear of the pole also supports Mr. Webb and the pilot wheel underneath. *Courtesy of Gene Webb*

Rear view of Gene "punch-in" header. Webb stands atop the pilot wheel (platform), steering when necessary using his feet and body weight to "pivot" the pilot wheel from left to right or vice versa. The vertical bar in front of him supports a lever for raising or lowering the cutter bar. The mechanism is operated with a set of springs, much like the springs used on the old-style garage doors. On the left is the header barge; center is the elevator that delivers the grain to the barge. *Courtesy of Gene Webb*

Header and header barge at work in the Northwest wheat belt. The average crew is pictured above. From left to right is a full header barge with loaders; the header puncher, and two empty wagons waiting to be loaded. Once the wagons were loaded they were then taken to the "set" to be threshed. Not every farmer operated the same way, however, as sometimes the headed grain would be stacked for up to ten days to insure a low enough moisture content. *Ritzville Library Archives*

Close up view of the ground (bull) wheel, the motive power for the header. From the inside you can see the brake strap on the small center hub, the springs that aid in header height adjustment, and to the far left, the "sunflower" gear. The link-chain lying atop the bull wheel originally gave motive power to the cutter bar, rollers, and drapers.

A group effort. Family and friends usually worked together in an effort to gather in the harvest. Though transient labor was also used, especially on the bonanza farms in California, the smaller concerns could pretty much get the job done with the locals. As pictured above, heading required a great amount of horsepower, and if the set up was done right, as one informant told me, an outfit like this could be hooked up and ready to go in less than twenty minutes! *Ritzville Library Archives*

This header is shown in motion. Note the elevator in the center of the picture. The cut grain was laid back on the platform by the reel, and then the endless canvass (draper) would carry the cut grain up to the elevator. The grain was then delivered to the header barge alongside the header where the waiting loader could easily disperse the grain evenly in the wagon. Header barges were also slanted, lower on one side, to accommodate the elevator. *Ritzville Library Archives*

Taking a break and giving a pose in the Ritzville area about 1918. This crew has covered a lot of ground judging by the looks of the stacks in the background. These stacks, often referred to as "ricks" were shaped, oddly enough, like giant loaves of bread. On the far left is the rest of the family and probably some visiting relatives out to watch the harvest. One thing the combine took away from the harvest was the social camaraderie, an event that was looked forward to by most and dreaded by others. Nevertheless, this type of harvesting defined the American wheat farm for generations. *Ritzville Library Archives*

Unloading on the main stack. Another thing that the combine did away with was these monstrous ricks. On the other hand, I've been told that the ground underneath these stacks probably yielded a higher bushel per acre in the years that followed. One local told me that you could always tell where the stacks had been the previous years, because the grain looked better there than anywhere else on the field. *Ritzville Library Archives*

Right
Generally speaking, most of the headers used in the West were McCormick-Deering machines. One who knows is Joe Jantz of Adams County, Washington. Joe's first turn at punching in header was at the age of nine. Forced into the job because the regular header driver had become "irregular," Joe was on top of the world. He said that the McCormick-Deering machines were everywhere, and even today remnants of the old headers can still be found, usually hidden from the casual eye in tall wheat grass. *Ritzville Library Archives*

The standard setup of the threshing set is the A. Krammers & Sons outfit at Roxboro, Washington, in 1914. From left to right is the cook car; steam traction engine with the flat belt stretched between 100 and 150 feet; and the threshing machine and derrick setup seen behind the threshing unit. Note the windstacker tube at the far right. This was used for stacking straw. Sacked wheat is visible in front of the thresher. *Ritzville Library Archives*

more versatile, less labor intensive machine was demanded by the market, and the harvester/binder would arise to fill that need.

Binding: The Humid Regions of the East and Midwest

Beginning in the early to mid-1870s the harvesting industry saw a rise in the production and use of the harvester/binder. Binders operated much like the early reapers with a few exceptions: the cutter bar, or sickle, was approximately seven to eight feet long; a reel rotated to lay the wheat down on an endless canvas; and the use of a hand raker or automatic raking arm was eliminated.

The binder cut wheat when it was partially green. This was a long-time practice in the humid regions mainly because of the erratic climatic conditions. Leaving wheat until "dead ripe" would often leave the crop open to high winds, hailstorms, or head shattering. Lodged wheat was difficult to harvest with the binder, hence the need to cut early. Binder crews consisted of one driver, two shockers, and four horses. This type of outfit could usually harvest anywhere from 12 to 18 acres a day. Once the grain was put up in shocks it remained in the field for six to 10 days; crews would then gather shocks into wagons and transport them to the threshing set.

In 1870, over 156 patents were taken out on the binder, and more were to follow in 1871. Though the reaper went through many changes by 1860, such as self-raker arms and automatic sweeping devices, it was still a slow process to hand bind grain in the field. The Civil War also managed to strip away much needed manpower, giving impetus to the development of the harvester/binder.

The durable early Holt 45 in 1912. Note the owner's name, "L.E. Ensor," painted on the canopy frame in front. Out of the picture to the far left is the flat belt trailing off to the threshing machine. The Holt machine was one of many that were used throughout wheat country and was the centerpiece of the set. These same rigs would be used to pull combined harvesters in the far West and Pacific Northwest during the early 1900s. *Courtesy of Harold Wegner*

An early threshing set in turn-of-the-century Montana. At the far left is the straw stack and straw elevator at the rear of the thresher. The men standing on the platform are "pitchers" who fed the grain into the cylinder. If the thresher came with a self-feeder, then the pitchers' job was to make sure the grain stayed on the conveyor on its way, "automatically," to the cylinder. In fact in 1912, Case was advertising a 24-foot side carrier that stretched from the threshing platform to waiting barges or wagons, enabling faster off-loading of grain. The side carrier was also used with the derrick fork and derrick wagons as well. Note the vertical boom above the straw stack and the derrick fork hanging parallel to it. *Courtesy of Harold Wegner*

Another view of the set where a horizontal steam traction machine is being used. In some cases the wind would whip to the point of almost taking the flat belt right off the fly-wheel. To remedy this problem the steam engine would be positioned either above or below the angle of the thresher, depending on which way the wind was blowing. *Courtesy of Harold Wegner*

The Marsh Harvester

The Marsh Brothers of Shabbona Grove, Illinois, were in the forefront of binder development with the invention of the Marsh Harvester in 1858. This type of harvester was much like the reaper in that it had a left-hand side draft, reel, and cutter bar. The platform, however, was fitted with an endless draper (canvas) that carried the cut grain to the right of the machine and then elevated it to the waiting binders. A platform was attached to the right hand side of the ground wheel housing, enabling two people to stand and bind the grain as it was delivered by the draper. This particular model was first displayed at the Iowa State Fair in 1867 by the manufacturers Gammon and Prindle of Chicago.

The Marsh harvester sounded like a good idea, but as the record shows, it encountered numerous problems early on. For one thing, production of the machine was done from three different locations: partly from Chicago, some from De Kalb County, and even some from the Marsh farm utilizing available blacksmiths. The result was inferior performance in the field. Unlike the reaper, the harvester became a more complicated machine for the average farmer to work on and service. Another problem for the harvester was that the reaper, during the 1860s, was perfected to the point of wide acceptance, making it more difficult for salesmen to convince farmers that they really needed a harvester.

One of the most famous teams in the field, the Case 20-40 tractor and thresher operating around Reardan, Washington, in 1921. Looks like most of the family turned out for this photo. The unit is hitched and ready for transport to the next set. The signature windstacker tube is folded over the top of the thresher. *Courtesy of Harold Wegner*

This amateur photo is a little fuzzy, but the gas tractor engine pictured could be an International Harvester Mogul. Though the threshing unit is out of the picture, the flat belt leaves little doubt as to where the threshing is taking place. *Ritzville Library Archives*

An example of the enormous straw stacks generated from headed grain. Note the derrick frame at the far left. When the stacks reached a certain height the derrick was moved on down the line to start a new stack. Once the threshing took place, the derrick was then used to bring the grain to the threshing platform. The photo was taken circa 1920. *Ritzville Library Archives*

Nevertheless, there was no stopping the Marsh Brothers from perfecting their machine. After their initial introduction of a mere 25 harvesters in 1864, total production by 1870 reached 1,000 machines annually. Oddly enough, the Marsh Harvester was the only one of its kind until 1875 when the Wood, McCormick, and Osborne companies had similar harvesters on the market.

The Marsh and other like binder/harvesters were clearly making inroads on the American farm. By the mid-1870s, reports from Nebraska stated that "binding on the ground was almost a thing of the past," and that nearly 100,000 harvesters of the Marsh type had been produced by the end of 1879.

Another turn-of-the-century steam traction machine idle in Montana. The large flywheel sent power to the thresher machine via the flat belt. Judging from the cleats on the steel tire faces, the machine was probably operating in soft, sandy soils. The make of this beast is unknown. *Courtesy of Harold Wegner*

An excellent close-up and personal shot of the pitcher loading grain into the threshing cylinder from the wagon. The gentleman standing atop the thresher is most likely the separator tender, making sure everything is up to snuff. The windstacker is in action at the far left depositing straw onto to the stack. *Ritzville Library Archives*

Note the sacks of grain stacked and ready for delivery to the warehouse. One source tells me that he made a whopping $7.50 per day picking up and stacking sacked grain from the field. At 10 cents a sack, he was doing 750 per day. Not a bad day's work, though he's the first one to admit that the introduction of the combine was a welcome sight. *Ritzville Library Archives*

Another view from the tractor angle of the same set. The straw stack is put into even better perspective in relation to the entire scene. The smoke from the traction engine was probably for the benefit of the photographer, as an efficient-running engine doesn't smoke. *Ritzville Library Archives*

This crew has either finished up or is just posing for the camera. This shot gives one a good view of the self-feeding process shown in the center of the picture. Notice the guy sitting atop the idle header elevator at the left, and the other fellow perched high above on the windstacker at the right. *Ritzville Library Archives*

Wire Binders

Harvesters such as the Marsh were complimented further with refinements in binding mechanisms that would soon replace the need for men to manually bind grain. Machines using wire and later twine to tie bundles of grain began to appear in the mid-1870s. In fact, one report in 1871 stated that 50 to 60 bundles had been tied by machine with no interruption; the feat being achieved by two horses, a driver, and a self-binding mechanism.

Wire was used first for binding, but it was soon discarded in favor of twine. There were several reasons for the change. First was the problem of wire fragments left in the field that often ended up in horses' hoofs, or worse, in the intestinal tract. Then there was the nuisance of pieces of wire going through the threshing cylinder. More often than not the wrath of a thresher man could be felt clear across the county when wire could be heard screeching in and out of a threshing unit. Lastly was the problem of wire being mixed in with the grain at the mill. It wasn't uncommon for a load of grain to be graded down, often as much as 10 cents per bushel because of "wire content." To remedy the problem, some warehouses resorted to the use of magnets in order to locate the wire in the grain before being milled.

Even with these problems associated with wire, by 1878 it was reported that close to 20,000 wire binders were in use. The Walter A. Wood Company is said to be the first to produce and market a commercial wire binder in 1873. Wood produced over 4,500 by the end of the decade while the McCormick machine maintained a

From stack to thresher, here is another view of the derrick in action transferring grain to be threshed.

close second for the same time period. D. M. Osborne & Company, C. Aultman & Company, and William Deering, all had wire binders in the field by 1878. Despite the disadvantages of wire, the wire binder became another stepping stone to a binder that would eventually tie with twine. By 1880 the price of twine had dropped considerably, making it more economical to make the change.

The Deering Twine Binder

The first successful production of twine binders on a commercial scale came from the Deering Company in 1878. The Deering binder was a combination of the Marsh-type machine with the Appleby knotter/binding mechanism.

William Deering was born in South Paris, Maine, in April of 1852. Initially, Deering was in the dry goods business with offices in Portland, Maine, and New York City. Though business was good, Deering had always had an interest in farming. This interest in farming, and the machinery that was doing a lot of the work, led him to link up with one-time Maine resident Eligah H. Gammon, who had since moved to the farm country of Illinois. Gammon had purchased the rights to the Marsh harvester and was beginning to produce machines on a small scale. Deering soon joined Gammon in Plano, Illinois, and formed a partnership around 1870. The union was short lived as Deering struck out on his own and moved the works to Chicago in 1880.

Deering was now sole owner of the company and, by 1883, incorporated with his sons Charles and James. Business was booming. At the height of production, over 9,000 workers were employed by the newly named Deering & Company. The company had also constructed its own steel mill in South Chicago and obtained coal fields in Kentucky along with iron-ore deposits in the Mesaba Range of Minnesota. By 1897, Deering & Company would be the largest producer of twine binders world wide. Though numerous firms would develop their own version of the twine binder similar to the Marsh/Appleby type, Deering & Company stood above them all. Other companies included: Easterly in 1880, Excelsior in 1880, McCormick in 1881, Buckeye in 1882, Champion in 1882, Osborne in 1883, and Wood in 1892. The John Deere product wouldn't appear until 1910.

The Growing Business of Twine

With a gargantuan binder market came the demand for twine. Twine for binding created a huge ancillary

A harvest crew on break in the early 1900s. The cook car stands behind the posed group. It's hard to tell whether the guy sitting down in the front is clowning with a wash pan or not, seeing as the other fellow at the far right is sporting the same kind of head gear. This particular group is made up of family and friends, a routine scene during the era of steam threshing in America. *Ritzville Library Archives*

The all-purpose wagon used for every task known to man, and woman, on the farm. This photo was taken in 1910 and shows the able crew atop with reins in hand and the animals that powered it. By the looks of the gentlemen aboard the wagon, they're probably part of the large population of German immigrants that made up the wheat belt of the Pacific Northwest in the 1880s and 1890s. Though this wagon does not appear to be sturdy enough to haul sacked wheat, you never know. *Ritzville Library Archives*

business that didn't really benefit fiber producers here in the states; twine was almost always imported. By 1911 close to 90 million acres of grain were being bound by twine, totaling over 190 million pounds of fiber. The number soared to 300 million pounds by 1918; 80 percent of the worlds consumption was of the Henequen fiber from Yucatan, Mexico.

It was essential that binder twine be strong, and not susceptible to damage from moisture, mildew, or insects. The best, according to the USDA back in 1911, was the Abaca fiber from the Philippines, a plant that resembled the familiar banana plant. Abaca was also the highest priced, costing anywhere from 5 to 10 cents a pound. Others included Sisal, Manila hemp, and varieties from Java, Costa Rica, and India. The U. S. did have a small share of the market from hemp and flax combinations grown in Kentucky. These fibers, however, were not only considered sub-standard because they weren't as strong as the imported fibers, they also proved to be a suitable diet for the grasshopper!

With just about everyone in the harvester business producing twine binders by 1890, the reaper and wire machines were beginning to fade away completely. In 1889 under 9,000 reapers were produced as opposed to over 125,000 binders and headers. The reaper was still being used on small farms in the East, where it could also be operated as a mower, but that was about it.

The twine binder was on its way to becoming one of the most commonly used machines of its kind for harvesting small grains. A study done in the latter part of the 1880s shows that production of all types of harvesting machines jumped from 60,000 in 1880 to 250,000 by 1885. What's interesting about these numbers is that wheat country was not really expanding at the rate that would

The calm before the storm? These two women pictured here represent those who probably spent more hours in the field than anybody else. Obviously this picture was taken either before or after the gargantuan meal of the day. In hot, dusty conditions potatoes were peeled, bread was baked, meat was roasted, and anything else you can possibly think of was prepared for the army of harvesters that never knew when to say when. The farm wife, and daughters, hailed the arrival of the combine to such an extent that they actually wrote to the manufacturers, praising them for finally coming up with something to liberate them from the fields. What would the farm wife say to the loss of community during the steam threshing era? Hogwash! *Ritzville Library Archives*

From the field to the warehouse, wagon upon wagon delivered sacked wheat to the nearest storage facility. It's interesting to note that the town of Krupp, Washington, pictured above, no longer exists. Actually, the name was changed during World War I. It seems that Krupp was also a German munitions plant, so in order to show their allegiance to the United States, the predominately German population of the town changed the name to Marlin, after the American arms manufacturer. Though no longer a wheat center, Marlin is still intact with a population of around 200 people. *Ritzville Library Archives*

A grand procession down Main Street with this steam traction machine pulling eight loaded wagons of grain in 1905. The wagon directly behind the engine is hauling straw for fuel. Note the hose draped over the front mounted tank. The make of engine could be any one of a dozen. *Ritzville Library Archives*

justify an increase in production and sales; more people were simply discarding their self-rakers and other harvesters for the twine binder. In fact, by 1891, wire binders were no longer being made.

The twine binder was further improved in 1918 when it became the first piece of farm machinery to be adapted to the power take-off (PTO) on farm tractors. Their popularity was still in vogue well into the 1930s, as the government reported that over 1. 2 million of them were still in use in 1938. Actually, twine binders were used well into the 1950s in the eastern farm regions, but the header was the harvester of choice in the semi-arid regions of western Kansas, parts of the Dakotas, California, and the Pacific Northwest. The sheer size of the ranches and the lack of rainfall in these regions necessitated the use of a harvester that required less manpower while at the same time eliminated the binding process altogether.

The Header: Dry Land Harvesting

The American header can be traced to the San Joaquin and Sacramento Valleys of California as far back as 1850. Vast wheat ranches, some in excess of 20,000 acres, required a more feasible way to harvest grain than with the binder. Because of the lack of rainfall in the summer months and the flat terrain in the majority of California's wheat belt, the header was almost exclusively employed. In fact, anywhere ranches tended to be a section (640 acres) or larger, and where grain grew short and stiff, the header was found. This was also the case in the sub-humid regions of the Great Plains. A survey done in the early 1900s shows that almost 90 percent of farms in western Kansas used the header while over 90 percent still used the binder on the east side of the state. Again, rainfall, terrain, and the size of the farm usually dictated the type of machine used.

According to some reports out of California it took only two headers, five wagons, and a large thresher to cut, separate, and sack 1,500 bushels of wheat in one day. That meant that around 40 acres a day was possible with the header; this was probably more the exception than the rule, however.

The header cut a swath of 12 to 16 feet wide, was propelled by six to eight horses, depending on slope, and could harvest on the average of 25 to 30 acres a day (though the header was often referred to as a "pusher," the horses actually pulled the machine, being hitched to a bar at the rear. They only appeared to be pushing because they walked behind the header). The driver, or "puncher," stood on a small platform to the rear of the machine; a pilot wheel was positioned underneath the puncher to keep the machine in line. The ground wheel at the left of the header provided movement for the pitman, reel, and drapers; it was also fitted with a brake that was positioned around the outside hub of the ground wheel.

Though less manpower was needed for the header, more horsepower was required as wagons were needed to load the cut grain. The header wagons, or barges, followed along the left hand side of the machine to receive the cut grain by way of the elevator. An endless canvas (draper) facilitated the cut grain up the elevator and into the wagon with a loader helping to disperse the grain evenly in the wagon. The grain could then be taken to the threshing set and be separated. Whether or not the grain was threshed right away or stacked to "sweat" depended upon the farmer. Eighty-seven-year-old header

The A-C Rumely All-Steel Thresher as it appeared in the Allis-Chalmers Yearbook of 1934. The platform is folded in the position for transport, as is the windstacker at the rear of the machine. The Rumely threshers were produced until the mid-1930s until they were discontinued by Allis-Chalmers which acquired Rumely in 1931. During the Heyday of threshing, the Rumely (Advance-Rumely) was one of the most popular machines in the field.

The Thresherman
THAT MADE THE
Biggest Run
In Adans County Last Year
was the man that had a
★ RUSSEL STEAM OUTFIT. ★
We have a Complete Machine now set up.
Examine it when in Town.
Remember we are headquarters for HARDWARE.
We Sell the
Famous Woodmanse
ENCLOSED GEAR WINDMILLS.
ST. CLAIR STOVES, BAIN & STOUGHTON WAGONS. HODGE HEADERS
and all other first class
Farm Implements.
Ritzville Hardware Company.

Advertisements like these were plentiful in weekly newspapers throughout the wheat sections of the country. In addition to steam engines and threshers, the local implement dealer handled windmills, stoves, wagons and anything else associated with the farm. This ad was taken from the 1899 edition of the *Ritzville Journal Times*, a weekly that still does a pretty fair job of reporting local news around the wheat belt.

veteran Joe Jantz of Adams County, Washington, said they used to cut two weeks before the grain was dead ripe and then stack it to insure a low moisture content; others tended to cut the grain when fully ripe and thresh as soon as possible. It all depended on the farmer.

Headers, like the binder, were manufactured by numerous companies; McCormick and Deering, under the International Harvester umbrella in 1902, would end up producing the lion's share well into the 20th century. But it was actually George Esterly of Whitewater, Wisconsin, who took out one of the earliest patents on the header in 1844. Esterly's initial product was reminiscent of Pliny's early stripper of the first century and would go through a few changes before evolving into the header. With the addition of canvas drapers and an elevator that would empty into waiting barges instead of into a small cart behind an elevated reel, the Esterly became a huge seller. Some sources suggest that the canvas conveyor and side delivery improvements were "borrowed" from Jonathan Haines of Pekin, Illinois, a header manufacturer in his own right.

Haines patented his famous "Haines Illinois Harvester" in March of 1849. His machine was popular throughout the West, and particularly in the California wheat fields where large tracts of grain could be harvested without interruption from rainfall. The vast majority of wheat in the Big Bend country of the Pacific Northeast, including the rolling Palouse, also used the Haines header. Because of the degree of slope in the Palouse, sometimes in excess of 50 percent, header barges were fitted with extended axles often up to 12 feet in length. In fact, an 1880 report from the *Martinez Gazette* triumphed the production of the Side-Hill Leveling Header Wagon by Taynton and Dickerson. The wagon bed moved on four friction rollers. The driver was in charge of governing the level of the wagon with the use of a "crank rod operating a worm pinion acting simultaneously at the bolster bearings, giving the bed any desired set to bring the load level on any side-hill angle." This worked well, even when the wagon had to make sharp turns, up or down a hill.

Another machine featured in the 1934 yearbook was this A-C Birdsell Clover and Alfalfa Huller. The sales literature touted the Birdsell as having the best rasp-type hulling cylinder on the market for opening up even the most obstinate pods. The self-feeder and windstacker were standard. Mainly found in the Midwest, the Birdsell was also discontinued by A-C in the 1930s.

Though the header would not enjoy the reputation and celebrity of the binder, its use continued in various regions well into the 1920s and 30s. This was the case in the Pacific Northwest, especially when there was an abundant supply of labor. The combine was used more often during World War I, but by 1920, more headers were in the field due to a fresh labor supply returning from the battlefields of Europe.

The header is an example of a machine that was built to adapt to a certain set of environmental and geographical conditions. The size of grain fields and the lack of moisture west of the 100th meridian created the need for a machine of this type in the same way that the windmill and the introduction of barbed wire were created to solve similar constraints in arid country. The header usually receives only scant mention when looking at harvest machinery on the whole, even though its basic principles of operation would lead to the birth of the combine in California.

Threshing: The End Product of the Harvest

The harvesting of small grains whether cut by reaper, binder, or header, needed to go through the threshing process. The threshing of grain is as old as time itself. Before the era of steam and horsepower, threshing consisted of beating, flailing, and winnowing by hand. Later, horses and oxen were driven into a circular corral where they stomped the grain into separation. The separated grain and chaff were then placed upon a sheet of canvas to facilitate throwing the grain into the wind. The wind blew away the chaff and only the kernels remained. Eventually horse-ground power was used to operate stationary threshing units. Obviously, a new technology was sought to lighten the burden of both man and beast; the advent of the "in-line" steam engine thresher/separator was the answer.

Most rural dwellers are familiar with the great steam threshing scenes that began in the 1860s and lasted well into the 1930s and 40s. The barber shop, grange hall, and the local coffee shop proudly display old photos of the "set," as it is sometimes referred to, from cook car to straw stack. The manpower, long hours, and dangerous working conditions that went along with steam threshing, not to mention the expense, are often taken for granted. Still, threshing time was a social event on par with the county fair.

Individual farmers rarely owned and operated their own units; threshing "rings" traveled from farm to farm acting as custom operators. The basic outfit was comprised of the engineer, fireman, and separator tender; all other manpower was supplied by the farmer and his neighbors or transient labor. The engineer in most cases owned the equipment, which included the steam engine, the thresher, water wagon, and the cook car. The farmer supplied horses and wagons, and up to 30 men for the purpose of hauling bound grain to the thresher. In the case of headed wheat, threshing could take place simultaneously to cutting, as the grain was hauled unbound, and usually dead ripe. The fireman was responsible for the early start-up of the boiler, often beginning at 4:00 am. During the course of the day the job could be delegated to a young kid who liked nothing more than to feed the boiler's fiery mouth with straw. The separator tender did just that, tended the separator. A good separator man with a watchful eye generally avoided problems and was responsible for any adjustments to be made to insure a safe, smooth run.

Unfortunately this was not always the case. Thresher and boiler fires just didn't happen occasionally they happened all the time, enough in fact, that state agricultural extension stations began to conduct investigations. It seems that in one particular area of Eastern Washington, over 300 thresher fires occurred in the 1914 season alone, totally destroying not only the thresher units, but also threshed and unthreshed grain. Conservative estimates of one half million dollars in losses were reported. Overheating thresher cylinders and smut in grain seemed to be the common culprit."Smut-air mixture" and static electricity was such a problem that grounding of the thresher cylinder alone was not enough . Some investigators suggested that a ground from all the main castings be employed to avert sparking. It was also found that most fires occurred in cylinders traveling between the speeds of 900 and 1100 rpm; the majority of the fires originating at or near the threshing cylinder.

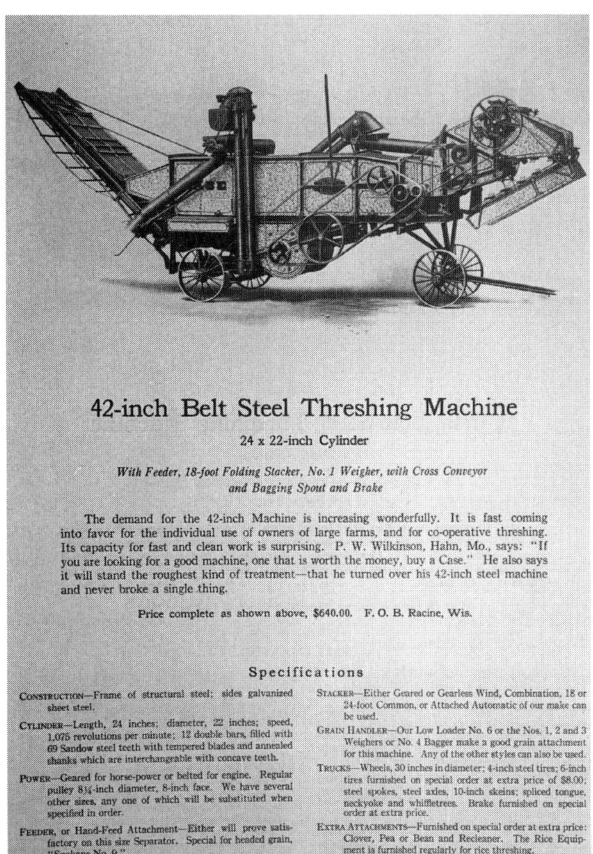

42-inch Belt Steel Threshing Machine

24 x 22-inch Cylinder

With Feeder, 18-foot Folding Stacker, No. 1 Weigher, with Cross Conveyor and Bagging Spout and Brake

The demand for the 42-inch Machine is increasing wonderfully. It is fast coming into favor for the individual use of owners of large farms, and for co-operative threshing. Its capacity for fast and clean work is surprising. P. W. Wilkinson, Hahn, Mo., says: "If you are looking for a good machine, one that is worth the money, buy a Case." He also says it will stand the roughest kind of treatment—that he turned over his 42-inch steel machine and never broke a single thing.

Price complete as shown above, $640.00. F. O. B. Racine, Wis.

Specifications

CONSTRUCTION—Frame of structural steel; sides galvanized sheet steel.

CYLINDER—Length, 24 inches; diameter, 22 inches; speed, 1,075 revolutions per minute; 12 double bars, filled with 69 Sandow steel teeth with tempered blades and annealed shanks which are interchangeable with concave teeth.

POWER—Geared for horse-power or belted for engine. Regular pulley 8¼-inch diameter, 8-inch face. We have several other sizes, any one of which will be substituted when specified in order.

FEEDER, or Hand-Feed Attachment—Either will prove satisfactory on this size Separator. Special for headed grain, "Spokane No. 9."

STACKER—Either Geared or Gearless Wind, Combination, 18 or 24-foot Common, or Attached Automatic of our make can be used.

GRAIN HANDLER—Our Low Loader No. 6 or the Nos. 1, 2 and 3 Weighers or No. 4 Bagger make a good grain attachment for this machine. Any of the other styles can also be used.

TRUCKS—Wheels, 30 inches in diameter; 4-inch steel tires; 6-inch tires furnished on special order at extra price of $8.00; steel spokes, steel axles, 10-inch skeins; spliced tongue, neckyoke and whiffletrees. Brake furnished on special order at extra price.

EXTRA ATTACHMENTS—Furnished on special order at extra price: Clover, Pea or Bean and Recleaner. The Rice Equipment is furnished regularly for rice threshing.

Prices Quoted on Pages 64 and 65

Pictured is the 42-inch cylinder thresher. The 42-inch featured an 18-foot stacker and self-feeder. These options could be had with just about all Case machines.

Another obvious danger was steam boiler explosions. This is the primary reason that threshing pictures of yore are often over a foot wide. The steam unit had to be situated anywhere from 100 to 150 feet away from the threshing unit as a good steam explosion could take out not only the immediate set, but might just burn up a few of the neighbor's harvests as well. Many explosions occurred when stream engines operated on uneven ground. Any condition that created loss of water level with relation to the crown plate of the boiler often spelled disaster as the plate would continue to heat to extremely high temperatures generated by the firebox. Remedies to this problem included installation of what the Waterloo Machinery Company of Waterloo, Ontario, Canada, called the "dry trough." Running nearly the full length of the boiler, this trough acted as a splash board that protected the opening into the dome and prevented water from interfering with dry steam while moving on uneven ground. Essentially the trough allowed steam to enter from both sides of the boiler regardless of up or down movement, resulting in fewer mishaps.

Still, nothing was 100 percent, and boilers would more often than not find a way to explode. One such incident in Antioch, California, in July of 1880 is a good example. This particular event was blamed on the fireman, for when the gauge registered 115 pounds of pressure everything went. The *Antioch Ledger* stated that the front of the engine was blown 125 yards from the force of the steam and tore up nearly 40 yards of ground. The recoil alone drove the entire machine backwards 16 yards. Two men were injured; their survival was considered a miracle.

Other Companies such as the Advance Machinery Company of Battle Creek, Michigan, claimed that the compound engine (two-cylinders in tandem) was not only safer but did the work of the "simple" engine (one-cylinder) on less fuel! According to the company's own literature in 1909, a compound engine, "will require less steam from the boiler, to do the same work, than the simple [engine] owing to its increased rate of expansion and decreased cylinder condensation."

Other common mishaps at the thresher sets included people getting caught in flat belts or getting tangled up in the machinery itself. Eighty-five-year-old Mel Hollenbeck recalls playing on the flywheel of a Rumely Oil-Pull Tractor on a Nebraska farm in 1918. When the tractor started, the nine-year-old was thrown like so much straw into the wind. Unscathed by the launching, he's avoided flywheels ever since.

The Steam Tractor

The first commercial self-propelled steam engine was produced by the Merritt and Kellogg Company of Battle Creek, Michigan, in 1871. It was extremely heavy and had just enough power to move its own weight at a slow crawl. Some of these "monsters," in fact, were reported to weigh as much as one ton per horsepower. Though one Case model was rated at 110 horsepower, this "lightweight" came in at a mere 20 tons! Most steam traction engines weighed on the average of 45,000 pounds, while generating more than 120 horsepower and creating anywhere from 150 to 200 pounds of pressure per square inch.

Dozens of steam traction machine companies paraded their wares through magazines like the *American Thresherman*, *The Threshermen's Review*, and *The Thresher World and Farmer's Magazine*. From the American Abell Engine and Thresher Company of Toronto, Ontario, Canada, to the Wood Bros. Engine and Separator Company of Des Moines, Iowa, and all the way to the Pacific Coast to the Daniel Best Agricultural Works of San Leandro, California, steam machines, whether stationary or otherwise, were aplenty. Engineering instruction was also offered through correspondence courses. Ads appearing in the various magazines like the *American Thresherman* promoted the Clarke School of Traction Engineering in Madison, Wisconsin, and asked the reader, "Why be the water boy, the bundle hauler, or work in the dust and chaff about a separator when in a few months' time you can fit yourself to be an engineer?"

Vertical portable engines were also popular for a time, mainly for safety reasons. One particular model was the Waterous "Fire Proof," a 12-horsepower portable, that supposedly had a fast but safe warm-up time in addition to a water type spark arrester. Though the threat of explosion was always a concern, sparks were more so. It didn't matter much whether the engine was vertical or horizontal; too much straw in the boiler along with a brisk wind often led to disaster.

Aside from occasional injuries and fires, threshing operations went relatively smooth. Countless threshers were on the market touting efficiency and safety. Self-feeding units devised in the 1860s were standard by the turn of the century, along with new ratings for threshing cylinders and separator chambers. Because the self-feeders tended to increase the amount of grain threshed, the separator section directly behind the cylinder had to be enlarged in width. Ratings of 30x36 simply meant that the cylinder was 30 inches wide and the separator width was 36 inches, creating better flow and higher efficiency. This method of rating the cylinder/separator size continued on with the combined harvester.

Like the steam traction companies, threshing manufacturers were also numerous, often producing both types of machines. The Rumely, Nichols & Shepard, Buffalo Pitts, and the Oliver Red River Special were just a few of the machines that dotted grain country from Kansas to California and points north and south. The Largest producer, however, was J. I. Case, who produced 100,000 threshers, the last of which rolled out of the factory in 1953. One of the earliest Case threshers was advertised in 1855 as a two-horsepower machine that could thresh from 200 to 300 bushels a day under the right conditions. Later models included extended grain elevators and

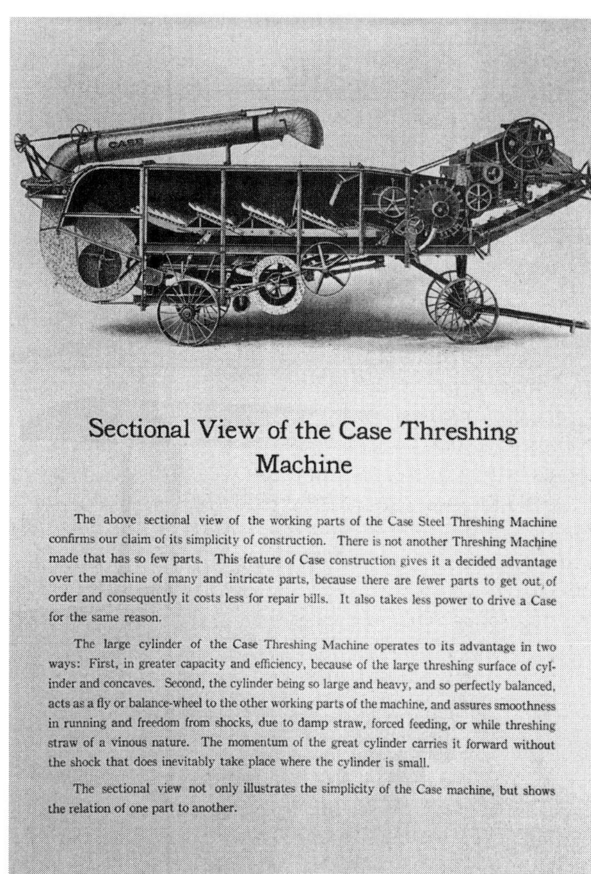

Sectional View of the Case Threshing Machine

The above sectional view of the working parts of the Case Steel Threshing Machine confirms our claim of its simplicity of construction. There is not another Threshing Machine made that has so few parts. This feature of Case construction gives it a decided advantage over the machine of many and intricate parts, because there are fewer parts to get out of order and consequently it costs less for repair bills. It also takes less power to drive a Case for the same reason.

The large cylinder of the Case Threshing Machine operates to its advantage in two ways: First, in greater capacity and efficiency, because of the large threshing surface of cylinder and concaves. Second, the cylinder being so large and heavy, and so perfectly balanced, acts as a fly or balance-wheel to the other working parts of the machine, and assures smoothness in running and freedom from shocks, due to damp straw, forced feeding, or while threshing straw of a vinous nature. The momentum of the great cylinder carries it forward without the shock that does inevitably take place where the cylinder is small.

The sectional view not only illustrates the simplicity of the Case machine, but shows the relation of one part to another.

The classic Case thresher. Producing a record 100,000 threshers, the last of which rolled out of the factory in 1953, the Case machine could be found coast to coast wherever harvesting was taking place. This is a factory cutaway view from the 1912 catalog.

swinging straw stackers. The higher elevators and the so-called "Double-tube Dakota Weigher," were made specifically for farmers in the Northwest where grain tanks tended to be taller. The Case Agitator, introduced in the early 1880s, was the precursor to the modern combined harvester with regards to its threshing and cleaning components. The Case company by 1900 also led the field with their steam tractors, producing three times that of their nearest competitor. As agricultural historian Graeme Quick points out, Case manufactured over 35,000 steam tractors during a 55-year run, more than any other competitor.

The Buffalo-Pitts Agricultural Works was yet another famous name in the threshing industry. In a marketing advertisement dated 1877, Pitts touted its threshers and cleaners as the best in the field, driven by water, steam, or horsepower. Craftsmanship was also stressed. In fact, one might think the ad was promoting fine furniture instead of a piece of agricultural equipment when elaborating about "woodwork made of carefully selected woods, free from knots and checks and thoroughly seasoned." The Buffalo-Pitts came in cylinder sizes from 24 to 40 inches

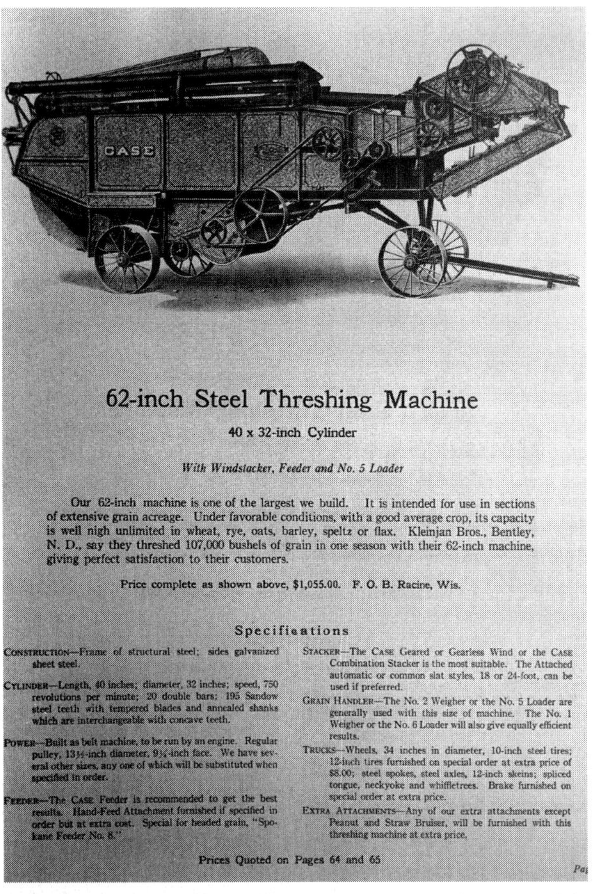

62-inch Steel Threshing Machine

40 x 32-inch Cylinder

With Windstacker, Feeder and No. 5 Loader

Our 62-inch machine is one of the largest we build. It is intended for use in sections of extensive grain acreage. Under favorable conditions, with a good average crop, its capacity is well nigh unlimited in wheat, rye, oats, barley, speltz or flax. Kleinjan Bros., Bentley, N. D., say they threshed 107,000 bushels of grain in one season with their 62-inch machine, giving perfect satisfaction to their customers.

Price complete as shown above, $1,055.00. F. O. B. Racine, Wis.

Specifications

CONSTRUCTION—Frame of structural steel; sides galvanized sheet steel.

CYLINDER—Length, 40 inches; diameter, 32 inches; speed, 750 revolutions per minute; 20 double bars; 195 Sandow steel teeth with tempered blades and annealed shanks which are interchangeable with concave teeth.

POWER—Built as belt machine, to be run by an engine. Regular pulley, 13½-inch diameter, 9½-inch face. We have several other sizes, any one of which will be substituted when specified in order.

FEEDER—The CASE Feeder is recommended to get the best results. Hand-Feed Attachment furnished if specified in order but at extra cost. Special for headed grain, "Spokane Feeder No. 8."

STACKER—The CASE Geared or Gearless Wind or the CASE Combination Stacker is the most suitable. The Attached automatic or common slat styles, 18 or 24-foot, can be used if preferred.

GRAIN HANDLER—The No. 2 Weigher or the No. 5 Loader are generally used with this size of machine. The No. 1 Weigher or the No. 6 Loader will also give equally efficient results.

TRUCKS—Wheels, 34 inches in diameter, 10-inch steel tires; 12-inch tires furnished on special order at extra price of $8.00; steel spokes, steel axles, 12-inch skeins; spliced tongue, neckyoke and whiffletrees. Brake furnished on special order at extra price.

EXTRA ATTACHMENTS—Any of our extra attachments except Peanut and Straw Bruiser, will be furnished with this threshing machine at extra price.

Prices Quoted on Pages 64 and 65

This is the 62-inch Case. Threshers such as these would enjoy use all over grain country, even after the introduction of the combine. In fact, many farmers who farmed less than 320 acres didn't make the switch to the combine until the small self-propelled model was made available in the late 1930s.

and could harvest anywhere from 300 to 3,000 bushels per day.

A late-comer to the threshing game was the International Harvester Company (IHC). Not until 1909 did IHC begin to market the Belle City thresher, and later in 1913, gain a selling arrangement with Buffalo-Pitts to market that product. They would also handle the Sterling and New Racine threshers until 1925 before producing their first all-steel McCormick-Deering models. Various models with different functions were available, from the standard stationary to the barn-floor type, as well as those set up for threshing beans, peas, and rice. Production of all IHC threshers ended in 1956.

The threshing era has long since past even though to some it seems like only yesterday that the crew was assembling and the machinery was being loaded onto the fields for yet another harvest. The age of the thresher was still being played out well into the 1950s while a new era of mechanized harvesting had begun in the golden state of California in the early 1880s. Early concepts of a combined harvester had been cultivated in an area that would make its use almost impossible. From the state of Michigan in 1836 came rumblings of a colossal machine, pulled by 24 to 36 horses; of a machine that could harvest up to 40 acres a day, and up to 2000 acres in a season. Even in an era dominated by the binder, new techniques in harvesting were right around the corner. Oddly enough, these achievements would not come from the Deerings or the McCormicks, but from a new breed of inventors that would build on an idea from one region and apply it to another. By way of the "Horn" came the long awaited solution for harvesting California's monolithic fields of grain.

Chapter Two

Early Combines of California and the Pacific Northwest

Beginning in the early 1850s, California was on its way to becoming the largest wheat producing state in the nation. By the 1870s and 80s, the spread of wheat cultivation would be tied to national as well as international markets, made possible by an extensive railroad system. In a way, "wheat followed the rails" down the Sacramento and San Joaquin Valleys from Stockton to Merced, an area that encompassed over 600 square miles of wheat country. Bonanza ranches of 10 to 20 thousand acres were common. Some spreads, like the Glenn Ranch of Colusa County was made up of seven to nine farms that contained over 55,000 acres and employed 700 laborers. It was on the giant farms of California that the combined harvester would flourish and change the face of harvesting small grains.

Although the combined harvester would mature on the West Coast, it was born in the Midwest. The exact origin of the combined harvester is debatable, but most agree that the first prototype was the 1836 Moore & Haskall machine from western Michigan. Patents were filed by Samuel Lane of Hallowell, Minnesota, in 1828 and Ashmore and Peck in 1835, but neither resulted in a successful machine. This is also true of the 1841 D. H. Church machine and the 1846 Darling combine patent. A combination of a lack of capital, weather, uneven terrain, lack of animal power, and small acreage all contributed to keeping these early machines from succeeding. How the Moore machine found its way to the California could be considered luck, if not for the tenacity of its inventor and those who had a stake in its success. Nevertheless, the machine was shipped around the horn to San Francisco in the early 1850s, where it met the fields of grain at Mission San Jose and later in Alameda County.

The Moore-Haskall combined harvester can be traced to the Prairie Ronde region of Kalamazoo County,

One of the many ads appearing in the *Pacific Rural Press* during the 1880s. The names Houser, Shippee, Minges, Powell, and Matteson & Williamson were all separate companies during the early to mid-1880s but were later consolidated under the Stockton Combined Harvester & Agricultural Works umbrella by decade's end. Most of these machines operated the same way; employing the tight-gear method from the bull wheel for motive power.

Probably the most recognized combined harvester ever is the Holt Standard. Stopping work just long enough for a pose, the photo above shows the header-tender standing with his hand on the wheel, the mechanic off to his right, and a couple of sack sewers seated under the canopy. In the picture you can clearly see the bull wheel and the Holt innovation of Link-Chain. This photo was shot in the late 1880s, probably in California where combine production at that time was in full swing. *Caterpillar Company Archives*

Michigan. The first of the triad who would eventually get the harvesting machine on track was John Haskall, lawyer, originally from Utica, New York. In 1820, Haskall was implicated in a Freemasonry scandal and felt the necessity to go West. When his attempt to open a law practice in Kalamazoo County failed, Haskall turned to farming wheat. The rest of the Haskall part of the story is best described by A. Y. Moore (no relation to the inventor) in a published letter that appeared in the *Pacific Rural Press*, dated October 2, 1886:

"On viewing the Prairie Ronde, in Kalamazoo County, of some 20,000 acres, seeing that it was good for wheat and thousands of acres uncultivated, he, Haskall, thought if he had a team, perhaps he could hold the plow and put in wheat. He knew that he could not harvest it, and there were no men to hire. He spoke of it in the family, and it caused his wife to dream; so one morning thereafter she stated to her husband that she saw in her dream a large machine going over the prairie, drawn by horses and harvesting wheat, describing its appearance and motion. Mr. Haskall related the dream to Hiram Moore (no relation), of Climax Prairie, knowing him to be of an inventive turn of mind."

Enter Hiram Moore, the second of the triad and eventual builder of the machine. Moore, born July 19, 1801, in New Hampshire, came to Western Michigan in 1831 and settled in the small village of Climax, Kalamazoo County. At the start, Moore brushed off the dream, and quite frankly, the whole idea espoused by Mr. Haskall, though the thought of inventing such a machine nagged him for over six months. Eventually Hiram decided to seriously consider the invention and, by 1834, had a model sent to the patent office in Washington, D. C.

Moore was awarded the patent in 1834, and he constructed a temporary machine that was tested at Flower Field, Michigan, in the harvest year of 1835.

This first trial was conducted without the separator and cleaner mechanisms because only the cutter bar was to be tested. Although "something broke" after several rods, the initial report on the cutter was good, and improvements were made. Again referring to the letter of A. Y. Moore in 1886:

"The next season he [Hiram] intended to perfect a machine for further trial. My brother Abner did the carpenter work, and, I had sowed some wheat when I came to Prairie Ronde in 1835, he asked me to let three acres stand for trial. It being late in the harvest season, so that he could make a fair trial, so I did so, and the harvester cut it and thrashed it in good order, but the cleaner was not yet attached. He asked me to take the time of its work and figure the cost per acre, at the going rate for men's labor and the hire of horses. Twelve horses were worked on the machine at that time, besides the team hauling to the barn. I took the exact time for cutting the three acres, and made the actual cost of 82 cents per acre."

Eighty-two cents may not mean a whole lot until you compare the cost per acre harvested the standard way at the time. A. Y. Moore wasted no time in comparing the costs between the two forms of harvesting and found that the operation of cradling, raking, binding, shocking, stacking, thrashing, and cleaning came to a little over $3.12 per acre. One must also keep in mind that the reaper at this time was still in its infancy. In the words of A. Y. Moore, "The contrast was so great that I took an active part in its [the combines] future."

Between 1835 and 1843, Hiram Moore would continue to fine tune his machine. A. Y. Moore assisted him on more than one occasion, driving the machine as adjustments were made for better cleaning and separating, and also giving Hiram the time to invent the Angle Edge Sickle in 1841. It was also in 1841 that Hiram journeyed to Rochester, New York, to find able mechanics that eventually helped him build two more machines for the harvest of 1842, one of which A. Y. Moore bought for himself. The machine was used on the Moore place utilizing 16 horses, hitched two abreast, and cutting a 10-foot-wide swath. According to Moore, the machine cut, threshed, cleaned, and bagged 25 acres per day, and did so with little trouble until the harvest of 1853. At that time, an interest in the machine was sold to George Leland, and the harvester was shipped to California by invitation of farmer John Horner. The Moore combined harvester reportedly cut 600 acres in Alameda County for the harvest of 1854. In 1855, the machine stayed idle as Leland decided to try his luck at mining. Leland's son, however, put the machine in the field for the harvest of

One of only two pictures in existence of the Moore-Haskell combined harvester, the first one of its kind to be operated successfully in California wheat fields in 1854. The machine actually dates back to 1836, about the same time that the reaper was being perfected. The machine above is one of five that was built by inventor Hiram Moore of Kalamazoo County, Michigan . Moore is seated on top of the machine wearing the stove-pipe top hat. The picture is actually half of a stereopticon slide that, according to Hal Higgins' caption work, was discovered by the inventor's granddaughter in the 1940s. Records vary on the date of the photo, but most accounts state that it was taken in the 1840s. After a season of harvesting in California, the machine was lost to fire, apparently due to inadequately oiled bearings. *F. Hal Higgins Collection*

G. W. Haines, vice president and general manager of the Houser & Haines Manufacturing Company. Haines was the inventor of the "Baby" and "Junior" side-hill combined harvesters that were used extensively in California and the Northwest. The company was founded in 1889 and opened up shop at the corner of Scotts and Aurora Street in Stockton. The Holt Manufacturing Company later acquired the company in 1901. *1908 Haines*

1856, where it was promptly set ablaze do to unoiled bearings. California now had the dual distinction of not only having the first combine in history operating in its fields, but also the first recorded wheat fire caused by a harvesting machine!

"Thus ended the machine business with me," wrote A. Y. Moore, but the event also began a new era in California with a potential boon for mechanized agriculture. John Horner had not invited Leland and his machine into the region out of pure curiosity. In fact, Horner was something of an inventor himself. According to F. Hal Higgins, the late agricultural historian, no drawings or photographs exist from the United States Patent Office on the invention of Horner's push-type combine of the mid-1850s. Only a hand sketched recollection from Horner's son, acquired in the 1930s showing the placement of the horses, proves that indeed the machine was of the push style.

Much like the Idaho National Harvester that is discussed at the end of this chapter, the Horner was built as a push machine for various reasons. Because farm labor was scarce in California at the time, it was essential that a harvester of the combined type be operated with as few

Below
The Jantz Brothers Houser-Haines working the field in 1909. Uncle Andrew is driving the combination mule/horse setup along with his pet Dalmatian barely visible at his feet. Nephew Joe Jantz explains that both horses and mules were used because the mules could "take the heat," being hitched on the inside close to the bull chain. This outfit is pulled by 16 animals and two leaders up front. In this case the leaders are mules, so only one rein is used, often called the "jerk" line. With one jerk, the leaders would move to the right, two jerks would signal a turn to the left. Commands of "gee" and "haw" were also used, especially with well-trained leaders. *Courtesy of Joe Jantz*

NO MORE

HEADERS,

NO MORE

THRASHERS

REQUIRED IN THE

HARVEST FIELD.

THE

"SHIPPEE" COMBINED HARVESTER

WITH SHIPPEE and GRATTAN IMPROVEMENTS.

......MANUFACTURED BY THE......

STOCKTON COMBINED HARVESTER AND AGRICULTURAL WORKS,

STOCKTON, SAN JOAQUIN COUNTY, CAL.

ACCOMPLISHES ALL THE WORK OF HARVESTING, CUTTING, THRASHING, CLEANING AND SACKING at one and the same time, at the rate of from 20 to 30 acres per day, at an expense of less than one-fourth of the old method of Harvesting, and enabling the farmer who buys a machine and owns his team to harvest his crop at a cost not to exceed two cents per bushel, doing all the work himself, with the aid of a boy.

IT IS THE ONLY LIGHT DRAFT, COMBINED HARVESTER.

It is the only Harvester that has been Successfully Worked by two Persons and ten Animals. It will pay for Itself in one season's run, and cuts more Grain than a Header. The only Harvester having an Elevator to run Straw into Header Wagons, thereby saving all the Straw if desired. Can be run with half the expense required to work any other Harvester. Received all Premiums

An early ad for the Shippee Combined Harvester. The literature on this machine claimed that it was the first to be operated by only two men and 10 animals. The Shippee was also part of the Stockton Ag Works family and bore the name of its founder L. U. Shippee. The entire company was bought out by Holt in 1892.

An elegant shot of the Daniel Best combined harvester at work in the fields of California circa 1890. Obviously posed, the harvester is powered by 18 horses and two leaders (note the double instead of single rein). The driver, header tender, mechanic, and sack sewers are shown in their proper positions. The rest of the gang is probably there for the picture. Best had a fairly long run with the horse powered harvester until he too sold out to Holt in 1908. Between 1890 and 1908 just over 1,200 Best harvesters were produced, primarily for the California fields. *Caterpillar Company Archives*

Daniel : Best's : New : Steam : Harvester.

[SHOWN AS AT WORK IN THE FIELD.]

Awarded First Premium at California State Fair, 1890.

I am now prepared to build on orders only my

NEW -:- STEAM -:- HARVESTER

Much like Holt, Best was usually preoccupied with the development of steam traction power for the farm. This photo comes from the Daniel Best Agricultural Works catalog of 1891. The above shows his new steam harvester, a machine that was limited to the extremely large bonanza wheat ranches. The harvester derived its power from a flexible pipe coming off the main boiler. *F. Hal Higgins Collection*

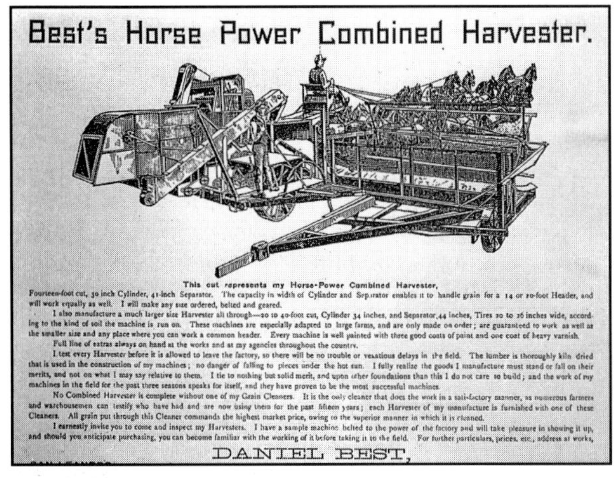

Another ad from the 1891 sales catalog. The Best horse-powered combined harvester was available with 20- and 40-foot cutter bars and a 34-inch threshing cylinder. The tires were anywhere from 20 to 26 inches wide, depending on the soil that the machine was to be used on.

men as possible. Operators on the front-driven combines would often experience the nightmare of bolting horses when the machine was thrown into gear, sometimes leaving the machine in pieces over the field. This was also true when a machine operated on a downhill slope. Bunching of horses and mules alone could cause a runaway, injuring men, animals, and equipment, hence, hitching animals to the rear of the machine "became the order of the day."

Horner's combined harvester was operated by three men: one to drive the horses from behind the machine, another out in front of the machine to raise and lower the cutter over uneven ground, and a sack sewer. The horses were hitched to a timber roughly 22x12x30 feet long, three to four horses next to the unharvested grain, and four horses on the other side behind the machine. Horner also held a patent on the cylinder teeth. Apparently, he had the only one of its kind and if anybody wanted it, they had to purchase it from him. According to Horner's son Robert, two of the old machines were left in a stable yard when they left California in 1879. So intriguing were the machines, eastern entrepreneurs traveled to take measurements for future developments prompting Robert to write, "I suppose

Need something to till the family garden? Both Holt and Best machines were outfitted with these enormous extended wheels for work in soft soils. This may be the reclaimed Tulare Lake bed in California. This Best Steamer was built for the Middle River Farming Company of Central California. Even these large wheels were no match for these saturated fields. Note the timber beams used to try to get the machine unstuck. These guys don't look very happy at all. *Caterpillar Company Archives*

that the present-day harvesters are more or less styled after father's machine."

The first Horner machine was built in 1859 at a cost of $20,000, with later harvesters being produced at least until the late 1870s. Public trials were held in August of 1868 claiming that the Horner Monitor No. 2 would save the farmer, "one-half the expense of harvesting," and do away with the total cost of threshing. Horner's was most likely the "first advertised demonstration of a combined harvester in history."

Not all were impressed with the "Monitor" and similar machines, especially those whose livelihood depended on the man-consuming style of harvesting of the times. The threat of a combined machine replacing the old form of heading, hauling, stacking, threshing, and bagging created near pandemonium among farm laborers. In fact, one of Horner's machines became the first casualty when it was deliberately burned in July of 1869. Horner was not the only one who suffered at the hands of the malcontents. The threat of fire and other types of vandalism was so real that barn-stored machines were put under armed guard!

Though Horner suffered some setbacks, he continued to build several more harvesters until his departure from California in 1879. What he left behind in that stable yard near Stockton eventually awakened the inventive curiosity from the lowly blacksmith to the most well known farm machinery people in the area. Soon, adaptation of the Horner combined harvester, in one form or another, created a new industry in the Stockton area, producing no fewer than 12 combined harvester companies between 1880 and 1892. Several of them are worthy of a brief history.

In July of 1880, J. S. Kerr of Lockeford completed a mammoth pull machine that reportedly had three sets of fans, the first one of its kind, housed in a 30-foot separator to increase better separating and cleaning. The number of machines built is unknown as they were constructed at his farm. Also in 1880 was the Huffman Harvester. This particular machine was operated by four men, 20 mules, and regularly cut, threshed, and sacked up to 40 acres per day. Huffman's machines were also produced at his farm. Others, such as R. R. Wise and John Mott, were building larger and larger machines in an effort to accommodate

Daniel Best's Field Locomotive.

Awarded FIRST PREMIUM at California State Fair, 1890.

This Cut represents my 30-horse Power Field Locomotive.

Engine, duplex, 5 x 6; drive wheels, 7 feet in diameter; tires, 20 inches in width; and is constructed upon the same principle as the larger size engine, with the exception that the engineer handles the engine from his stand in the center instead of at the rear of the engine, as shown in cut of the larger size. This size engine weighs 6½ tons, and is mounted on springs, making it a fine roadster.

Orders are increasing very fast from small farmers who farm 400 to 1000 acres. This engine, like the larger one, is very easily handled, and is capable of pulling eight to twelve plows or twenty-five to thirty feet of harrows at a speed of three miles per hour, and can be used as a stationary engine if desired, having a fly wheel to belt from, the same as the larger size. There are a number of them at work in different parts of the State, and all are giving entire satisfaction. Address,

DANIEL BEST, San Leandro, Cal.

Best advertised his 30-horsepower Field Locomotive in 1891. The engine weighed 6 1/2 tons and sported drive wheels that were seven feet in diameter. The machine was capable of pulling up to 12 plows or 25 to 30 feet of harrows at three mph.

the ever increasing bonanza wheat ranches in the area. In fact, 18–to–24-foot cuts were pretty much standard in the early 1880s. These "companies" were short-lived, rarely surviving for more than a couple of years, as the larger firms already established in the implement trades had the capital to produce on a larger scale. One such company was started up in 1880 by Daniel Houser.

Between 1880 and 1881, Houser was already experimenting with a combined harvester on the Moss farm outside of Stockton. With a bevy of anxious onlookers, his machine, pulled by 10 horses and operated by three men, successfully harvested an average of 25 acres without a hitch. The following year, Houser opened up his first plant on Center street in Stockton, later setting up shop in a larger factory building at Hazelton and Sacramento streets. The mechanics of the machine were not unlike all that were being produced at the time; the tight-gear driven mechanism from a gear on the main wheel, transferring power by way of a countershaft, then to a cylinder shaft, and then to a separator drive. In 1888, this type of drive was changed to a belt system (an early Holt innovation). In 1886, Houser would sell out to the Shippee Harvester Works, lending his name to several other combine manufacturers that were absorbed by the Stockton Combined Harvester & Agricultural Works. The Houser name would reappear in 1889, as Daniel's son, John, teamed with George Haines to form the Houser-Haines Company, only to again be acquired, this time by the giant Holt Manufacturing Company in 1901.

By 1890, only three major combined harvester companies were standing when the dust settled: the Stockton Combined Harvester & Agricultural Works, Daniel Best Agricultural Works, and Stockton Wheel

Company (Holt). But before the incorporation of Stockton Combined Harvester & Agricultural Works took place, the name Shippee stood alone, and that story deserves some attention.

The Shippee Combined Harvester

The Shippee combined harvester took its name from the enterprising Stockton capitalist, banker, and farmer L. U. Shippee. Recognizing a good thing, Shippee wasted no time jumping on the harvester bandwagon. He started out in 1883 by acquiring the rights to manufacture the "Parish Header and Thrasher" from W. H. Parish of Salem, Oregon. Shippee paid the handsome sum of $20,000 for the Parish. It was money well-spent. The Parish machine's advantages were light weight, low cost, and easy operation as it required only two men and six to eight horses for operation. The machine came in both 10- and 12-foot cuts and weighed a mere 2,400 pounds as opposed to 8,000 pounds, which was normal for other machines. Though not the ideal machine for large bonanza-type ranches, it was a good deal for the smaller farms at half the cost.

Shippee's machine was first demonstrated at the Agricultural Park in the San Joaquin Valley in July 1883. With a crowd of about 100 people in attendance, the Shippee harvester proved to be "entirely satisfactory," and plans were made to produce as many machines possible for that harvest year. Shippee also had a factory location in mind for immediate production of 200 to 300 harvesters for the following year. *The Pacific Rural Press* reported that farmers were "highly elated over the success of the harvester as it is so cheap—costing about $1,000—that any farmer of 160 acres of land can afford to purchase one for his own use."

By 1884, the Stockton Combined Harvester & Agricultural Works was up and running with 140 employees on the factory floor and more to be employed when the

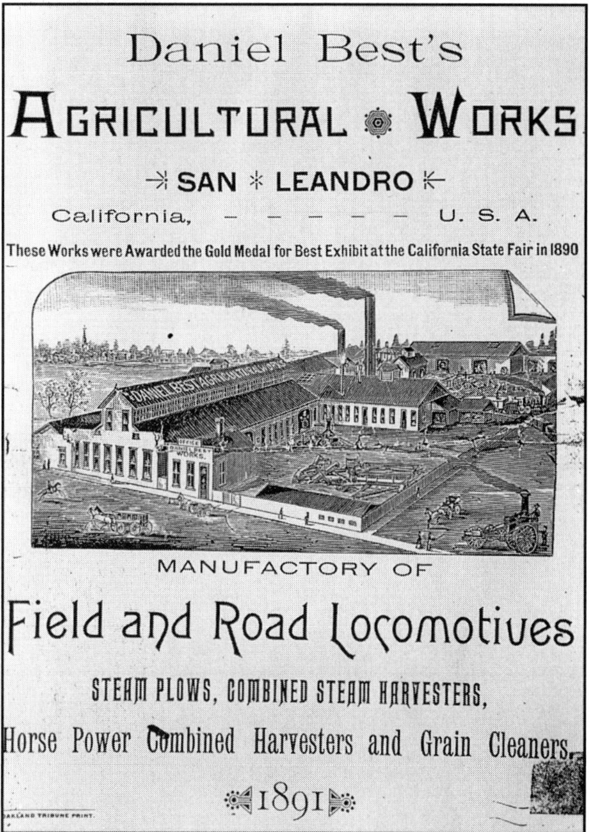

The Best Agricultural Works as it appeared in the early 1890s. Steam plows and harvesters, horse-drawn harvesters and grain cleaners were produced at the San Leandro plant well into the 1900s. After the Holt acquisition in 1908, Best's son C. L. took to manufacturing the steam and later gasoline powered traction machines on his own. C.L. Best and Benjamin Holt would later form the Caterpillar Tractor Company in 1925.

A tractor pulling four John Deere grain binders in Southern California. Note the bundled wheat in the foreground. Oddly enough this team would come together again in the 1930s, when the Caterpillar Company and John Deere entered into a joint tractor dealership scheme. Deere would also be the recipient of the famous Holt 36 hillside harvester, getting Holt out of the harvester business for good. *F. Hal Higgins Collection*

Unfortunately, this scene was one of the downsides of the extreme weight associated with early traction machines. More than a few bridges gave way, giving impetus to the construction of concrete reinforced bridges. This is a gasoline-powered Best machine in the early 1900s. It's not certain whether the structure collapsed while this picture was being taken, but judging from the motion of the people around the front wheel, it must have been darn close. *F. Hal Higgins Collection*

The world's first self-propelled steam harvester developed by George Stockton Berry of Stockton, California, in 1886. The Berry machine had a 22-foot cut that was extended to a 40-foot cut in 1888. The Berry was also the first combine of its kind to use straw for fuel. The machine was capable of harvesting over 50 acres per day. Though innovative, only four of the Harvesters were built and production ceased entirely in 1902. *F. Hal Higgins Collection*

Reportedly the first Holt combined harvester in Adams County, Washington, in 1889. This machine is powered by 33 horses. The header tender is standing on top of the combine. To the right is a good view of the balanced beam behind the header itself, for the purpose of easily raising and lowering the cutting level. The header was also hinged for cutting on uneven terrain. Also shown at the left is the sacker platform. *Ritzville Library Archives*

main building was completed. In no way skimping, Shippee made sure that only the finest wood and iron machinery would be used, enabling literally all parts for the combines to be made on site. The newest building to be completed measured 100x345 feet and three stories. They even had a 160-foot artesian well where water was pumped to elevated tanks for the outbreak of fires.

Shippee was also on his way to cornering the market on patents. In May of 1884 it was reported that the company had purchased all the patent rights of any standing for combined harvesters for manufacture in the state of California. In all, 10 patents were purchased with four more in the bag. This meant that all other manufacturers would have to go through Shippee and submit to their rates for a manufacturing right. All seemed to be going well until the bottom fell out with respect to machine performance. In 1884, 90 machines were built, but only half were sold, and those that were sold performed poorly in the field. Lawsuits were brought against the company for damages in late 1884, with a decision in favor of the plaintiff, John Fox, in 1888.

Best steam harvester in Southern California around 1900. Note the three sections of header. Oddly enough, the smoke stack is without a spark arrester. This could be an early promotional photo; that being the case, the arrester could have been removed to allow a greater amount of smoke to be emitted for photo purposes. Besides, what's that auto doing in the path of the cut anyway? *F. Hal Higgins Collection*

Above is the giant Holt steam harvester outfit in 1900. This particular machine is one of the largest models offered by Holt, as evidenced by the size of the separator. Like the Best machine, the Holt harvester portion of this tandem received its power from flexible pipe that ran from the main boiler. The traction engine is also aided by extension wheels with timbers affixed to help support the main axle. Another feature with the steam engines in wheat country was the spark arrester so noticeable above the canopy of the tractor. You never could be quite sure when or where an errant spark would take off, and the arrester shown in this picture was probably double- or triple-lined for that reason. *F. Hal Higgins Collection*

Since 1886—"HOLT COMBINED HARVESTER"— 40 years

"HOLT" COMBINED Harvester

A Pioneer in 1886, the "HOLT" Combined Harvester has been constantly improved through 40 years' exclusive combine experience.

There is no substitute for experience. Think before you buy—study Combined Harvesters seriously.

Ask us for catalogs and prices

David Hoefel

Ritzville, Washington

A testimony to the longevity of the Holt combine, this ad was taken out of a weekly newspaper in the year 1926, 40 years after Holt introduced his first harvester. Besides the main factory in Stockton, the company would soon branch out with offices in Los Angeles, Walla Walla, Spokane, Portland, and Calgary, Canada.

The monster Holt No. 574 in the 1890s with its record 50-foot cut header, made up from the 26-foot main header and two 12-foot extensions. The harvester is being pulled by a steam traction engine. Note the American flag flying overhead. *F. Hal Higgins Collection*

The Shippee Company continued to manufacture, however, building not only their own machines but adding the Minges in 1885, and purchasing the Houser Harvester Company in 1886. In 1889, combine manufacturing would begin another round of consolidation as Holt bought out the Stockton Shippee interests in 1889, narrowing the field and bringing Holt and Best to the forefront of the industry by 1890. The rest of the California combine story concerns three main companies: Best, Holt, and Harris.

Daniel Best & G. S. Berry: Harvesting With Steam

Daniel Best, inventor and manufacturer, was born March 28 1838 in Crawford County, Ohio. Best spent his early years on the move with the family, living in

A factory photo of an early Holt harvester circa 1888. This looks like one of the small Standards or could even be a "Baby." This was a horse-drawn model, as the drivers platform extends out front. The signature "Link-Chain Drive" is visible in the center of the machine. The turn-table front wheel was another Holt first, enabling easy turning for much better operation. Unfortunately most of the wooden machines are long gone due to the need for iron and steel during World War II. Most machines throughout wheat country were burned for salvaging metal parts. *F. Hal Higgins Collection*

The Holt at the harvest in the Northwest, 1909. Only a small handful of individuals can relate the feeling one gets while operating one of these horse-drawn outfits. Imagine being perched out on that drivers platform, especially in hill country. It has been said that when the harvester is going up a steep grade the drivers only view is the sky above, in many cases not even knowing what direction he is traveling. The opposite effect of being in the bottom of a draw while the horses are ascending a hill is even more spectacular. At this point the driver need only to drop his hand off the side of the platform to pat the head of one of his horses. *Ritzville Library Archives*

Ohio, Iowa, and later in the town of Steptoville, Washington (now Walla Walla). It was in Steptoville that Best started in the lumber trade, later moving on to Portland, Oregon, to continue logging and working in a sawmill. Though he became head sawyer, he soon became restless for a challenge. To quench his thirst for adventure, Best farmed for three years and also worked in the mining trade on the Snake and Powder rivers in the early 1860s. What brought him to California, a trip that would eventually make the Best name synonymous with harvesting and steam power, was to visit his brother Henry.

Here, Best noticed the considerable distance and expense that farmers had to deal with to have their harvested grain recleaned, as many states required the process by law. In 1870, Best had built a portable grain cleaner/separator and secured a patent for it in 1871. He initially set up shop in Marysville, California, and after a brief interlude that took him back to Oregon for almost eight years, returned to operate a grain separator plant in Oakland. Around 1884, Best purchased the San Leandro Plow Works, renaming it the Daniel Best Agricultural Works.

The grain cleaning machine story is something of legend, told and retold concerning the lack of space in

A similar factory photo taken in the late 1880s. Though these models enjoyed their greatest success in California and the Pacific Northwest, the Holt Company also shipped to Kansas, Seville, Spain, Bozeman, Montana, Mexico, and Argentina. *F. Hal Higgins Collection*

A Holt level-land model powered by 24 mules in the early 1900s. The canopies seen on most of the very early machines were homemade. This helped a little bit to block out a searing sun that could send temperatures into the triple digits. However, dust and chaff was a different story. One has to live in wheat country to appreciate the closed, air-conditioned cabs of the modern combine. Open conditions while harvesting could be murder; a literal hell on earth, but harvest they did. *Ritzville Library Archives*

Harvesting near Lind, Washington, in 1916. Literally reams of harness, rein, collars, and hames were employed to keep the animals in line and insure that the load they were pulling was shared equally. Eveners, double-trees, and triple-trees were one thing, but not until the Shandoney hitch was introduced did the aligning of animals and weight distribution become an art. The Shandoney was a clover leaf type hitch that was situated in a way that even the smallest of horses could pull his weight in relation to his size while not over burdening the other horses. *Ritzville Library Archives*

one particular building Best had at the time. Apparently he had so many grain cleaning machines that he had to store them on the city streets, prompting local police to step in and ask that they be removed. This is when Best made the move to San Leandro and also the time period that he began to seriously experiment with the combined harvester. His first combine was probably built around 1884, was sold in 1885, and by 1886, he had over a dozen in the field. There was nothing especially unique about these harvesters as basic principles for motive power still persisted with a tight-gear design. In addition to the horse-drawn harvesters, Best also produced disc plows, mowers, reapers, and binders. But his passion would be the successful operation of the steam-powered harvester, which by 1889, became a reality.

Auxiliary steam power for the combined harvester actually pre-dates the Best with respect to threshing and separating. The "Pritchard Combined Steam Harvester," built by B. F. Pritchard of Oakland, California, in 1885 was successfully tested on the farm of Joe S. Gibsot of Colusa, Colorado, in June of the same year. The machine harvested 18 acres, being cut, threshed, cleaned, and sacked in six hours. One barrel of crude petroleum was sufficient to run a whole day. As the *Pacific Rural Press* reported, "The boiler is made with return flues, and so constructed as to burn oil or straw; the engine and boiler is 15 horsepower, and made very light for this combination." The machine was pulled by ten mules.

One of the advantages of auxiliary power for threshing and separating is that no matter how fast the horses are traveling, the threshing stays at a constant speed, unlike machines powered by a ground wheel. Whether on uneven ground, turning corners, or getting a wheel stuck momentarily, the threshing process could go on uninterrupted. The Pritchard machine cut an average of 25

At least three early Holts harvesting the Northwest in 1908. Massive horsepower was needed for the larger operations as anywhere from 24 to 40 horses and mules were employed. There was a story going around at one time that the large fields of California were so large that one could start harvesting a row in the morning and not finish that same row until sundown. The harvesters would then bed down and start the second row in the morning and on and on. Maybe a stretch of the imagination, but you never know. *Courtesy of Marciel Cronrath*

This early Holt has stopped momentarily for the camera in the fields of Eastern Washington. The driver is on the platform, the duo under the top canopy are the mechanic and the header tender; those four off to the right are sack sewers and baggers. Note the slanted sack ramp used for "windrowing" bagged grain for later pick-up. *Ritzville Library Archives*

acres a day, but the larger machine with a 16-foot cut could do 40 acres a day.

Though auxiliary power would see widespread use, Dan Best wanted to take the harvest process one step further; a steam traction engine supplying power to the harvester and eliminating animal power altogether! In 1889, Best designed and developed the first successful steam tractor of ample power for drawbar work. According to the records, Best sold his first tractor in 1889 and developed the first steam-powered combined harvester at about the same time.

The two chief components of the combined harvester were the traction engine, which gave the motive power to the whole outfit, and the harvester's cutting and cleaning mechanisms that were operated by an auxiliary engine. The auxiliary motor took its steam from the main boiler by way of a flexible pipe. This design made the harvester portion of the team independent as the speed of locomotion had nothing to do with separation. The first engine Best used was patented by D. L. Remington of Oregon and as time went on, Best included important patents of his own.

By far the most important part of the machine was the boiler. The engines were made almost entirely of steel; the upright body measured four feet in diameter and housed 160 two-inch flues, five feet long. The horizontal firebox was 6 1/2 feet long, 44 inches wide, and 36 inches high. Another important feature, which by the way is similar to modern EPA-approved wood burning stoves, was the combustion chamber. Here the smoke was burned and cinders and sparks caught, making boiler operation much safer. The problem of weight displacement was also solved with the Best design. In his model, the vertical boiler was placed upon the axles and between the two eight-foot–in–diameter drive wheels. The power was applied directly to the rims that contained segments of cogs. This meant that "grabbing" power was increased with the increase of load, and the added differential gearing insured better traction as well as sharper turning. Turning the "square" corner was a piece of cake. The machine fully loaded with water weighed 11 tons!

Obviously this type of outfit must have been something to see let alone operate. The shear size alone caused a look of amazement where ever it traveled, engaging even the most hardened of equipment operators. One May morning in 1889, a couple of writers from the *San Leandro Reporter* ventured out to the Henry Best Ranch to watch the "beast" in action. They logged this report:

"The floor of the pilot-house is about seven feet from the ground, thus raising the eye of the pilot or engineer from 12 to 13 feet high, giving him the most complete view of the surroundings. It takes five men to manage the monster—two with the engine, a sack sewer, one to manage the lever by which the cut is regulated, and one who is loose to oversee the machinery. One man and a team are required to draw wood and water. The water wagon is driven alongside, and the huge roadster, like an elephant, drops his trunk (hose) into the tank and fills his own reservoir therefrom while moving at the rate of three miles an hour. Cottonwood was being used for fuel. ."

When Holt shipped a machine it came with explicit instructions so—hopefully—the new owner wouldn't screw anything up. Besides oiling and greasing, another important part of operation was getting the horses used to the machine. In Holt's 1912 catalog, the owner was urged to start with as few animals as possible. The reason being that if the horses bolted at start up, the driver would have an easier time controlling the team. Holt also urged his new owners to come up to full operation in steps so as to get the animals accustomed to the noise. The initial clutch to be "thrown in" operated the header, shoe, cleaner, grain carrier, and pickers. Once the animals were used to that level of noise, then the main clutch could be thrown engaging the cylinder, feeder, and beaters. A process that usually took up to an hour could mean the difference between a pleasant harvest or a brand new Holt in pieces all over the field. *Ritzville Library Archives*

The Holt combine with an auxiliary four-cylinder engine in 1915. The auxiliary engine replaced the need for a ground wheel. Though horses and later the tractor was still needed for actually pulling the combine, the auxiliary engine drove the cylinder and separator. Holt first produced the auxiliary-powered combine in 1904, with the motor mounted in front of the machine. *Courtesy of Harold Wegner*

The Caterpillar 75 pulling a Holt combine with auxiliary engine in 1919. Holt's greatest success was in the West because of the soft soils. Just about everyone, even today, owns and operates the track-laying type "Cat" in the western wheat fields. The 75 pictured above weighed nearly 24,000 pounds, was eight feet wide and nearly 20 feet long. *Courtesy of Harold Wegner*

With reviews like this, the Best machines had no trouble at all finding a following for their use. Out of 28 harvesters constructed, all but six were sold for the 1889 harvest year. By 1892, orders for the new traction engines were coming in on a daily basis from all over the state, with 40 combined harvesters being made for that year, the largest number in history. An increase in the horse-powered combines was steady as well, with over 70 men employed and more applications being sought all the time. By the end of 1892, payrolls had climbed to over $6,000 a month.

In addition to the California trade, Best was receiving orders for traction engines and harvesters from all over the place. Eastern Oregon had requested a "load" of harvesters while Denver, Colorado, was practically begging for the traction engines to power ore wagons. In 1897, two traction engines were sent to the interior of China, with other orders coming in from Salt Lake, St. Louis, and Arizona. The Best Works became second only to the Union Iron Works of San Francisco in terms of total capacity.

By 1896, the inventor's son and future president of the Caterpillar Company, C. L. Best, became involved in the combined harvester business until the rights, patents, and business interests were sold to the Holt Manufacturing Company in 1908. Thus ended another chapter in the combined harvester trade in California. With Best now out of the combine game, Ben Holt of Stockton would assume the enviable position of dominating the combined harvester market for almost 40 years. Though Holt would make his mark with regard to steam and gasoline-powered harvesters, one would be remiss not to mention the inventor of the first self-propelled steam combine, G. S. Berry.

George Stockton Berry of Visalia, California, is credited with building and operating the first steam self-propelled combine in 1887. Originally cutting a 22-foot swath, Berry had increased the capacity to 40 feet in 1888. The traction wheels measured five feet in diameter, with a 25-horsepower Mitchell-Fisher engine placed directly over the wheels. Like the Remington-Best design, the wheels carried the greatest weight but did not bog down. This main engine furnished the motive power and operated the header, where the smaller Nagle engine drove the separator. Both engines received steam from the same boiler. This particular machine utilized straw for fuel. When the straw was separated from the chaff and grain, it passed through a chute and on to a platform near the furnace, where it could be readily shoveled into the firebox.

It took seven men to operate this gargantuan enterprise, including one to haul water and another to gather sacks of grain that were dumped on the field. The Berry machine would cut anywhere from 90 to 100 acres per day. In the words of one who recorded such a day: "it may enter a wheat-field of 100 acres in the morning and at night have all the wheat produced by it in sacks and piled snugly together."

Obviously this machine was designed for the big bonanza ranches that were so prolific in the 1870s and 1880s. By the mid to late 1890s, however, the reduction of such large ranches was the norm as wheat became less of a cash crop. Berry only built four machines that were manufactured by the Benicia Agricultural Works at a cost of almost $7,000. Shortly after the turn of the century production had ceased.

King Combine: The Holt Manufacturing Company

Born January 1, 1849, in New Louden, New Hampshire, Benjamin Holt was an experienced woodworker

In the mid-1910s, the gasoline-powered traction machine began to replace the horse for pulling the combine. Above is a Holt Caterpillar pulling a Holt combined harvester in the Washington wheat belt. *Ritzville Library Archives*

early in life. The seventh child of William Knox Holt and Harriet Parker Ames, Ben was schooled much like anyone else at the time, learning the three "R's," then joining the family business. In Holt's case, this was his father's hardwood lumber mill located in New Louden, where his skills were honed from 1865 to 1875. Shortly after 1875, his father moved the business to Concord, which was a transportation center at the time and a good place to manufacture and market wagon wheels, buggies, sleighs, and a variety of other items. Though the Holt Brothers Company of Concord would enjoy a successful run from the late 1870s to 1945, four of the eldest brothers decided to leave the lucrative business early on and travel to California.

Close-up view of the Holt 75. They sure don't make them like they used to. Note the decorative awnings and flags on the canopy. *Ritzville Library Archives*

It was in 1865 that elder brother Charles Holt opened up C. H. Holt & Company on Beale street in San Francisco. From this business, Charles imported and sold fine lumber for stage coaches, boats, and wagons, much of it being purchased from his father's mill in Concord. The Holt California company was truly a success. But what of Benjamin?

According to Holt biographer Reynold M. Wik, it took almost 20 years after Charles had started the San Francisco business for Ben Holt to come West. Traveling on the newly completed transcontinental railroad, Benjamin finally met up with his brothers and decided that he, in cooperation with Charles, would open a wheel company in Stockton, a growing community on the fringe of California's soon to be agricultural dynasty.

Holt knew a good thing when he saw it. The boom days of the bonanza ranches in California in the 1870s and 1880s meant that agricultural technology would out of necessity take center stage. The establishment of the Stockton Wheel Company in 1883 was not just another lumber and wagon shop, but the beginning of a shift in agricultural mechanization. Holt was well aware of the experiments of Shippee, Myers, Powell, and Matteson & Williamson with regard to the combined harvester. In fact, two years after the establishment of the Stockton Wheel Company, Benjamin Holt built his own combined harvester.

In 1885, the Stockton Wheel Company began experimenting with the combine. Right off the bat they went against the grain by toying with the idea of changing the standard method of motive power. Virtually all combined harvester manufacturers at the time were using the tight gear

Holt's wheel-type Steamer No. 77 in 1903. Machines similar to this one helped clear away the rubble after the devastating San Francisco Earthquake in 1906. The 77 was a good all around heavy construction traction machine and was later used to lay cable for San Francisco's cable car system in 1900. In 1904, the 77's wheels were replaced with tracks. *Caterpillar Company Archives*

This huge Holt steam traction machine was important in furthering mechanized agriculture in the state of California. Machines like these, however, were not cheap, costing between $4,500 and $5,500. In reality, the vast majority of farmers at the end of the 19th century still relied on horses and mules for power farming. The photo above shows the Holt during tillage operations in central California. *Caterpillar Company Archives*

method of transferring power from the ground wheel to the separator and so on. Knowing that the tight gear method was clumsy and noisy, Holt was the first to use the link chain and V-belt method, and it became the industry standard.

With a large ring sprocket bolted to the main wheel, the link belt from there ran to the main countershaft and then to the cylinder countershaft that was fitted with a 44-inch v-pulley. The V-belts consisted of a three-ply riveted leather belt two inches wide, which was tapered to fit the v-shaped pulley. According to Thomas Luke, a contemporary in the combine industry for over 40 years, "the V-belt was gradually done away with and a band was shrunk over the v-pulleys, changing from V to flat belt for cylinder drive." By 1890, the flat belt was adopted by all manufacturers. Holt had also put a ring sprocket on the right hand wheel to power the header only.

This wasn't Holt's only first in combined harvesters; the hinged header added flexibility. Coupling the header by hinges to the separator allowed for closer cutting by the sickle bar and easier raising and lowering of the header. With the aid of weights for balancing movement by a header wheel (instead of a lever), the header operator could be placed upon a platform to observe cutting performance and make adjustments as necessary. Previous designs placed the header tender behind the separator, where the person was unable to get a full view of the cut and steer clear of obstacles. The header raising wheel was incorporated in 1887.

By 1892 the Stockton Wheel Company was incorporated as the Holt Manufacturing Company, taking most of the competition with them. Just about all the companies producing combined harvesters between 1882 and 1892 had been absorbed by Holt, with the exception of the Best line, which stood alone until 1908. Holt continued to advance the technology of the combine, possibly doing more for the industry than anyone else. The list of firsts are quite impressive:

- Development of Link-Chain V-Belt drive (1885)
- First to adapt hinged header (1885)
- First to use single front wheel with turn-table (1886)
- Improved sack hook and header-raising wheel (1887)
- Improved sheet steel separator shoe (1894)
- First to implement double drive (grain wheel-assisted separator drive) (1892)

Pictured above is Holt's steam powered crawler, the No. 122, produced in 1908. Interestingly enough, Holt bought back the machines that were resold to area concerns. *Caterpillar Company Archives*

• Widest cut from harvester #574, 50-foot cut and 150 acres per day (1893)
• First to introduce side-hill harvesters (1891)
• First to implement steel wheel frames on side-hill machines (1898)
• First auxiliary gasoline engine used (1904)
• First self-propelled harvester introduced (1911)
• First all-steel harvesters constructed (1913)

It's quite possible that the development of the side-hill harvester was one of Holt's greatest achievements (the track-laying tractor being the other). While the wheat boom was beginning to fade in the Central Valley of California during the 1890s, the Pacific Northwest was just getting started as an important wheat region. One of the most fertile areas for wheat production was the Palouse region of Eastern Washington. The problem, however, was that much of the region had steep hillsides, some with slopes up to 60 percent, and harvesting with anything other than the old style header was unthinkable. Although Holt initially developed the side-hill for the hilly terrain around Oakdale, California, the Northwest was clearly the market of the future.

The problem with trying to operate the standard combined harvester on hillsides was obvious; without being able to level the separator portion of the harvester to the incline of the hillside the cut grain would fall to one side, bunch up and fail to be properly threshed and separated. To remedy this Holt came up the idea for an auxiliary frame. This frame was positioned inside the main frame that supports the driving wheels, allowing the separator to be carried level to any degree of elevation. It worked horizontally on two upright racks and pinions, enabling one wheel to be raised while the other was lowered.

The Holt side-hill machines were an instant success in Washington, Oregon, Idaho, and Montana, as well as in California. According to an article in the *California Farmer* dated May 15, 1954, Holt had even visited Russia to determine the potential of the market in that country.

One of the first tractors to be completed at the East Peoria plant. This particular machine had an "A" frame that came to a point at the tiller wheels in front, the only model to feature this design. *Caterpillar Company Archives*

An interesting side note to the hillside combine is that of Franklin S. Holly, a native Vermonter and Civil War veteran, who patented his own combine leveling device in 1904. One-time Holt office manager "Ollie" Eccleston related that the Holt Brothers paid Holly royalties on, "all Holly combines built by Holts for the hill country of California and the Northwest." In fact, if you look real close at some of the early Holt field scenes, you can see the Holly name on the canvas housing at the rear of the machine. Holts built the Holly combine for 20 years.

Though Holt had also produced steam harvester outfits, the push for gasoline auxiliary power welled to the forefront in the early 1910s. In fact, up until 1915, just about two-thirds of all combines produced were ground-driven. But, as the *Caterpillar Times* boasted in that same year, more than two-thirds of the Holt harvesters being produced were equipped with auxiliary engines. Essentially, the gasoline engines was more efficient and cheaper to run, requiring up to 40 percent fewer horses. The threshing and separating process as well was more even and prevented further grain loss. But probably the greatest advantage was the ability to harvest downed (lodged) grain. With auxiliary power, the harvester could stop in heavy stands without the worry of straw choking. The engine would continue to run and thresh out on an even keel.

The final triumph in motive power for Holt was the introduction of the self-propelled gasoline-powered combine in 1911. According to Tom Luke, large numbers of self-propelled combines were built in both the prairie and side-hill models. The self-propelled was introduced in the Northwest in 1912 and into Kansas in 1918. Though a proven machine, the self-propelled caught on slow especially in the Pacific Northwest because it was still more economical to employ the crawler tractor for pulling sidehills up until around 1930.

Holt gained a virtual monopoly in the combine industry with the acquisition of the Best Manufacturing Company in 1908, but didn't stop there. A branch factory

Another view of the Holt steamer, this time in South Africa. It appears that the machine may be taking on water out of the creek. Note the man in front with the hose. Behind is a wagon loaded with rock. *Caterpillar Company Archives*

An act that might be considered blasphemy to some is this photo of a McCormick-Deering crawler tractor pulling a medium hillside Holt combine. This photo illustrates the leveling action of the machine. Note the wheel on the outside being raised by way of the screw-type mechanism located near the exhaust of the auxiliary engine. This was accomplished by using a swing wheel frame within the main frame. The wooden Holt sign in the center of the photo is quite unusual and is probably being used for promotional purposes. *Ritzville Library Archives*

Looking like something out a futuristic motion picture comes this Holt self-propelled combine at the Wegner Ranch in 1917. This is the hillside model, first built in 1911. Large numbers of the self-propelled were built but the machine was clearly ahead of its time. Most farmers stuck with the pull-type. These machines were introduced in the Northwest in 1912 and into Kansas in 1918. *Courtesy of Harold Wegner*

was acquired in Walla Walla, Washington, in 1902, a branch office in Spokane in 1908, and a Northern Holt company in Minneapolis in 1909. Holt also incorporated the Aurora Engine Company in 1906 for the production of gasoline motors. This was followed by a Peoria factory in 1910 and the Canadian Holt Company LTD of Calgary, Alberta, in 1914.

Beyond the Holt combined harvester story is the organization of the Caterpillar Tractor Company in 1925. Besides the combine business Holt was also developing the track-layer tractor, some say, because of the soil, topography, and large acreage on the Pacific Coast. He would build and test his first steam-powered machine in 1890 and, later in 1904, demonstrated an improved version utilizing three clutches; one master clutch and two track clutches for pivoting. With only eight steam track-layers produced, he was already making the transformation to gasoline power, the first being manufactured in 1906.

The combine became a sideline to Holt in the true sense of the word, as his preoccupation with crawler tractors and heavy equipment dominated his priorities. The

Another view of the medium hillside machine with the screw-type leveler seen at the far right, extending from the top of the triangular wheel housing. This is probably a Model 36, the same model that was acquired by Deere & Company in 1935. By this time all-steel construction had replaced the wooden separator bodies, a switch that actually took place in 1913. Note the grain elevator and spout to the waiting sack on the bagging platform. The Holt is being pulled by a McCormick-Deering T-40 TracTracTor. *Ritzville Library Archives*

The end of an era. This is the medium hillside Model 36. The 36 was probably one of the most famous combines ever made and without doubt the longest running model ever made. Holt (Caterpillar) was finally out of the combine business but was well aware that its legacy would be passed on to a company that was, in its own right, a symbol of excellence in agricultural America. *F. Hal Higgins Collection*

The Harris side-hill near Ritzville, Washington, in 1930. The Harris machines were quite popular in the Northwest, and many can still be found on abandoned homesteads throughout the region. The Harris Manufacturing Company was founded in 1904 and initially rebuilt machines to their own style; only later in the teens did they create a combine that could be distinguished from all others. The side-hill like the one in the photo was truly their bread and butter. *Ritzville Library Archives*

The Harris pictured here was originally a ground-powered machine. This particular machine was modified with an auxiliary engine added, and a bulk tank replaced the sacking mechanism. You can see the radiator and exhaust pipe next to the bulk tank. When Harris finally did come out with an auxiliary engine, it was located in the usual position, behind and above the front wheel. *Ritzville Library Archives*

building of tractors was undertaken at both the Peoria and Stockton plants while the Western Harvester Works in Stockton and the Northwest Harvester Works in Walla Walla produced the combined harvesters. By 1935, the Holt/Caterpillar Company got out of the combine business for good selling its side-hill, the famous model 36, to Deere & Company.

Caterpillar literally gave the hillside combine to Deere, lock, stock, and barrel. As early as 1926, Caterpillar had approached Deere with an offer to sell the harvester business for a reported $1. 2 million. The combine business had been generally restricted to the West coast and Pacific Northwest, with efforts to expand in the Midwest not very likely. Besides, according to Deere historian Wayne Broehl, the harvester line was "actually getting in the way of their aggressive moves into the industrial construction and road-maintenance areas." At the time the deal was struck, Caterpillar was producing two level-land and the hillside versions. Deere, who was lacking a hillside in their line, would now be in a good position to take advantage of the lucrative Northwest market.

With the hillside model gone to Deere and the remaining level-land machines discontinued, Holt-Caterpillar was finally out of the combine business. By 1935, the Midwest had finally begun to accept the combine,

A loaded Harris hillside combine ready for delivery by the Farrier Springs Transfer Company in the early 1930s. Note the leveling mechanism and hinged frame on the ground wheel. The unit was operable on either side of the machine, using these racks for raising and lowering. The header is being pulled on the trailer behind. There is only one totally restored wooden machine around these parts that I know of, and it is quite spectacular to stand next one of these giants as they run about 11 feet from the ground to the top of the leveler's platform. In fact, the feeder house is so big that the average person could stretch out and use it for a bed. *Ritzville Library Archives*

The lone Harris unloading grain from the bulk tank into a waiting truck. This outfit is powered by 15 horses. With the sacking platform removed, the truck could easily back-up under the spout from the bulk tank. You may also notice the reduction in manpower when harvesting with the bulk method. Pictured is the driver, header tender, and truck driver. The truck will most likely unload the grain at a nearby elevator and return to take on more grain. This scene was captured around 1930. *Ritzville Library Archives*

Two auxiliary-powered Harris combines in the Pacific Northwest. The gas auxiliary machine was introduced in 1912. At that time, the level-land model with 10-foot cut and four-cylinder 45-horsepower engine could be had for around $5,000. The "Harris Gas Side-Hill Combined Harvester" with a 14-foot cut ran for just over $3,700. *Ritzville Library Archives*

with eastern old line companies supplying the demand once held exclusively by the Californians. Besides, John Deere, International Harvester, Allis-Chalmers, J. I. Case, Rumely, Gleaner, and later Massey-Harris, would all build a combine or two. But the California legacy would not end with Holt. One last company held out well into the 1950s, producing both level-land and hillside models, mostly for the Pacific Northwest.

Last of the Californians: The Harris Combine

Seven years after Holt bought out the Matteson & Williamson Company, former manager George H. Harris decided to strike out on his own. In 1902, Harris opened up a small factory at Park and Ophir streets in Stockton for the purpose of converting combines to the Harris type. By 1904, Harris had an associate from none other than the Holt Manufacturing Company, Chas. Cullums, and together they would form the Harris Manufacturing Company. They continued to restyle harvesters, while also building new models from the ground up.

A closer look at the "bulking" of grain. The off-loading spout could be swung out from the side of the combine by the cables running from the tip of the spout to the machine. The combine unloading in this picture could be either a Deere or Holt machine, a medium hillside, because of the out of focus "screw" pictured along the left-hand side of the photo. This was part of the leveling device. *Ritzville Library Archives*

A level-land Harris being pulled by a diesel McCormick-Deering TD-35 TracTracTor. You might notice that these machines were still being made primarily of wood. Harris did not change from wood to all steel construction until after WWII. There's no real rhyme or reason to it, that's just the way Harris wanted it. This particular machine's separator is being powered by an engine. Posing on the combine is the mechanic and the header tender. *Ritzville Library Archives*

A close-up view of a Harris on the Dugger Farm outside of Ritzville, Washington. This was a hillside model as the hinged frame can be seen running from the center of the ground-wheel to where the ladder is attached. Also still visible are the drive chains with nearly all the sprockets intact. One feature unique to the early Harris machine was the use of three separator fans, one of the first companies to employ them.

This is the Harris Model 30-38, the last pull-type model made before Harris entered the self-propelled market. This is the hillside combine operating in the 1940s. Note the "ladder" type racks on each side of the machine to enable leveling the separator body. Harris veteran owner-operator Walt Nissan of Adams Company, Washington, still misses the harvest with his giant twin bulk-tank Harris. The machine still sits outside of town in almost operable condition. *Ritzville Library Archives*

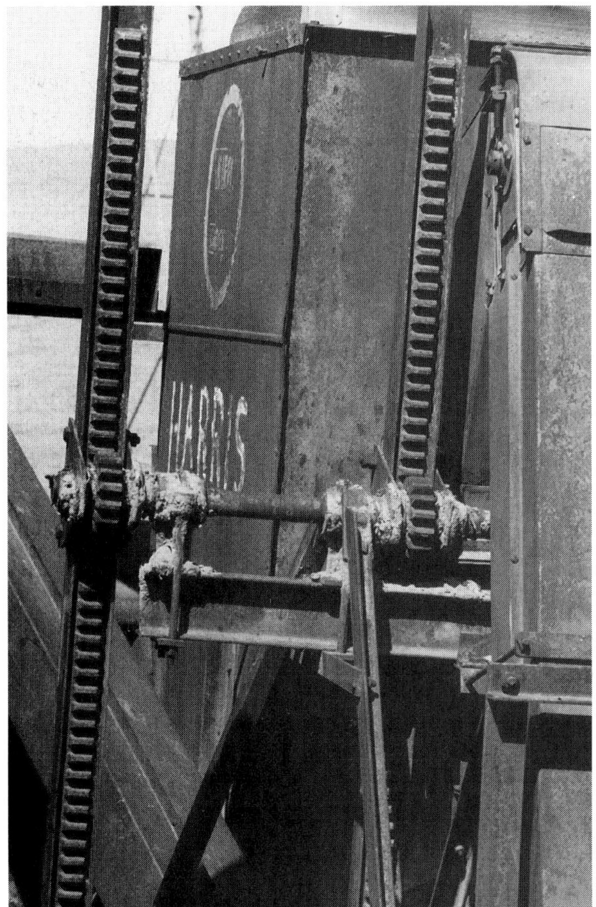

Close-up view of the 30-38's rack-type leveler. Both rack assemblies had a lever to control the raising and lowering of the separator body, as well as a foot pedal braking system for each side.

The Harris hillside model was extremely popular in the Pacific Northwest. In fact, it's not very hard to find one even today, abandoned in the numerous dry coulees throughout eastern Washington. Most are of the steel frame type that were introduced after 1945, although I do know where a wooden frame machine is (many of the wooden frame machines were burned for metal salvage during World War II). By 1912, Harris offered three different model combines; a ten-foot Standard pull-type with a four-cylinder 45 horsepower engine; a 24-foot Standard with a four-cylinder 55 horsepower engine, and the Harris "Gas Sidehill Combined Harvester" with a 14- and 18-foot cut. Separator sizes ranged from 26 to 54.5 inches.

One of the most popular Harris models was the 30-38 hillside produced in 1937. The 30-38 had a 30-inch spiked tooth cylinder and featured three separator fans. The separator was of the raddle type and had fore and aft pendulum leveling. An operator platform was placed on top of the separator almost directly over the cylinder. From here, the lateral leveling of the machine was operated by two levers, one for each side, with foot pedals for brakes. With a seat provided for the operator, he had a bird's-eye view encompassing at least 180 degrees. The leveling mechanism on the 30-38 was attached to the main frame and featured racks on both sides of the machine for raising and lowering. The leveling "A" frame was hinged at the rear of the main frame. The 30-38 came with rubber tires, the Hercules gas-powered auxiliary engine, a turntable type front wheel, and straw spreaders at the rear of the separator housing.

Though the decade of the 1930s was considered the heyday for pull-type combines, the 1940s was a different story. The production of hillside models had stopped due to World War II. In fact, the last pull-type combine built

At left is the Harris Model 88. As early as 1946, the company had been experimenting with a self-propelled, along with just about everyone else in the business. Harris had put 10 pre-production self-propelled models in the Northwest in 1950 and continued production with several hundred more until 1953 when the company went out of business. This particular combine was operating around Reardan, Washington, at the Wegner Ranch in 1957. *Courtesy of Harold Wegner*

The leveler operator had his own seat on top of the separator body along with two levers and two brake pedals. The photo above shows the rear of the right side leveling rack, the operator's seat, and a partial view of the foot pedals. The hand operated levers have since been removed. The bulk tank sits in front of the operator's seat.

The Harris 88 and, later, the 98 pictured above, was manufactured first by the Harvesters-Implements Company of Fresno, California, and later by the Case Company from 1959–64. Case decided not to renew the production contract, and the machine was discontinued for good. The photo above was taken at harvest in 1976. The machine operated with a 38-inch separator, and contrary to the industry's shift to rasp bars, the Harris stuck with the spike-tooth cylinder. *Courtesy of Harold Wegner*

When a farmer suffered from acute illness at harvest time, the neighbors would combine forces and help out the family in need. This is a scene that wasn't all to uncommon. Above shows the numerous machines involved; some Harris, a few Deere, and even some IH were showing their stuff in the wheat belt of eastern Washington. Note the towering grain elevators in the background. *Ritzville Library Archives*

was the Case V2. By war's end, the Harris Company, among others, began experimenting with the self-propelled combine. Ten Harris pre-production models were put in the Pacific region in 1950, a number that swelled to 150 in 1951 and 225 in 1953. The Harris 88, as it was called, featured an advanced hydraulic control system along with the normal Harris innovations, with the larger Model 98 in the field by 1959.

The Harris self-propelled 98 came equipped with a 16 1/2-, 18 1/2-, or 20 1/2-inch header. The powerplant was the Hercules six-cylinder, gas or diesel, 339-cubic-inch engine. The leveling mechanism was of the automatic controlled hydraulic type; cylinder was the tapered spike, V-belt driven with a speed range of 650-1100 rpm. Harris also stuck pretty much to the raddle type thresher.

But the self-propelled combine market was extremely competitive, causing the original Harris company to close its doors in 1956. Shortly after this date, the company was purchased by Harvester-Implements Inc. of Fresno, California, where the Model 908 was produced in 1962. The J. I. Case Company marketed the Harris 98 in an arrangement with Harvesters-Implements in 1959 and continued to do so until 1964, opting not to renew the contract. It was also in 1964 that the Mathews Company of Crystal Lake, Illinois, purchased the rights for the Harris from Harvester-Implements and continued production into

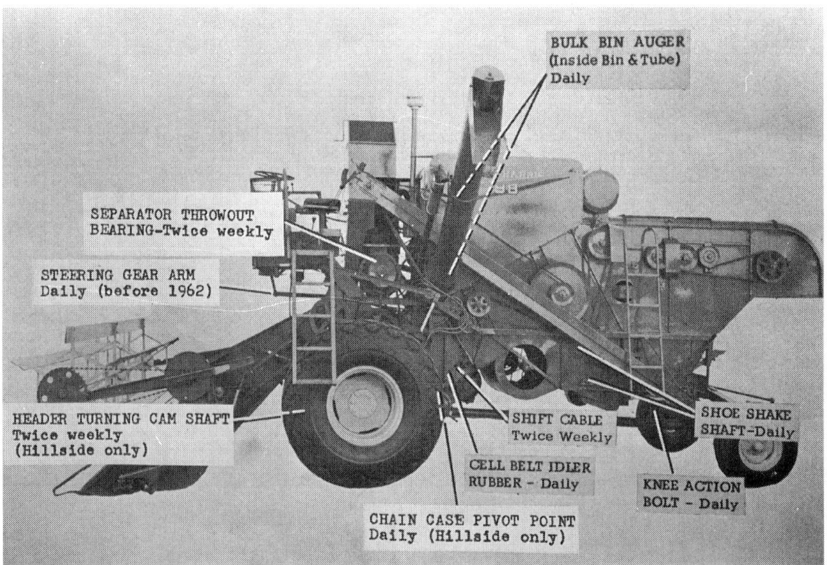

View of the left side of the 98 from the operators manual.

1967, with 50 machines produced in Fresno. Shortly thereafter, the Harris combines were discontinued.

The end of the Harris Company was the end of the California combine industry. Combine manufacturing would become an Eastern concern, serving not only the West and Pacific Northwest, but also the newly opened humid Plains regions. New information and technologies, state and federal investigations, and manufacturers who were listening to potential customers created a new domain to be conquered by the once forbidden machine from the West.

Small Companies In the Northwest

By 1889, California's combines began to find their way into the Big Bend region of Eastern Washington state.

Three-quarter front view of the 98 from sales brochure. Note the peaked radiator screen above the drivers platform.

From the 98 operator's manual is this up-front view of the spike-tooth cylinder that was to be a part of the Harris machines for over twenty-five years.

The Dunning-Erich Harvester circa 1912 in the field being powered by 33 mules. The Harrington took its name from the town where it was produced from 1915 to 1923. The machine above is the early ground driven model. None of these machines exist today, not even in a museum. However, one individual does have the only auxiliary engine in existence. *Courtesy of Marciel Cronrath*

Though not of the bonanza type farms of California, many ranches in and around the region could exceed 2,000 acres. In fact, the town of Ritzville briefly had the distinction of being the "greatest primary shipping wheat point in the world, shipping over 2 million bushels of wheat per year." With generally flat terrain, although 30 percent slopes were not unheard of, the region was well suited for the combined harvester.

Holts and Housers were found in this region as early as 1889. As usual, these monster wood-framed harvesters were met with amazement, prompting tourists to venture out to a farm and watch as 24 to 36 horses and mules hauled around equipment the size of a small home through the dead ripe grain. One such "tourist" was an editor of the *Harrington Citizen* , who in 1899 described his experience aboard a Holt Standard:

"The grain is headed, threshed, and sacked by a combination which does the work in a smooth, clean, and expeditious manner. The combination machine weighs 11 tons, is drawn by 32 horses in five rows six

The Gordon & Troop Draper Factory housed the Dunnong-Erich Harvester Company from 1905 to 1915. Notice the steam engine on the far right. This was probably used to power various types of machinery for the factory. In the center of the photo in the foreground is where finished headers were stored, later to be affixed to the harvesters. *Courtesy of Marciel Cronrath*

A rare look at the inside of the Dunning-Erich Harvester Company in around 1910. Pictured in the center is a Blewett Harvester and at right the Harrington. The Harrington Company not only built their own machine, but also, according to local historians, manufactured some components for the Holt machines. There is no information on the Blewett Harvester. *Courtesy of Marciel Cronrath*

Another view of the Harrington in the assembly stage. You will notice that the header wheel appears to be located at the rear of the separator housing. Don't be deceived, as the wheel is actually part of another harvester directly behind it. You'll also notice that the motive power on the Harrington was transferred from the bull wheel by the Link-Chain method pioneered by the Holt people 30 years before. The view of this picture shows the header side of the combine. *Courtesy of Marciel Cronrath*

abreast and two leaders. The two leaders alone have reins to guide them, the rest follow with military precision. The big wheels of the side-hill are so adjusted that the frame remains level while the machine is working on a side hill. The machine man attends to this feature, raising and lowering a wheel as the ground justifies and the header by another contrivance, raising and lowering the sickle to accommodate the blades to uneven ground."

It wasn't long before ambitious farmers of the area were sounding the death knell of the header and thresher machine and trumpeting the arrival of a new era in harvesting. California transplants to the Big Bend region like J. F. Green, an experienced combine operator from the California Land and Livestock Company Ranch, thrilled the locals with unheard of records of 750 sacks of barley harvested in one day. Large local farmers such as J. A. Talkington of Harrington reported in 1907 that with "20 to 30 combines in the famous wheat belt this season," the thresher in a few years would become a mere curiosity. Even M. A. Carter, resident agent for the Houser-Haines company, believed that in just a few short years, "the farmers of Adams County will use nothing else but the combine." Obviously, the thresher would enjoy close to another 50 years of use on the American farm, but the combine had definitely made inroads in a surprising way.

California manufacturers were not to be the only ones in the business of making combined harvesters. In the early 1910s, several Pacific Northwest harvester companies began to appear, one from the town of Harrington, Washington, and two others from the Palouse region of Moscow, Idaho. These particular companies didn't last for very long, but their impact on the regions they served helped to increase the acceptance and use of the combine.

The Harrington Harvester

In April of 1908, Lewis A. Dunning and Charles A. Erich formed the Dunning and Erich Harvester Company in the small eastern Washington town of Harrington. With an initial start-up of $800 and "one lathe, a drill, and some wood and blacksmith tools," the two harvester men immediately bought up the old Gordon & Throop draper factory building in 1909 and began experimenting with what would soon be known as the "Harrington" harvester.

These Harrington factory workers are posing on the railroad loading dock behind the Harrington works, probably sometime between 1915 and 1922. Somebody knew who all these guys were at one time, unfortunately that information is long gone. Apparently the Harrington's were only shipped within a fifty-mile radius, so not many of them ever left the eastern Washington region. *Courtesy of Marciel Cronrath*

The end of an era. On September 8, 1923, all hell broke loose as the Harrington Harvester Works burned to the ground destroying valuable patterns, blueprints, and castings vital to the future of the combine. Apparently, a piece of coke got away and landed on the tarred roof. A track-laying tractor and several harvesters were also lost, not to mention every piece of equipment that occupied the building. *Courtesy of Marciel Cronrath*

The first machine was tested at the Fink ranch outside of Harrington in 1910. By successfully cutting over 250 acres, four harvesters were slated for production for the harvest of 1911, and by 1913 no fewer than 22 were built. Demand for the Harrington wasn't restricted to the local farm trade. Although the vast majority of machines were sold within a 50-mile radius, the Advance Rumely Company purchased a Harrington and later lured Erich away to develop a hillside model. Dunning bought out Erich in 1915 and renamed the company Harrington Manufacturing. After 1913, ten harvesters a month were being built with a price tag of $1650 to $2050 per machine. By 1918, the company employed 65 people with a payroll of over $15,000 annually, and had $200,000 worth of equipment. Close to 60 machines had been produced for 1918 alone.

Improvements were also being made on the Harrington. The 1921 model was actually 1000 pounds heavier than earlier machines, but was also a great deal stronger. The improvements in the leveling system allowed the Harrington to lean left and right, and remain level on slope of 40 percent. These later models were also

Rebuilding began shortly after the fire, but the harvester company soon faded away. Today one can still drive through Harrington, a town of around 400 people, and see a small remnant of the old harvester factory where a local welder now plies his trade. *Courtesy of Marciel Cronrath*

One last field view of the old Harrington Harvester somewhere outside the town of Harrington, Washington. Quite similar to the Holt, the Harrington operated much the same. This may be because the inventors, Erich and Dunning, were from the Marysville, California, area where they both had an interest in a machine shop. One never knows, they might have even crossed paths with Benjamin Holt himself. *Courtesy of Marciel Cronrath*

equipped with gasoline auxiliary engines. The 50-bushel capacity hopper was a feature in 1921, designed by Robert Sheffels and enhanced by the Erich-designed elevator. The system enabled the transfer of grain from combine to truck in one motion, an operation that was unheard of up until that time. One of the last models built operated with a 28-inch cylinder, 44-inch separator, and a 24 foot cut. The ads boasted over 100 acres per day when pulled by a 75-horsepower tractor.

Just as the Harrington company was enjoying a lucrative business, disaster struck on September 8, 1923. Due to an errant piece of coke that landed on a tarred roof, the harvester factory was burned to the ground, destroying over $200,000 of equipment including two harvesters, a track-laying tractor, and vital patterns that represented 14 years of work. The Harrington had become so successful that telegrams poured in from Spokane, Walla Walla, and Seattle, offering the devastated company a new home. Spokane and Walla Walla may have been interested because the Holt Manufacturing Company had a branch office in the former, and a production facility in the latter. Oddly enough, parts for the Holt models were produced at the Harrington factory for a short time. Nevertheless, the Harrington factory was rebuilt at the site where it had burned but never regained its commercial success.

Meanwhile, just over 100 miles south of Harrington came the invention of the Idaho National Harvester in the town of Moscow. Initially designed in 1904 by Cornelius Quesnell and A. M. Anderson, the Idaho National was a push-type combine developed specifically for steep slopes in the Palouse region. With a patent granted in 1905 and only $1,000 to begin their venture, Quesnell and Anderson, with the help of an influential implement dealer, secured the funds needed to start production.

The first machine built cut a four-foot swath and required two men and four horses; both cylinder and separator were also four feet in width. This first model, put out in 1905, sold for $700. Not a bad deal, considering that the average combine of that time was between $1,500 and $2,000, and required 24 to 33 horses for operation. Though the Idaho National was primarily a push-type machine, there were occasions when the harvester had to be pulled as well as pushed. Steepness of slope dictated this method. This was probably because of the long tradition of using headers, as pulling the machines on steep slopes required the horses to be walking in uncut grain. Hence, on the steepest of slope the machines were both pushed and pulled, as sliding often occurred.

Later models offered an eight-foot sickle and cylinder with the use of six to eight horses; the average cut per day was approximately 15 acres. By 1912, 52 Idahos had been sold with more orders on the way and more improvements as well. The usual process of grain carried to a table was retained while three fanners were added and the cut was increased to ten feet enabling over 150 acres harvested in a ten-day period. Another engineering innovation was the introduction of a threshing design that did not require leveling.

CORNELIUS QUESNELL
INVENTOR
ANDREW M. ANDERSON
INVENTOR
The first machine built in 1905, was a 4½ ft. cut and run with 4 horses. This machine cut and threshed several sacks. It gave the inventors the encouragement out of which has developed the greatest harvester of the age.

Above is the early Idaho National push-type combine along with its founders. Produced up until World War I, the little Idaho caught the eye of the Midwest farmer almost before it became popular in the rolling hills of the Palouse. *Photo number 14-140, Historical Photograph Collection, University of Idaho, Moscow*

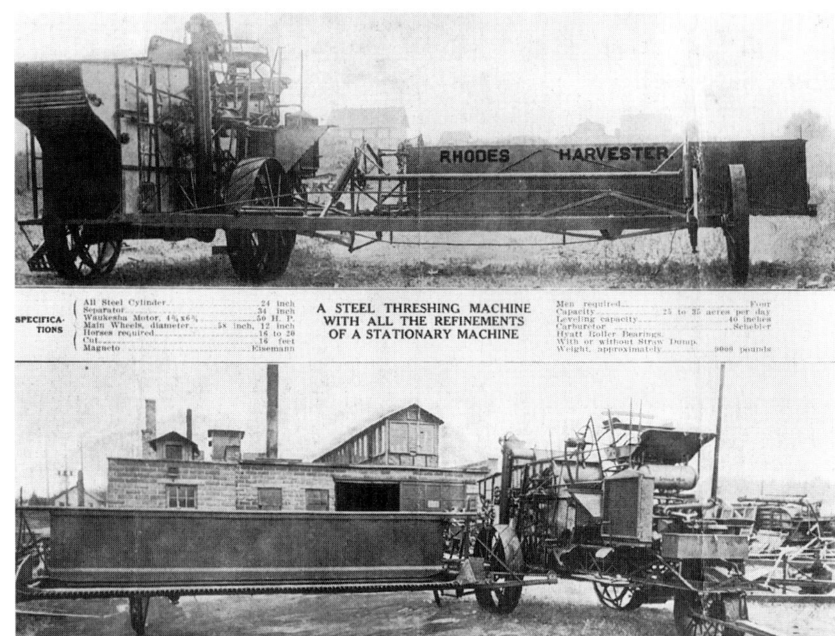

At right is the Rhodes combine outside the factory at 808 South Main Street in Moscow, Idaho. Willis M. Rhodes came to Moscow in 1898 where he established his iron works. Oddly enough, the Idaho National was built at the location until new facilities could be erected not far from the Rhodes Works (1907–09). Shortly after this time, Rhodes developed a combine of his own like the one pictured here. *Number 14-85, Historical Photograph Collection, University of Idaho, Moscow*

As in the case of the Harrington harvester, others outside the region became interested in the work being accomplished by the men in Moscow. The International Harvester Company was acutely aware of the achievements in the hillside design to the degree that they tested the leveling and frame strength of their McCormick-Deering line of combines in the Palouse region. Still, the interest didn't stop there. It was reported that the Minister of Agriculture from southeastern Russia pushed for an Idaho Harvester factory to be built in his country after being convinced of their superiority in field tests. Even the skeptical Great Plains had an eye on the "Little Idaho," as it was often referred to.

Indeed, the "Idaho" was a engineering success by virtue of its patents alone; 12 in the U. S. and one in Canada. They included a draper-equalized cutting device, corrugated threshing tooth, tilting device, pneumatic separator, and a self-leveling sickle bar. The corrugated threshing tooth is said to have had 10 times the threshing surface of the average tooth at a much lower speed, while the pneumatic separator aided in better wind circulation under pressure.

The engineering success of the Idaho National Harvester, however, was overshadowed by the lack of production capabilities. Though the company had what some called the best-equipped machine facilities in the Northwest, it could not meet the market demands in 1912 of 10 to 20 machines per day. Finances and cramped quarters restricted production to just two machines per day, with a selling price of $1,100 per machine. The last models rolled off the factory floor in 1916, with two train car loads being shipped to Arizona wheat farmers. Oddly enough, grain growers in Argentina had purchased the largest number of "Idahos."

The final blow to the company came with the outbreak of World War I. With restrictions on raw materials and the draw on labor, not to mention the collapse of wheat prices after the war, the end was near. Some have also said that the company could not adapt to the changing market of gasoline-powered harvesters. The company did manage to stay afloat manufacturing camp stoves and a patented automobile steering gear, but their harvester days were over. The Idaho National Harvester company closed its doors in May of 1921, and in 1923, the buildings were sold to the University of Idaho.

The Rhodes Harvester Company

One other harvester company established in the Moscow area was the Rhodes Harvester Company. Founded by Willis M. Rhodes in 1898 as the Rhodes Iron Works, the first combine was built and tested in 1911. Like the Idaho National, the Rhodes was designed specifically for the hilly terrain of the Palouse region. It was reported to be the lightest all-metal constructed combine at the time, weighing in at just 9,000 pounds. One of the first models cut a 16-foot swath with a conveyor to carry the cut grain to a 24-inch threshing cylinder and 34-inch separator. According to the literature that exists on the harvester, it had the first leveling device used on a separator. The separator also stayed level traveling up and down hills with the use of a simple pendulum, similar to the ones used on McCormick-Deering models that appeared in later years.

Because the header and separator were powered by a 50-horsepower Waukesha engine, only 16 horses were required to pull the machine. Manpower was also limited to four men; one to drive the horses, one to regulate the header, another to operate the leveling device, and a sack sewer. Like most other models of the day, the Rhodes was also set up with a sack carrier to enable windrowing the sacks for easy pick-up.

A parting shot of the Holt combine being pulled by its newest sibling, the Caterpillar tractor. By the end of the 1930s, the tractor for all intent and purpose replaced horse-powered harvesting and was breaking ground in the newest region for combining, the Midwest. Though the Holt machines appeared in the humid region well before the 1930s, it wasn't thought practical to use the combine due to weather and acreage limitations. The tractor would change all this along with better strains of wheat and field tests that proved that the combine could be used wherever grain was grown. *Ritzville Library Archives*

Unfortunately, the Rhodes would suffer a similar fate as that of the Idaho National. Finances as usual plagued the small outfits and with the coming of the war, materials were in short supply. The Rhodes, however, found a new home, if only temporary, in the town of Colfax, Washington, just over the state line. The small company would make a final move to the tiny community of Dishman, outside of Spokane, before shutting down completely in 1924. It was at that time that the Case company took over the patents on the Rhodes leveling device. Remarkably, only 25 to 30 Rhodes harvesters were produced from 1911 to 1924.

No matter how small these companies may have been, they all had something to contribute to the harvester industry. Holt came out with the first side-hill combine in 1891, but it was the small manufacturers that furthered the technology in leveling devices, mainly out of necessity for the markets they served. They also had the small farmer in mind when developing their machines. After all, it was the "Little Idaho" that had first caught the eye of the Midwest, the region that was the last to be convinced to employ the use of the combine.

Chapter Three

The Combine Moves East

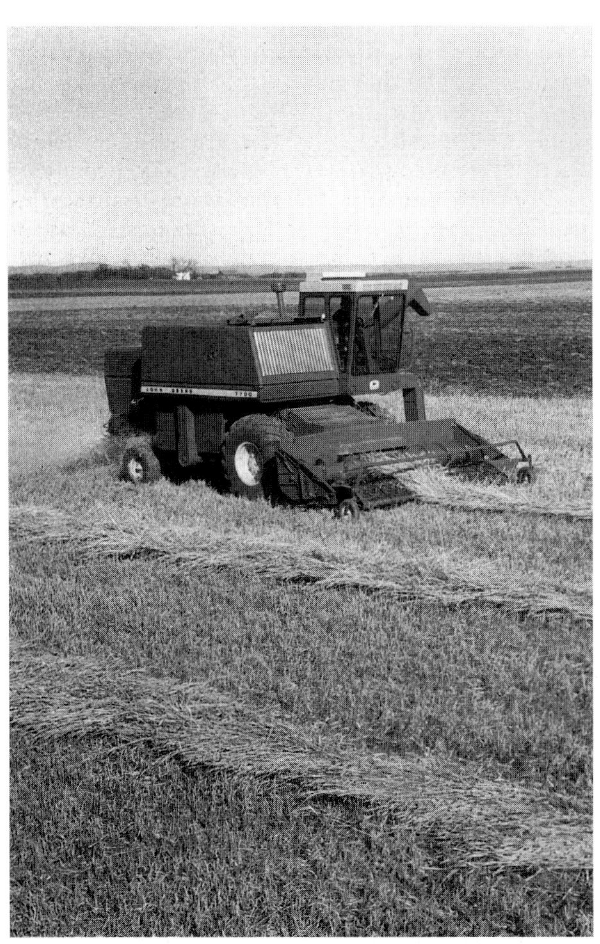

Far from the early machines that offered windrowing and pick-up attachments in the 1920s is this scene in 1969 of the John Deere 7700 combine with the three-roller belt pick-up in Grand Forks, North Dakota. *Deere Archives*

In December of 1926, the Farm Power and Machinery Division of the American Society of Agricultural Engineers (ASAE) met at Chicago to discuss the use of the combine in the Midwest, the Southeast, and Eastern states. The group discussed four specific concerns about combine use in these regions: adaptability of the combine to various crops, acreage limitations, relations to climatic conditions, and mechanical problems of the combine. Engineers from both the public and private sector attended, with representatives from John Deere, Massey-Harris, Western Harvester Works (Holt-Caterpillar), J. I. Case, and engineers from the smaller combine firms.

It was decided early on that the only way to find out about the combine's advantages and/or limitations was to go to the source; the farmer and his machines that were already in the field. For the purposes of obtaining general information about the combine, a questionnaire was prepared for interviewing owners and operators at the end of the harvest season. The areas where the combine had been used for the longest time east of the Rocky Mountains were done first, mainly in wheat producing regions. It was also important to utilize areas in which binding, heading, and combining were done on an equal basis for the purpose cost analysis. The Panhandle section of Texas; Alfalfa County, Oklahoma; Ottawa County, Kansas; Grant County, Nebraska; and the Judith Basin of Montana were the areas selected for the trials. Field crews from the cooperating bureaus started in the Panhandle of Texas in early June of 1926 to begin the task of collecting data.

Information was gathered while the harvest was in progress. Careful attention was paid to the ripening of various crops in each region, weather conditions and losses of grain incurred by each method of harvesting. Even before all the information was in, C. D. Kinsman, an

In order to use the combine effectively in the humid regions, a small machine that could be pulled by a general purpose tractor was highly desired. The photo at left comes from the Midwest in 1927. The mid-sized John Deere Model D tractor pulls its sibling, the No. 1 combine. The combine is stopped for off-loading harvested grain into the wagon. You might also notice the long cleats on the rear wheels of the tractor. The "sticky" texture of soils in these regions necessitated the use of cleats to avoid getting bogged down completely. *Deere Archives*

agricultural engineer for the USDA, claimed that after only four months of observations in 12 different states, the combine was proving to be successful. The traditional argument that the combine couldn't be used in regions of heavy rainfall during the harvesting period was proved to be a misnomer. In fact, Kinsman's report went on to say that as more information becomes available regarding the proper operation of the combine, there's no reason why they could not be "used successfully wherever grain binders are now used, and that the manufacturers of combines may consider all of this territory as a possible field for sales." This was not to infer that binder use would be supplanted entirely, but outside of extremely small acreage, the combine would become widespread.

Although wheat was the primary crop harvested in the Great Plains region, reports were coming in about the harvesting of oats, barley, rye, and flax, with one farmer using the combine to cut grain sorghums in the

Though predominately used in the West, the crawler tractor wasn't exactly a stranger to the fields east of the Rockies. This McCormick-Deering No. 8 combine is being pulled by a TD-35 crawler. The International Harvester Company answered the call of concerned Midwest farmers in 1928 by offering new options for the No. 8 including straw spreaders and attachments for harvesting rice, flax, and soybeans. The long-awaited pick-up attachment also appeared in 1928. *Courtesy of Joe Jantz*

This Gleaner six-foot machine is operating in a Kansas field using the pick-up attachment. Just about any type of crop could be windrowed and picked up later. Even today, crops such as seed peas and beans grown under irrigation in the West are windrowed mainly to let the leafy part of the plant dry up for easier combining. In the photo above, the previously windrowed crop is now being picked up and threshed through the combine. *AGCO*

This early model Case combine is stopped for a pose. When and where this photo was taken is a mystery to me, but it affords a look at how the early combines of the Midwest were set up. Though the crawler looks a little out of place (unless you're farming in the western reaches of Kansas), the right side view of the combine shows the sacking shelf and stacked up bags to be filled by the kid off to the far right. Sacking would soon be a thing of the past. *Ritzville Library Archives*

Panhandle of Texas. The news got even better when it was learned that in the more humid areas of the eastern plains, sweet clover, aslike clover, alfalfa, and timothy was falling under the cut of the combine. In most cases it was found that harvesting costs were much lower with the combine than with either the header or binder. It was estimated that, in 1926, the average loss of winter wheat harvested with the combine was 2.6 percent. Fields that were harvested with the header had a loss of 3.3 percent, and almost double that with the binder at 6.1 percent. Putting it another way, the average loss of grain per pound per acre was 32 pounds for the combine, 40 pounds for the header, and a whopping 74 pounds for the binder. News like this prompted many in the Midwest to further investigate the combine.

Most problems with the combine came from poorly trained operators not adjusting the cutting and threshing mechanisms with different crops. In many cases, all it

This Advance-Rumely No. 3 hillside combine didn't frequent the plains states, but the prairie models with twelve horses pulling them often did. Beginning in the early 1920s some farmers were experimenting with machines like the one pictured above. As a matter of fact, numerous Midwest companies were purchasing western made combines to see just how well they could be adapted to their region. Both Holt and Best had shipped their machines back to Kansas as early as 1917. It wasn't until the late 1920s and early 1930s, however, that the combine was widely accepted, and by that time the tractor had replaced the horse, especially on the average farm. *Ritzville Library Archives*

This Gleaner 12-footer is picking up a windrowed crop in East Texas. Note the rollers and retractable fingers underneath the pick-up platform. As you can see, the grain is being "rolled" over the top onto the platform where an auger feed delivers it to the feeder house and then on to the threshing cylinder. For the average farm east of the Rockies, this kind of outfit was ideal, simply because various crops could be harvested at different times. The pick-up attachment could be changed for conventional cutting, or the machine itself could be used as a stationary thresher. Also, because combines like the one pictured tended to be lightweight, a small tractor could be employed without having to invest in a second machine. *AGCO*

Here again is another view of the old McCormick-Deering No. 8 in 1938. A little fuzzy, but nonetheless frozen in time. This right side view shows the sacking shelf and dump off ramp for "windrowing" grain sacks onto the field. The No. 8 became even more popular in the humid regions when the 30-bushel grain tank was introduced, requiring only one man to operate the whole show. *Courtesy of Joe Jantz*

Though the California-style combine was considered alien to areas east of the Rockies, it did make some headway in the header regions of extreme western Kansas and in the Dakotas. The couple pictured in front of the crawler tractor must be the owners of the ranch, possibly out on a Sunday drive checking up on the harvest crew. *Ritzville Library Archives*

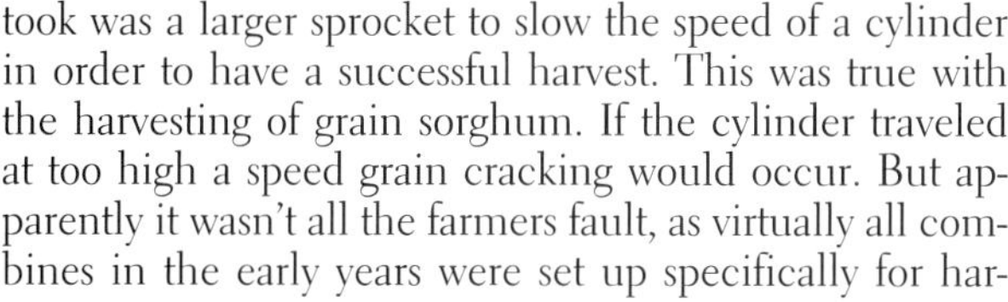

took was a larger sprocket to slow the speed of a cylinder in order to have a successful harvest. This was true with the harvesting of grain sorghum. If the cylinder traveled at too high a speed grain cracking would occur. But apparently it wasn't all the farmers fault, as virtually all combines in the early years were set up specifically for harvesting wheat. Dealers had to take some of the heat as well. In one particular area of Oklahoma, only one dealer had ever heard of switching sprockets for a particular crop, the vast majority having to be shown by government investigators where the information was in their own catalogs.

The Harris hillside could also be found in the hilly regions of Montana. Here the machine has stopped for a photo. Note that the reel is turning, evidence that while the combine is at a standstill, the auxiliary engine is still running. *Ritzville Library Archives*

Beyond these problems, the combine performed admirably in most areas throughout the humid Midwest. The early field tests in Illinois are one such example. The first combine on record in the state was owned by the Garwood Brothers of Stonington, purchased for the 1924 soybean harvest. Soybeans had become such a nightmare to harvest that every machine conceivable was employed. After two seasons of unusually wet weather, the combine was put to the test and did surprisingly well. I. P. Blauser, instructor from the Department of Farm Mechanics at the University of Illinois, stated that in 1927 there were between 60 and 70 combines in the state, up from a mere dozen the previous year. The feeling was that even more would appear in the fields the following year "given the amount of grain that rotted in the shocks this year." At the time there were only three makes of combines in the state, and a fourth, the Fordson tractor-mounted Universal Gleaner, had just finished trials of its own. The Fordson differed from the others as it was somewhat of a "self-propelled," with the combine being mounted on the tractor.

The initial tests in soybeans was so good that some wondered how the combine would fare in small grains like wheat. If performance proved satisfactory, then the combine could be considered the harvester of choice on the small farm where labor is often scarce and overhead can eat into profits. If the combine operated in small grains like it did with soybeans, the farmer who had various crops to harvest would truly have a reason to invest in such a machine. Because of this possibility, feasibility tests were run with the combine in the field.

According to Blauser, the tests were made by "catching the straw and chaff in a canvas and at the same time catching the grain in a bag. The loose and unthreshed grain in the chaff and straw was recovered by re-threshing the material in a 16-inch double-cylinder thresher...the yield per acre was determined by measuring the width of cut, and the distance covered in the test." In soybeans harvested by the usual methods, up to 45 percent of the crop could be lost, not to mention that if the weather was bad enough, most of it would simply rot in the field. With regard to wheat, losses totaled less than 9 percent. It was also found that in fields with heavy weeds, Canada thistle in particular, the toothed cylinder should be replaced with the rasp bar as the bar cylinder didn't mash the berries, putting more moisture in the grain.

The Illinois tests of 1926 began the fall of long-standing opposition to the combine. The concerns of too much moisture, weeds, uneven growing grain, and weather related problems became groundless arguments with regard to a harvester that was restricted to dry, semi-arid conditions. The majority of combine owners in the state of Illinois were very well satisfied with the combine

Companies like John Deere answered the call early on to produce a combine with windrowing and pick-up capabilities. Pictured above is the No. 3 windrow combine being pulled by the Model D tractor in 1929. Note that the cut grain is being elevated on to the canvas platform (later replaced by the auger) and then delivered to the feeder house for threshing. *Deere Archives*

and were excited about the possibilities. Most of the objections came from those who did not own or operate a machine, still convinced that the combine should remain west of the Rockies.

Nevertheless, by 1927, it was apparent that the combine had been successful in almost all areas where studies were done. Even in the state of Virginia, where one might find it hard to imagine a combine being used, the combine had a very successful run, especially in soybeans. D. C. Heitshu, an agricultural engineer from the Virginia Polytechnic Institute, reported on observations of the four machines operating in his state. One combine had been operated under the control of an experiment station while the other three were running in other parts of the state. Results showed an overall satisfactory performance in all of the small grains with the exception of barley, only because the machine was not used in that crop. Heitshu did make some recommendations for design changes, as the combine was still a bit "unbalanced" for Eastern use. His recommendations were: cutter bar ex-

The John Deere Model 95 windrowing an oat crop at Saginaw, Texas, in 1958. *Deere Archives*

tensions for proper sizes; for harvesting soybeans the cylinder speed should be increased to 2300 feet per minute; the use of the hinged header in hilly country where soybeans are usually planted; complete enclosure of the feeder housing; and increased ground clearance.

Others in the field gave numerous suggestions to manufacturers for improved performance. Like Heitshu's recommendations, most of the ideas relayed to manufacturers had to do with cutting and separating. They included: adjustable reel; easier sieve adjustment; increased separator capacity; shoes on the cutter bar to permit floating during operation; and a platform design to allow cutting lower to the ground. Literally all areas reporting had some kind of improvement idea for his particular region. Unlike the West, the Plains and humid regions required specific modifications due to the variety of crops grown. If the combine was to be a hit, the manufacturers would have to modify existing machines for this new market, a market that would eventually prove very lucrative for combine makers in the near future.

Inasmuch as refinements were needed, the lack of them didn't slow the use of the combine. In Iowa, some 27 machines were sold within the harvest year of 1927 to bring in the oat crop, that state's most important small grain. The various Iowa varieties of oats yielded ten percent more with the combine than with the binder for a period of three weeks, thereafter the yield was at least equal if not greater. Again, moisture wasn't a problem, and rainfall records over the past ten years showed that Iowa actually had more suitable days for combine use than the state of Kansas. And speaking of Kansas, a report was filed in 1926 comparing the cost of combining the

The John Deere Model 55 windrowing in 1957. *Deere Archives*

state's wheat as opposed to using a cradle. To achieve this feat via the scythe and cradle, you would need 775,000 harvest hands working 20 days to bind and shock, utilizing the entire male population in the state from 15 to 60 years of age, and all females between the ages of 20 to 37 to complete the harvest! If this wasn't good marketing, I don't know what was.

Whether it be Indiana, Kansas, the Dakotas, or Iowa, the "Spread of the Combine" was hailed as being more important to mechanized agriculture than the reaper. This was indeed a mouthful, but probably true. The combine began to show up in the most unlikely places, the state of Pennsylvania is a case in point. Apparently the oldest combine on record belonged to Ralph Brinser in 1920, who farmed on an island right in the middle of the Susquehanna River. Brinser routinely combined 100 acres of wheat, 70 acres of barley, 40 acres of buckwheat, and even some rye. He reported to investigators that his entire crop was easily harvested "with no loss of grain and no trouble in taking care of threshed grain." Brinser was also of the opinion that, "the combine is just as applicable in Pennsylvania as to any other state." Harold Short of Delaware shared these same sentiments. Delaware? Short bought his first machine in 1924 and almost at the outset offered his services as a custom cutter. Using a 12-foot machine, he cut all the various crops that Brinser did and contended that standing grain dried out much faster than shocked grain. Though this was all good news, more work had to be done in order to bring the combine up to 100 percent for use within the Plains region. To do that, modifications would have to be made.

Engineering Advances With the Combine

Two refinements being discussed concerning the combine for Midwest use consisted of the windrower and the pick-up attachment. The windrowing method was used in areas where grain crops were extremely weedy or where uneven ripening grain was prevalent. The crop was cut and then left in rows for drying. After four to eight days the cut grain could then be " picked-up" and combined in the usual manner. The down side was the need to perform two operations. The pick-up attachment was mounted in place of the header platform and operated

continued on page 78

Rear view of the Case prairie-type combine, probably in the late 1920s to early '30s. This machine is being pulled by a Case tractor. Note the 60-bushel bulk tank and the straw spreader. The scene pictured here was taken in South Dakota. *Courtesy of J. I. Case Archives*

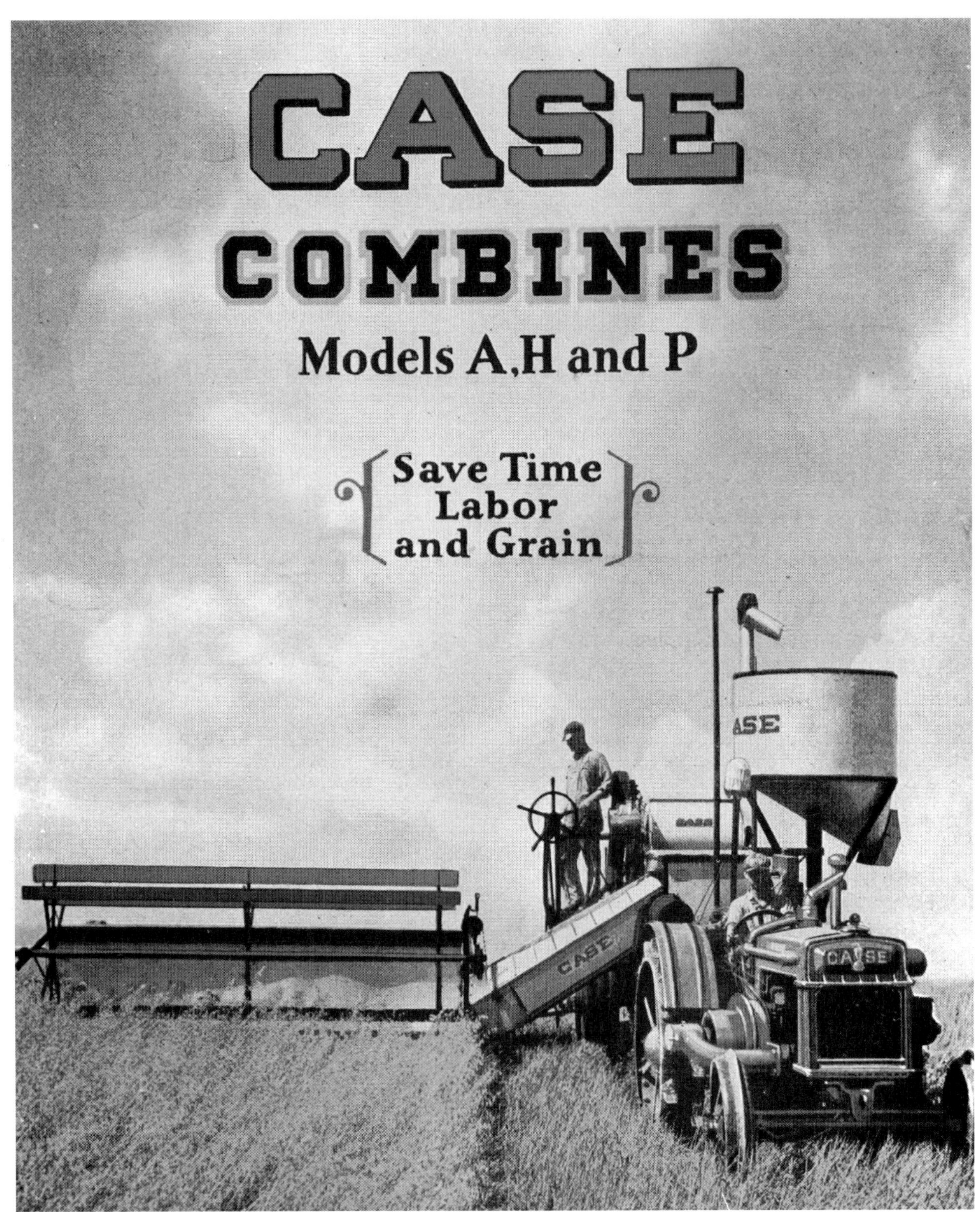

From the cover of a Case sales brochure circa 1925 is this Model H combine with a sixty bushel bulk tank. An extra wheel was attached to the outer side of the tank frame for better weight support. Stretching all the way above the bulk tank elevator is the exhaust pipe from the Case four-cylinder engine, a necessity to avoid sparks in the field. The Model H could also be fitted with equipment for the use of horses for motive power. Equipment included a horse pole, driving platform with spring seat, and a brake assembly. Case initially introduced the prairie model combine in 1923.

Case Combines

During the mid-1920's there was a proliferation of combine manufacturers, and with the further acceptance of the combine in the humid regions it only seemed fitting for the J. I. Case Company to join in the fray. The legendary thresher manufacturer by 1923 had nearly 84 years of experience with the threshing/separating process. Now, Case was determined to apply its know-how to the development of its own "traveling" harvester.

Case initially brought out a prairie model in the early 1920s, with a hillside model being added later on. The hillside model looked a lot like the Holt's and Harris' of that same time period and operated much the same. Unlike the many current models, however, the leveling device on the Case machine was situated between the separator body and the header instead of on the left side of the combine. One of the primary reasons the leveling device was placed in this location was because of tip-over problems. Case claimed that if the combine did start to tip on a steep grade, the machine would lean toward the hillside instead of away from it, thereby eliminating a roll-over on the downward side.

The early hillside machines didn't have a bulk tank; the bagging platform was built out off the left-hand side. There the bagger could sit and perform his duties in relative comfort and also have the convenience of a sack chute for the dumping of sacked grain to be picked up later. The header size on the early hillside combine was 14 feet and could be adjusted to cut from four to 36 inches depending on the stand; the reel was eight slats and was worm gear-driven.

Like most of the combines at this time, the Case hillside model operated with an auxiliary engine, mounted sideways up front behind the turn-table front wheel. The Case four-cylinder engine (the same engine used in many Case tractors) had a rated brake horsepower of 20 at normal engine speed, with 25 horsepower at maximum speed (normal engine speed was 1050 rpm). One interesting aspect of the Case engine was that at times it could become "portable." With the use of suitable frame with wheels, the combine engine could be taken off its steel frame to be used as a handy power source for silo filling, corn shredding, and grinding feed. In fact, the Case engine could be used for any type of belt pulley work.

Throughout the 1920s and early 1930s, Case combines sales were on an upward climb. By 1932, the company introduced its "'one-man'" machine with power take-off (PTO) and soon thereafter started production of a straight-through-feed six-footer. The straight feed machine was probably introduced to counter the John Deere No. 6 and the Allis-Chalmers All-Crop that was introduced in the mid-1930s. Whatever the reason, by 1933 Case had eight different combines to offer in three different styles.

With the expansion of the combine line came the acquisition of the Showers Brothers furniture factory in Burlington, Iowa, in 1937 for the future production of the models A-6, G, and F combines. These were small machines to answer the demand of that particular market in the Depression ridden 1930s. Case also brought out a corn picker in 1930; a windrow pick-up hay baler in 1932, and a sliced hay pick-up baler in 1940 (it's interesting to note that Case literally dominated the baler business in 1941...until New Holland came out with a better machine that baled with twine. According to company history, Case failed to respond and literally found themselves out of the baler business overnight).

In addition to the hillside, A-6, G, and F models were the A, H, and P model combines. These particular machines were pull-types, similar to the previously mentioned models operated by either horse or tractor, and all had auxiliary engines to run the thresher/separator. The A, H, and P models differed mainly in their width of cut and cylinder size. The "A" model was the smallest, offered with either the eight-foot or 10-foot header; a four-cylinder Case auxiliary engine rated at 1250 rpm; bagging spout or square holding tank and an all steel 22-foot cylinder. The "H" model combine was similar to the "A" but offered a header width of either 10 or 12 feet. The same four-cylinder engine was used operating at 1200 rpm engine speed. The "P" was the largest, offering the 12- or 16-foot width of cut and operated with the valve-in-head type four-cylinder engine. Both the H and P were also equipped with a round, 60-bushel bulk tank.

Case also made available add-on items such as pea and bean attachments, chaff carrier attachments, a header truck for transporting the header when not in use, grouter plates for the rear wheels to avoid slipping on hillsides and a windrow header with pick-up attachments. Like most companies in the late 1930s and early 1940s, Case had become a full-line company, catering to the needs of the humid regions and beyond.

With the expansion of the Case line came the development of the self-propelled combine in 1954, along with two new pull machines and a corn harvester. The Model 120 self-propelled was initially introduced as a "rice special," with high-cleated drive wheels and specialized pick-up reel for harvesting in wet fields. The company had also introduced its Model 88 tobacco harvester built in Anniston, Alabama, prior to the model 120 combine and had large scale plans to develop the Southeastern market. However, Case, like other companies of that era, was beginning to see the post-war boom turn into a bust. In the words of one company historian, "The 400,000 unit years were over." Shrinking sales and profits took its toll on the company, even though management was introducing new tractors and implements. Unfortunately, timing worked against Case.

Case continued to produce combines throughout the 1950s. In fact, the company obtained the rights to manufacture the Harris combine product in 1959, an arrangement that continued until 1964. During the 1960s, Case manufactured the model 800 and 1000 self-propelled combines, followed by the 1660 and 1665 that continued to be produced until 1972, at which time

continued on page 78

Continued from page 77

Case got out of the combine business. The cruel fact was that Case had dropped to less than a seven percent share of the combine market. With a combine design that was outdated by more than ten years, it just seemed to proper to drop the line altogether.

Case didn't offer a combine again until 1985, the same year that the company acquired the International Harvester implement, tractor, and combine lines. With the combine now known as the Case-IH, the company continued the pioneering of the Axial Flow system that has the threshing cylinder sitting in a longitudinal position, a design that was developed by IH in the 1970s. More importantly was the future 1600 series combines on the drawing board at the time that Case acquired the IH line and the huge dealer network already in place, numbering more than 1800 in all. Case was again a full-line company and continues to manufacture the inherited combines, tractors, and implements, as well as their own equipment.

Continued from page 75

much like a hay loader, the windrowed grain being lifted by forks (tines), dropped onto a canvas conveyor and then separated by the combine.

This then was the task for engineers representing their respective companies at the symposium of the ASAE Power and Machinery Division meeting at Chicago in 1928. Just about everyone in attendance realized the importance of producing an efficient pick-up attachment for windrowing purposes. Opening the discussion was B. S. Harris, chief engineer of the Massey-Harris Company, LTD. Harris urged his counterparts to take seriously the further improvements regarding "pick-ups" simply because certain regions can't be harvested otherwise.

Frank P. Hanson, sales engineer for the Western Harvester Company, started out with a slide presentation showing windrow and pick-up attachments produced by his company. When windrowing, the header was provided with a bull-wheel that supported the drives and cutting/conveying mechanisms. Instead of the grain falling upon a platform in the usual fashion, the grain was conveyed up over the bull-wheel and dispersed in a loose row on top of the

Above is the early Case hillside combine. The leveling device on the Case was situated between the separator body and header to avoid tip-overs on steep grades. Instead of rolling down a hill, the case design allowed the combine to fall toward the hill. Pictured are the driver, header tender at the wheel, the mechanic standing behind, and the sack sewer seated. Note the sack chute near the rear wheel. This allowed the sewer to drop sacks on the ground for later pick-up. The scene was captured on a dry land wheat farm in Rosalia, Washington, 1929. *Courtesy of Case Corporation Archives*

Harvesting head-high wheat on the hillsides of Thornton, Washington in 1929. This hillside crew consists of the driver, header tender, mechanic, and an assortment of sack sewers. *Courtesy of Case Corporation Archives*

stubble. The pick-up device replaced the standard reel, consisting of a canvas conveyer with slats and steel fingers. During operation the steel fingers would comb the stubble, lifting the windrow onto the moving canvas, then to the platform to be delivered to the threshing cylinder. These two improvements would have to be perfected in order for the combine to be a complete success.

To illustrate just how important the windrowing method was, Tom Campbell, president of Campbell Farming Corporation, Hardin, Montana, purposely left windrowed grain in the field during some 63 rainstorms from July through October. An area with shocked wheat was also left nearby. With the use of a side-delivery rake, Campbell had no trouble picking up the windrowed grain, and the losses were minimal. Even though the windrowed crop had been struck by hail, the grain heads remained in the straw. The shocks, on the other hand, had grown together in the field and could not be salvaged. Campbell estimated the loss of the windrowed grain at not more than 25 percent.

W. F. MacGregor of the J. I. Case Company reiterated the need to develop the windrow and pick-up method as well but had other improvements in mind. MacGregor felt that the combine, like all other farm machinery, should be standardized. In his opinion, a trend toward the auxiliary engine for the primary drive of the combine, grain bins, and straw spreaders should be standard equipment. He also felt that two sizes of machines should be concentrated on. Others like J. T. Ashton from Nichols & Shepard felt that machines, especially for the Midwest market, should be a lighter weight and also emphasized the need for anti-friction bearings (something that the Gleaner Company would offer very soon). Ashton also stressed the importance of pick-up and swathing devices in order for the combine to be used in newer territories.

John Mainland, engineer from the Advance-Rumely Company addressed concerns from Eastern and Midwestern combine users about increased separator capacity. Separator capacity needed to be substantially larger in the humid regions to permit "full-swath" operation in heavy yields of long-strawed grains. The problem with increasing separator capacity was the machine would have to be larger as well as heavier, something manufacturers wanted to stay away from. Seeing that a larger machine would be more costly, excessively heavy, and less efficient in the field, it was determined that a reduction in width of swath was a better route to take. This is one of the reasons why early combines in the Midwest often cut a swath of only seven to 10 feet.

In addition to design changes and refinements, simple adjustments to the existing combine were recommended; for the harvesting of oats, the operator was instructed to cut down on wind, open up the chaffer sieves, and remove the small wheat screen. When harvesting rye, the heads are often thrown out of the combine reel. Widening of the slats usually remedied the problem. The harvesting of grain sorghums with the combine always presented problems, mainly because of the thick stalks

Factory photo of an early prairie-type combine set-up for the horse. *Courtesy of Case Corporation Archives*

and uneven ripening. Because of this, the recommendations were to cut the grain with 12 to 20 inches of stalk along with the heads and then windrow. If the operator still wanted to combine in the usual manner he was urged to: install wider reel slats; use screens at the back of the platform; reduce the speed of the cylinder, and lower or completely remove the concaves. For soybeans and peas it was important to lower the cutter bar to four inches above the ground and reduce the cylinder speed by 50 percent to avoid cracking the bean and pea pods.

One last area of discussion concerned the cost of operating the combine on the small farm. According to a 1927 USDA report, combines could cost anywhere from $1,000 to $3,000, with the average length of service being eight years. The benefits of operating the machines on large farms had already been established, but little attention was paid to the small farmer. It was generally assumed that anything over 150 acres was well suited for combine use. Some even felt that 60 acres was feasible because most of the acreage in the early years were custom cut. In some cases family members went in on a machine together, cutting there own grain then offering their services around the area. As a matter of fact, the ASAE stated in 1927 that close to 90 percent of all combine owners in the Midwest were custom cutters.

The combine versus the header/binder also figured into the equation of whether to switch machines because costs were so greatly reduced when crops were harvested with the combine. One had to calculate the savings in manpower, horsepower, food and lodging for transient labor, and fee's for the thresher set. Four to five men could operate the combine with little trouble. By the late 1920s, the tractor was the motive power of choice, freeing up crop land that was usually set aside for animal feed. The labor issue was another determining factor in the transition to the combine. Often times the shortage of workers could delay a harvest and, in a worst case scenario, cause complete ruin of the unharvested crop. With a properly trained combine operator, the harvest could commence at the farmers choosing.

There were many variables involved when it came to purchasing a combine in the Midwest. Tradition more than anything else had a good deal to do with putting off making a change, even though in the long run the farmer would save some money. Refinements to the machine that were mentioned above and the manufacture of the small combine specifically for harvesting the humid regions became the most important innovations that led to its acceptance, though in many areas the transition was slow. Eventually, though, manufacturers of combines would find that the central part of the US would become the new horn of plenty for their machines. It has been estimated that in 1920 only 5 percent of the nation's wheat crop was being harvested by the combine; by 1938 the number soared to over 50 percent, the majority being used in the Heartland. Companies such as Deere, Baldwin-Gleaner, and International Harvester, among others, would cater to the region and give them what they wanted.

Chapter Four

The Gleaner Story

While California and Northwest companies continued to service their respective regions in the mid-1910s, others in the Midwest had begun to fashion harvesters to their own needs. As discussed in the first chapter, combined threshing and separating was an almost impossible task in the humid regions given the problems with weather, small acreage, and the cost of operating a seasonal machine like the combined harvester. It just wouldn't pay considering the expense of feeding and keeping livestock alone. What the Midwest needed was a small machine, at low cost, and one that would require minimal labor. Curtis Baldwin attempted to give them what they wanted.

Kansas-born Curtis C. Baldwin knew the drudgery of binding and heading, a task that was only half of the harvest process. As a kid, he put in back-breaking 10-hour days of stacking and pitching grain into the mouths of threshing cylinders, often collapsing into a straw pile at the end of the day. Through the years, Baldwin would gain practical experience and end up operating his own threshing rigs that worked from the Kansas plains to the Canadian wheat fields. All the while he toyed with the idea of perfecting an economical combined harvester, and in 1911, he achieved his goal at the age of 23 with his first patent for the "Standing Grain Thresher."The

One of Gleaner's key products was the Fordson-powered combine. This photo gives a look at the factory where these combines were built and fitted to the Fordson. *AGCO*

Upper photo is
win. Lower is
and Earnest B
go much of th
of the GLEANI
COMBINES.

The Gleaner story starts here with founder Curtis C. Baldwin (top-center) shown with brothers and sometime associates Ernest and George. Although Curtis would start over a half dozen different companies, the Gleaner enterprise is his most noteworthy. The Baldwin Company was established at Nickerson, Kansas, in 1911 with the production of the Standing Grain Thresher, initially tested in 1910. The push-type combined-thresher lasted until 1918 when a second factory facility at Sparta, Michigan, closed its door that same year. Curtis would eventually move on to the Savage Company in Denver, Colorado, and later develop a pull-type machine for the Gleaner concern. Baldwin was an intermittent figure throughout much of the Gleaner's history. At about the same time Baldwin was working on the tractor-mounted Savage, brothers George and Ernest were developing the Fordson-mounted combine back in Kansas. *AGCO*

One of the earliest photos taken of the Standing Grain Thresher in the field in 1910. Many of those who actually operated one of these machines compared it to a carpet sweeper in that it "cut" the grain with a blast of air, generated by an overhead fan. *AGCO*

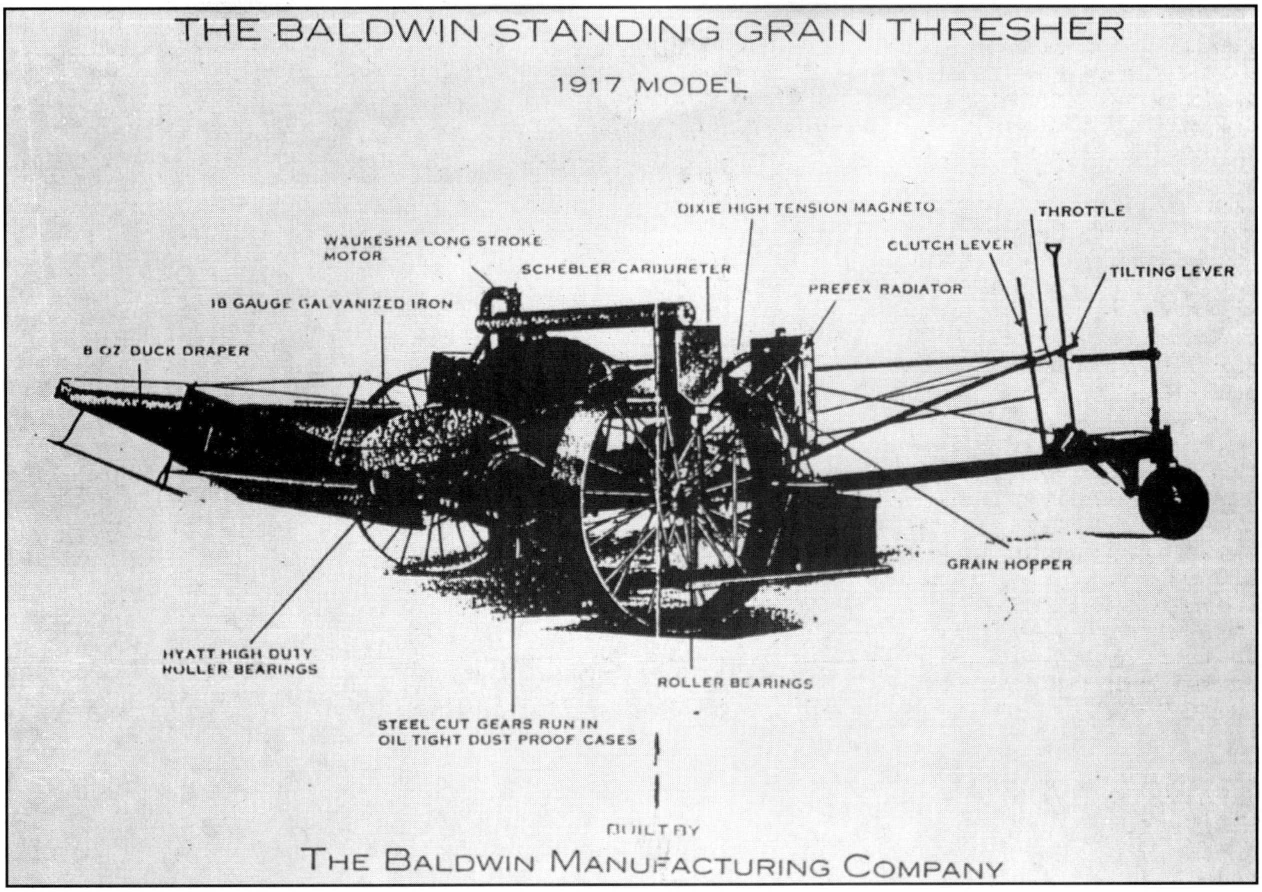

THE BALDWIN STANDING GRAIN THRESHER

1917 MODEL

DIXIE HIGH TENSION MAGNETO
THROTTLE
WAUKESHA LONG STROKE MOTOR
CLUTCH LEVER
SCHEBLER CARBURETER
TILTING LEVER
PREFEX RADIATOR
18 GAUGE GALVANIZED IRON
8 OZ DUCK DRAPER
GRAIN HOPPER
HYATT HIGH DUTY ROLLER BEARINGS
ROLLER BEARINGS
STEEL CUT GEARS RUN IN OIL TIGHT DUST PROOF CASES

BUILT BY
THE BALDWIN MANUFACTURING COMPANY

Looking almost like a push header from about the same time period, the Standing Grain Thresher appears here from the 1917 catalog. The machine could be operated by one man and four horses. According to Baldwin one could harvest grain at a mere two and a half cents per bushel. It's interesting to note that the Standing Grain Thresher was the first of its kind in the Midwest and led to early acceptance of this type of harvesting in various parts of the region. *AGCO*

Baldwin Company was established that same year in Nickerson, Kansas.

The Baldwin machine was a "pusher" much like the early Idaho National but differed greatly from all other combines in how it cut the grain. Powered by four horses (eight without the auxiliary engine), the machine traveled through the fields and swept the grain to the threshing cylinder. The earliest version had a canvas draper that extended at an angle out in front of the feeder. This angle could be manually adjusted by the driver at the rear of the machine using a lever like those on the early headers. Baldwin later perfected a blower of sorts that actually bent the grain stalks rearward to the cylinder. This was achieved with an overhead fan. Once the grain had entered the toothed cylinder an auger lifted the grain again to be re-threshed. Testimonials often equated the Baldwin machine to an early carpet sweeper.

Always on Baldwin's mind was the savings achieved by using his machine. In a 1915 catalog, Baldwin shows a comparison of costs between his standing grain thresher and the header-thresher method. Based on a 30-acre day, the heading/threshing method came to over $75, while harvesting

BALDWIN STANDING GRAIN THRESHER
One man with four horses threshes the standing grain at a cost of 2½ cents per bushel, dispensin with harvest and threshing crews, and leaving the straw on the ground for fertilizer.
Manufactured at Nickerson, Kansas

A closer look at this unconventional harvester in the early 1910s. Here one can see the hood that rode over the grain platform. First, a canvas draper would draw the grain heads back to the spike-tooth cylinder, then a blast of air from the overhead fan would help in the threshing/separating process. The grain spout at right above the platform delivered the cleaned grain to either sacks or waiting wagons. *AGCO*

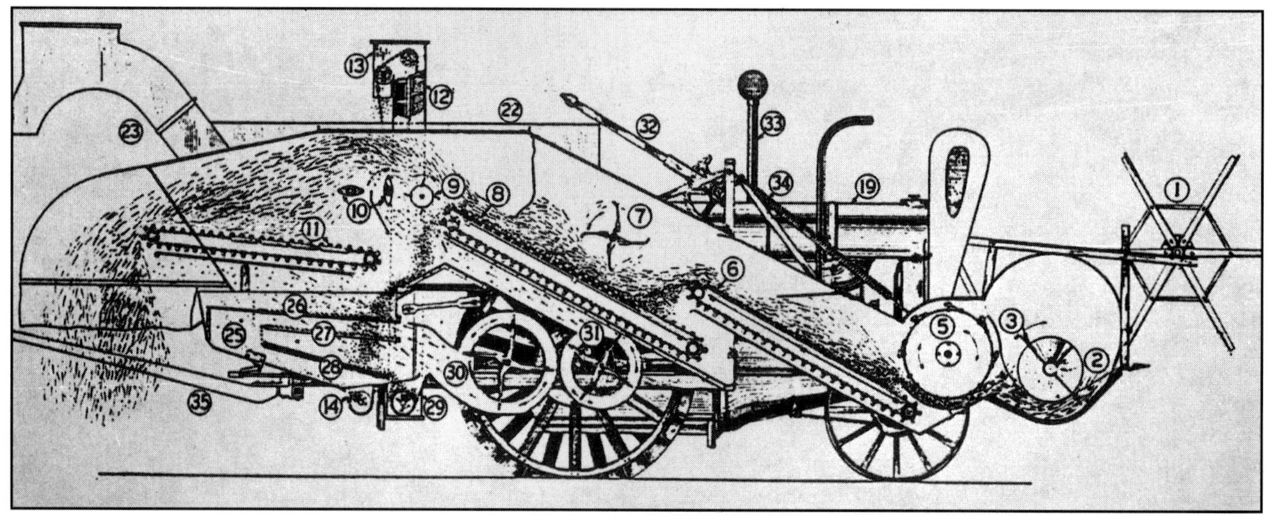

Touted as the first "self-propelled" combine was the Fordson tractor-mounted Gleaner Universal Harvester Thresher in 1923. Above shows the right side view of the Fordson in a factory cut-away. The combine literally rode on top of the tractor. It's interesting to note that the Gleaner signature down-low cylinder design that became standard on all later combines is employed here on the Fordson.

and threshing with the Baldwin machine barely totaled $16! But cost was only one advantage. In his own words, Baldwin describes the superior threshing method of the harvester:

"With the ordinary thresher, as well as ours, the threshing is done principally by the cylinder. With the ordinary thresher it is estimated that the grain passes the cylinder at the rate of one mile per minute. With the Standing Grain Thresher the grain passes the cylinder only as fast as the horses walk, which is two and a half to three miles per hour, a ratio of 20 to one, so you see that

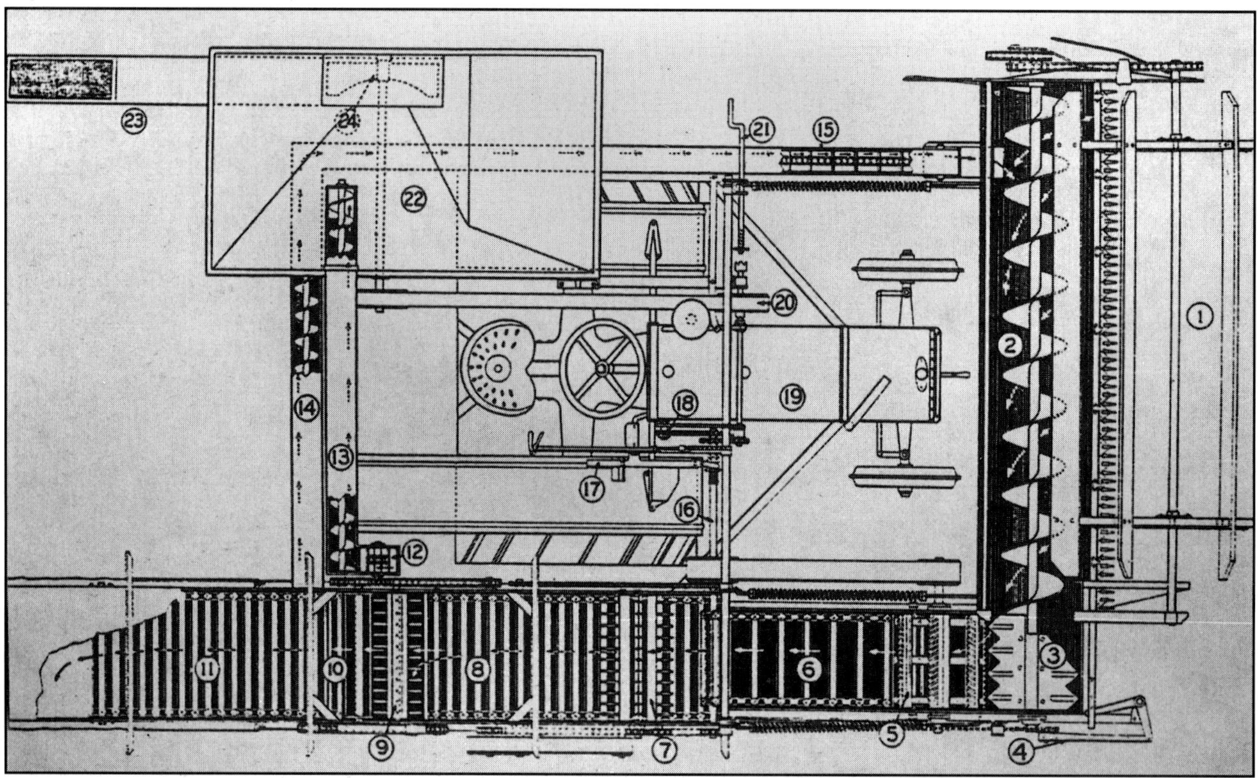

Top view of the Fordson. Gleaner was early in its use of the auger feed, replacing the conventional canvass feed for gathering grain in to the threshing cylinder. This particular photo also shows the raddle-type separator unit located at the bottom of the picture. *AGCO*

with our machine the cylinder strikes the heads 20 times where the ordinary thresher strikes them once."

In other words, the more times that the grain is beaten the better it's threshed. And all of these points had hit home to those who wanted an economical and mechanically sound machine in an area where skepticism ran high with regard to a combined harvester. The added benefit was that not too much labor was needed for operating the machine. With an auxiliary engine to power it, the Baldwin only required two men for the chore; one to drive the four horses and one to tie the sacks and keep an eye on the engine. The capacity of the machine was 25 to 30 acres per 10-hour day. In 1913, Baldwin claimed that by using his machine, the cost of harvesting could be reduced from 14 to 2 cents a bushel.

Although the Standing Grain Thresher performed admirably, Baldwin knew the machine still had its shortcomings. The stripper-type system he had devised often ran into problems with lodged wheat, weeds, and gathering losses at the stripper drum. After all, the stripping method of harvesting in humid regions frequently encountered problems. To help remedy this, he replaced the air-blast over the stripping drum with a slotted reel to reduce excess power.

With the Baldwin Manufacturing Company well established in 1915, Curtis took on Clarence A. Stevens as a partner and soon left for Denver, Colorado, to develop the Savage Combine. The Savage Harvester Company's combine was a side-mounted type on a 44-horsepower Savage tractor. It had a 16 1/2 foot cut and featured a

Front view of the Fordson showing sickle bar, reel and bats, and auger feed. The whole show was powered by a direct drive consisting of three belts and three roller chains. Dumping the canvas-style feed aided in a more positive, smooth feed and was easier to power through a single drive unit. *AGCO*

Rear view of the Fordson with the separator at right and discharge elevator on the left. Though farmers were a little leery about combining in the humid regions, the Fordson tractor-mounted became quite popular and gained quite a following until Ford's decision to discontinue the tractor was announced in 1927. *AGCO*

Two views of the factory that produced the Fordson-mounted combines in the 1920s. *AGCO*

Following the demise of the Fordson came a series of pull-type combines beginning in the late 1920s. By this time the Midwest was just about convinced that the combine could be adapted to their region and be profitable at the same time. Above is the Model A Gleaner combine produced from 1928–35 operating in the fields of Kansas. Complete with roller bearings, balanced straw walkers, and spiral conveyer feed, this 12-foot machine could cut 600 acres of rye and wheat at a cost of fifty cents per acre. The tractor pulling the combine is none other than the Fordson. *AGCO*

Baldwin-patented chaff cutter bar. Literature of 1921 claimed that with the use of this cutter bar the separator size and weight was cut in half. The success of the Savage is vague, but the initial combine design was acquired by Advance Rumely of La Porte, Indiana, in 1921. Baldwin went along with the deal for a few years and remained in Denver to work on the Savage.

The Fordson-Mounted Combine

Meanwhile, back in Kansas, Baldwin's brothers Earnest and George were working on a tractor-mounted idea of their own. The brothers were assisted by C. A. Stevens and designer George Michael. By 1923 the first Fordson-mounted combine became a reality. With successful operation in the harvest year 1923, five of the tractor-mounted combines were produced for the following year. The Fordson-mounted machine killed two birds with one stone in that it could be operated as a self-propelled combine and also be utilized as a tractor around the farm when the combine was not in use. So bright was the future of the Fordson that heavyweights such as oil promoter Stephen H. Hale of Independence and W. J. Herman of Wichita joined the group of inventors and designers in 1924.

Curtis Baldwin also became involved with the tractor-mounted machine, often accompanying the combine in various locales for demonstration purposes. One company history has him assisting in a demonstration in Hayes, Kansas, walking along the header portion of the machine with a cane in order to force the heavy stand of wheat down against the conveyor and then into the cylinder. Five machines were built in 1924 with four sold to farmers and one kept for demonstration purposes. George Baldwin was responsible for following the other combines around to rate performance. He was also responsible for developing the angle in the back of the pan that held the grain down where the auger could catch it. It's interesting to note that the Gleaner Manufacturing Company later sued J. I. Case for using this method on their combines.

Testimonies during the harvest year of 1924 were numerous, all praising the work of the little Fordson-mounted combine. One believer in the machine wrote to the company to express his appreciation by stating that, "the wilderness of weeds and sunflowers was too much for my binder, header, or even my mower machine." Mr. Smyser went on to say that the only competition to the Fordson was "my bunch of hogs, which was doing fine until you finished." As to the superb way that the machine "picked" the wheat from the stalks, Smyser ended his correspondence by saying that if the machine was used through out the state of Kansas, "the Blackbird would have to carry a knapsack to cross the country." Testimonials like these, of which numbered into the hundreds, were successful in boosting the reputation of the fledgling company.

There were actually two companies formed in 1924. The Gleaner Company, a Kansas corporation and the Gleaner Manufacturing Company (GMC), a Delaware

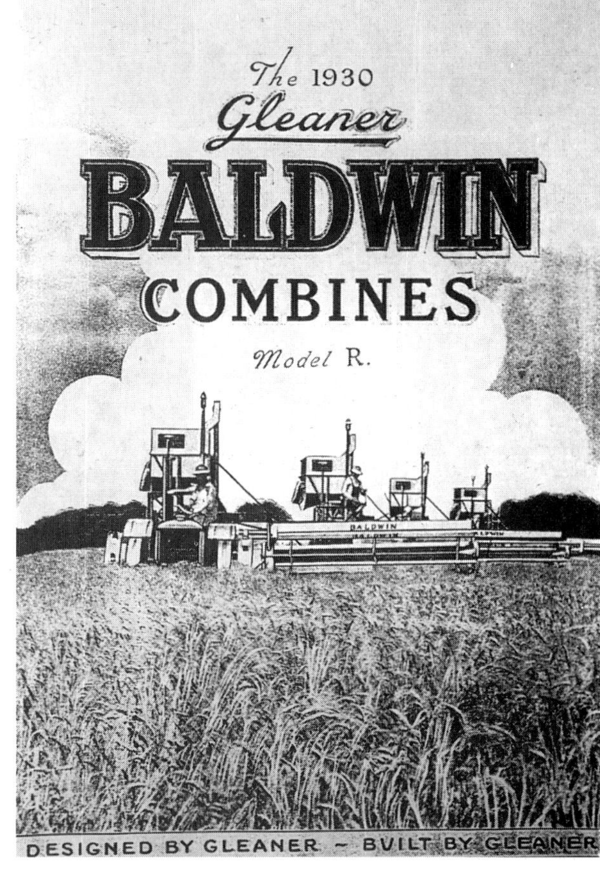

Model R sales brochure from 1930.

Tandem mounted Model Rs in 1931. A single tractor could pull two Gleaner combines enabling a 24-foot cut. Gleaner claimed that it was less expensive for a farmer to own two of their combines and a medium sized tractor rather than one large conventional machine. It was argued that two model R's weighed less than one 24-foot cut machine and that by using two machines grain capacity was increased so less stops were made for off-loading. Note the tandem hitch between the two combines in the center of the photo. *AGCO*

Factory photo of the Model R in 1930. Located almost dead-center on the combine is the Ford Model A industrial four-cylinder engine. Note the twin front wheels, a dead give-away that the machine is most likely operated in the Midwest. The Model R featured the rasp bar cylinder, the cylinder of choice for diversified crop regions. Unpainted galvanized steel became an early trademark of Gleaner combines. Even today their machines remain silver, with very little color. *AGCO*

A whopping seven tandems operating in the American Southwest. Would you believe a 168-foot cut? Depending on how these machines are aligned on the field, that's what you've got. *AGCO*

corporation that had an agreement with the Gleaner Company to use their patents on a royalty basis. The ever-present Curtis Baldwin became vice-president of the Delaware concern. Early in 1925, the GMC arranged to have the Butler Company of Kansas City build 100 machines for the harvest season. That the Gleaner machine was popular can't be understated, as it had been over sold at the Implement Show in Wichita in early February. After the first 100 were sold, the company took $100 deposits hoping that Butler would manufacture more combines. True to their word, Butler produced and sold 200 more combines for that year.

Curtis, on the other hand, was away in the fall of 1925 working on a pull-type combine. He felt that the tractor-mounted machine had too many pitfalls such as poor visibility, a dirty operator position, and a short usage cycle that tied up an expensive machine like the tractor. The latter reason Baldwin gives is debatable, as one of the advantages of the tractor-mounted combines was that it

Another popular pull-type was the Model R produced from 1929–35. The Fordson is ever-present once again, pulling this time in Nebraska. Auxiliary engines also became a permanent fixture with the Gleaner models from the twenties on. *AGCO*

eliminated the need for two separate machines on the farm for harvesting. Whether this was a case of "sour grapes" with regard to Baldwin is unknown. It should be remembered that while the Fordson-mounted machine was under development, Curtis Baldwin was in Denver working on the Savage machine.

In August of 1925, the Gleaner Manufacturing Company purchased the Baird P. Tool Company at Independence, and by October all the offices were moved to Independence from Wichita. While the new home of the Gleaner Manufacturing Company was as up to date as any other of that time, they still suffered from growing pains. Storage was a huge problem; raw materials were often simply piled outside of the main buildings, and steel bars had to be stored under the docks to protect them from the weather, creating extra labor costs when it all had to be moved. Even local transportation was hindered with the absence of pavement and drives from the buildings to the streets. Most of the outbound machines found themselves in a quagmire during the wet season, causing tractor drivers to spend time hauling trucks out of the mud.

But the show went on with 500 Gleaner machines manufactured for the 1926 harvest. The kinks were also being removed from a few production problems when it was rumored that the Fordson tractor might be discontinued. Seeing that the Fordson was the only tractor that the Gleaner could be mounted on, the move was soon made to develop a pull-type combine that could be pulled by a tractor. In the meantime, the Fordson continued to be a popular machine. Gleaner literature in 1926 reported that during the 1924 harvest season, one tractor mounted harvester traveled over 1000 miles, harvesting in 30 localities in three different states. Through the entire trip the tractor operated on smooth wheels to demonstrate that

The Gleaner Model T or Gleaner "Six" was produced from 1937–38 and reappeared again in 1940. The push was on for the development of a good solid six- or seven-foot combine during the 1930s and early 40s, and just about every other manufacturer was trying to do the same thing. This six-foot cut pull-type wasn't around very long but was handy for the small farmer with little acreage, especially during the Depression years when the small machines enjoyed their heyday. *AGCO*

"in the absence of the drawbar pulls, little traction is required." But even with a total production of 640 machines in 1926, the company was losing money. Over $33,000 was lost through the fabrication and assembly of combines by the Butler Manufacturing Company. Reorganization and increased financing was sought in an effort to keep the company afloat.

During this time, Curtis was still adamant about producing a pull combine, one that he had already built and demonstrated with great success. But with the Fordson going strong despite its rumored demise, the Gleaner Board of Directors turned Baldwin down flat. Curtis then left the company and formed the Baldwin Harvester Company. He then contracted with Standard Steel of North Kansas City to manufacture his pull-type combine. If that wasn't confusing enough, the Baldwin Harvester Company would be the sales organization for the Gleaner Manufacturing Company, which changed its name to the Gleaner Combined Harvester Corporation in December of 1926.

By 1927, Gleaner was still marketing its Fordson-mounted machine while Baldwin manufactured his pull machine. The Baldwin was equipped with a Model T Ford motor for the thresher-separator; motive power was to be derived from a tractor. According to company records, there were 415 Gleaners and 9,819 10- and 12-foot Baldwins sold in 1927. Actually, all the pull models sold in 1927 were the 10-foot cut except for a few that were increased to 12 feet with the use of a two-foot extension.

The Baldwins were clearly outselling the Gleaners, as was evident at the Wichita Show in early 1927. With so many orders taken by the Universal Equipment Company, Standard Steel Company of Kansas City would probably not be able to furnish an adequate amount of harvesters for the coming harvest season. Though the records are a little unclear, it seems that Baldwin and Standard Steel were not getting along. This prompted overtures from Hale of Gleaner to buy Baldwin out and at the same time acquire raw materials from Standard

A left side view of the little "Six" or Model S, denoting the straw walker separating unit. Note how the grain platform underneath the reel looks more like a bucket from a front-end loader rather than part of a combine. These machines were equipped with the small Wisconsin air-cooled four-cylinder motors for threshing and separating. *AGCO*

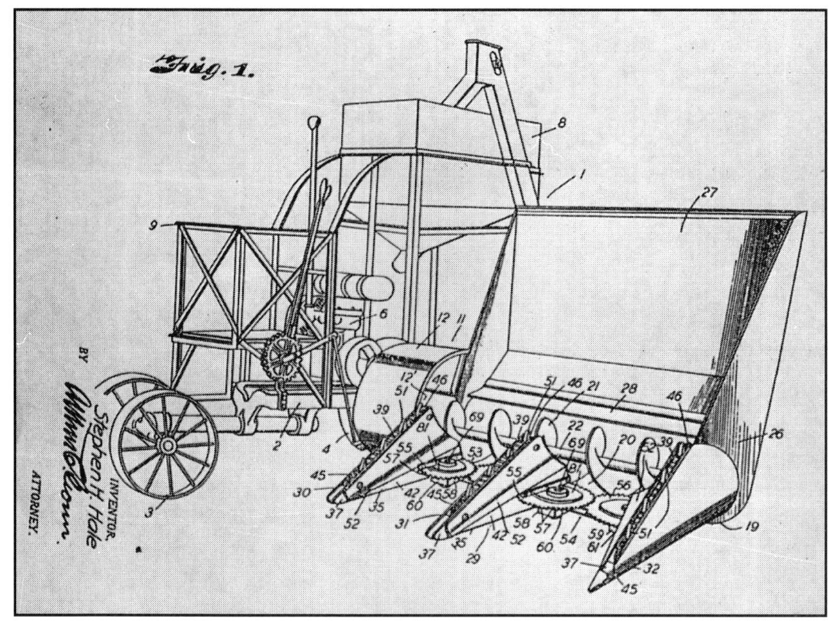

An early design from Steven H. Hale for a corn cutting mechanism in 1933. Gleaner attempted to vault into corn combining at a very early time, even though grain dryers weren't even devised yet. *AGCO*

Steel. With the former and the latter being accomplished, Gleaner settled with Universal Equipment for the orders they had taken. By the end of 1927, 1,050 Baldwin pull machines were built, the Fordson tractor was finally phased out of the United States market by Henry Ford, and Curtis Baldwin, who had sold off the Baldwin Harvester name to Gleaner, set off to start Curtis Harvesters, Inc.

Almost immediately, Baldwin set up shop in Ottawa, Kansas, where the Curtis Model 30 was built under the watchful eye of its proprietor. Baldwin apparently sold his machine directly to the consumer, eliminating the middleman. Unfortunately the Depression of the early 1930s did in what business he had managed to create in the small combine field. He did, however, continue his inventive ways by tinkering with rotary threshing models that would be built by Gleaner in the future.

Another tandem outfit operating in Oklahoma around 1932. The tractors appear to be Fordsons. *AGCO*

Things were different at the Gleaner plant, where the 1928 pull model was just coming into production. The 12-foot cut model proved more popular than the 10-foot, but for some reason the size of the separator was never increased, causing it to become choked. Another problem was the Model T Ford engines that powered the

Not just a picker, but a bona fide corn combine pictured here as the snow flies in 1930. Note the primitive looking snouts affixed to the platform in front of the auger. The reel is used instead of cutters for knocking down the stalks, something that Steve Hale would try to introduce three years later. Gleaner was so far ahead of the game when it came to corn combining that the resurgence of the idea didn't come to pass until the 1950s when corn dryers were perfected. Needless to say, the 1,500 corn attachments produced by Gleaner in the 1930s were shelved along with the corn combine idea itself. Not until the acquisition of Gleaner by Allis-Chalmers in 1955 did corn combining make a comeback. *AGCO*

Runs Smoother... Easier... With Less Chance of Costly, Time-Consuming Breakdowns.
Requires Less Power, Gives Longer Life
"Full-Jewelled" means that every rotating shaft, except the slow-turning reel and straw spreader, is mounted on anti-friction bearings. These anti-friction bearings—ball, roller and taper, many of which are factory sealed—are used to make your GLEANER BALDWIN last longer and run smoother. Only GLEANER BALDWIN offers this extreme degree of quality, which means, that after years of service, you have a higher trade-in value with a GLEANER BALDWIN.

Gleaner's "Fully Jeweled"" combines featured 71 Hyatt, New Departure, Timken, and SKF bearings. Gleaner was one of the first companies to introduce these anti-friction bearings, abandoning entirely the plain bearing. The company claimed that with the use of anti-friction bearings, lighter draft, greater smoothness, and less power for movement was required. *AGCO*

Gleaner machines were not powerful enough to harvest in the heavy Canadian wheat prairies. The answer was a more powerful engine. Apparently, three engines were used: the Continental, Waukesha, and Le Roi. Though these engines were more powerful than the Model T, other design flaws began to appear. In the case of the Continental, grit entering through the breather pipe and carburetor caused excessive engine wear. The result was over 2500 engines being brought in to the Gleaner works for reconditioning. Apparently longer breathing pipes and fuel strainers were not enough, so the Model A engine replaced all others in 1930.

In addition to the Gleaner 10- and 12-foot model was the Model R that was first developed in 1928 with a raddle-type separator. This model was quite successful and the first to use anti-friction bearings and roller chains. Model R literature referred to this a being "fully Jeweled," in that "all rotating shafts were supported by ball or roller bearings, except the reel shaft." Indeed, the technology developing was by no means a fluke, as some of the most inventive people in the business were embraced by Gleaner. A short list includes: P. H. (Pete) Hanson from J. I. Case in 1926; Norman E. "Pop" Bunting from International Harvester in 1927 (although "Pop" had been with Curt Baldwin at the Savage Company in 1921); Harper from Ford in 1928; Wayne Worthington from John Deere in 1928, who bought and disassembled a JD tractor in order to replicate a future Gleaner tractor; and H. C. Doss from Ford in 1930. And yes, Curt Baldwin was still around to form yet another company. In 1928, Baldwin along with C. B. Ruble and a Mr. O'Malley of the Universal Equipment Company formed the Baldwin Harvester Corporation to market the "New Baldwin" pull combine.

Gleaner had produced 1,039 Model A pull combines and 3,663 Model R's both with a 12-foot cut in

A 1930 Model A operating through wheat on the plains. These popular models could be found from Reno County, Kansas, to north of the Canadian border. Again, the dependable Fordson is pulling this "A" through the field. Note the bulk tank and the elevator running from the separator to the top of the tank. By this time, sacking was almost a thing of the past. *AGCO*

A front three-quarter view of the 12-foot Gleaner. The auger feeds the grain from left to right. The reel had six slats and a cutting range from 4 to 40-inches. The separator was an early rotary type (which Curt Baldwin had pioneered in the early thirties) that measured 32 inches wide and 13 feet in length. This model is also equipped with a 50-bushel bulk tank. *AGCO*

The tandem set-up was very popular in areas where extensive cropping took place. One report has the Carter Bros. outfit from Texas purchasing 13 Gleaner combines to harvest over 6500 acres of wheat. The 13 machines were pulled by seven tractors that harvested around 185,000 bushels of grain in twenty days. It was said that the two Gleaners could easily be pulled in tandem by a 20-35hp tractor. *AGCO*

With the self-propelled market exploding in the early 1950s, Gleaner wasted no time in unveiling its own SP in 1951. The Gleaner Model A SP featured a choice between a 12 or 14-foot cut and utilized the straw walker type separator. The "A" pictured above also continued the Centerline design with engine, bulk tank, and operator platform centrally located to enhance weight distribution and better traction. The machine is very similar to the Massey-Harris Model 21 as far as outward appearance. The Model R was also available with all the features of the "A" with the exception of the separator unit; the "R" came with the raddle-type. *AGCO*

Factory photo of the Model A in 1953. Hydraulics were offered on the 1951 model and were upgraded further by 1953. Note the extra long dividers on the outside of the grain platform. *AGCO*

1929. The company was also developing a corn head that proved successful in field trials in western Nebraska. By 1930, material was purchased for 1,500 attachments for the harvesting of corn. The attachments cut two rows of 40-inch corn, shelled it off, and delivered it to the grain bin. According to Gleaner, this corn combine was well ahead of its time. Unfortunately it wasn't feasible because grain dryers had yet to be developed. The machine was advertised not as a picker, but a *real* corn combine. Things were going well for Gleaner; by 1931, that would change.

The effects of the Great Depression were now being felt industry-wide, with unsold inventory piling up in Gleaner dealerships. With farmers unable to pay for equipment they had purchased, much less buy new machinery, the cash flow to the dealerships was severely curtailed. As a result, many dealers who handled the Gleaner product were unable to pay their accounts. The company coiffeurs were quickly emptied. To make matters

Left side view of the Gleaner 1955 Model A outside the production facilities in Independence, Missouri. After the acquisition of the Gleaner Company by Allis-Chalmers in 1955, the Model A featured the 70-horsepower Hercules Engine, automotive steering, unlimited propelling speeds, and dual control levers for "fingertip" operation. Because of the fierce competition in the combine market, every bell and whistle imaginable was included. *AGCO*

The first and last year that Gleaner offered the eight- and 10-foot cut Model T was in 1954. Smaller combines like the Model T were simply not in demand as in previous years. In fact, the six-foot machines were completely phased out in 1953. One reason for this move to the larger machines was that the SP could cover more ground with less manpower, allowing the farmer to open up more ground for crops. The smaller pull-types became more the exception than the rule, and to devise an SP with so narrow a cut defeated the purpose of the self-propelled. By 1955, the narrowest swath on all Gleaner machines was 12-foot. *AGCO*

Factory cutaway of the 1954 Gleaner Model A. Note the protective screen above the radiator located at the rear of the bulk tank. In later years the rotary screen would replace this stationary housing, a first in the industry introduced by Gleaner. Also note the straw walkers located behind the conveyor at the rear of the separator housing. *AGCO*

Field scene of the 1957 Gleaner Model A. Besides mechanical innovations, attention to comfort was also high on the priority list. These new models featured contoured-cushion seat hinges to enable the operator to either sit or stand "with ease." Notice the width of the slats on the reel. A far cry from the new Air-Reel systems used on today's combines. *AGCO*

Frontal view of the 1957 Model A on the open plains. *AGCO*

Bigger is better. The Model C made its debut in 1960 with options of 12, 14, 16, 18, or 20-foot cuts. The Model C, like the Model A, had the straw walker-type separator. From Hugoton, Kansas, to Vanceboro, North Carolina, the largest model Gleaner made at the time became extremely popular. These new model Cs were cutting everything from wheat to milo maize. The Model C, like its predecessors, offered the option of either the spike-tooth, rasp bar, or rubber-faced cylinder. *AGCO*

Still not satisfied that the small combine was long gone, Gleaner introduced its Model E in 1962. The photo above shows the Model E using the eight-foot header although a 10-, 12-, or 13-foot header could also be used. In addition to the Model E was the Model 2E, also introduced in 1962, for two-row corn harvesting. *AGCO*

Harvesting corn in Iowa with the 1965 Model E and two-row corn head. The Model E handled easily the 36- and 42-inch rows. The 1965 models also offered the "Quik-Tach" header system that allowed header swapping in a matter of minutes. Note the low-down snouts of the corn head. This extra low profile aided in lifting the even the most tangled stalks for threshing. *AGCO*

Gleaner's Model G was introduced in 1968. Referred to as "The Big One," the Model G offered the choice of three different engines; the power-crated gasoline model rated at 105 horsepower; the LPG 95-horsepower gas; and the turbocharged diesel with 109 horsepower. All were six-cylinder 301-cubic-inch engines. The Model G also performed well in corn harvesting using the six-row corn head for row spacings of 20, 30, 35, or 40 inches. The conventional grain header was offered in 13- to 23-foot cut. *AGCO*

worse, Gleaner owed the Agricultural Bond and Credit Corporation. When Gleaner was unable to pay up when the funds were demanded, the company was forced into receivership.

According to Gleaner records, the first receivers were a Mr. German, a lawyer, and a Mr. Patten from the infamous Pendergast political ring of Kansas City, the same ring that launched the political career of future United States President Harry S. Truman. German's son George was appointed general manager, whose job it was for the rest of 1931 to oversee the clean up of factory-field surplus. The receivers operated the company until April 6, 1932, and the sale of the company was scheduled for a week later. By the end of the day on April 15, 1932, the Gleaner Combine Harvester Corporation was owned by the newly formed Gleaner Harvester Corporation, a company created by the Commercial Credit Company, William J. Brace, Kansas City Banks, along with creditors and stockholders of the Gleaner Harvester Corporation. William J. Brace, the new General Manager, had just retired from the Hudson Motor Company. With the formation of the new company it was felt that a new model combine should also be developed to replace the successful Model R.

Before Gleaner could produce a new model, they had to find some business in the dismal market of the Depression era. Things were so bad that when Clyde Brown moved to Dodge City in 1932 to become Gleaner's only sales representative in the state of Kansas, exactly one new Gleaner was sold, and that was a 1930 model. The company didn't fare much better in 1933, as only existing inventory was used and service parts manufactured. But the tide began to turn in March of 1934 when 197 combines rolled off the production line, increasing the

Combining in Kansas with the 1968 Gleaner Model G. *AGCO*

following year with 523 Model R pull-type 12-foot raddle machines.

In April of 1936, the Model NR was introduced. Limited quantities were built, and it was shown at the Wichita Implement Show. Tentative orders were taken, an indication of an improving market. The NR had the "down front" cylinder and was tied to the pivotal Harvester-Thresher. The NR also came equipped with the exclusive steel conveyor and the auger over the canvas, first adopted by the Gleaner Company. By the end of the1936 harvest season, problems started to surface with cylinder bearings failing and headers breaking down between the 10-foot and 12-foot pan back area. Though costly to Gleaner, repairs were made on the previously sold NRs.

Excited with the prospects of entering the small combine market with a bang, Gleaner unveiled its six-foot combine models S and T (S denoted the straw walker type and T for the raddle type). Initially, the machine was equipped with a two-cylinder Cushman engine but was later replaced with the four-cylinder Wisconsin air-cooled engine. Again, the company rushed the machine into production with hardly enough time for trials. According to the record, the backlash was bad enough that Gleaner was stuck with "a graveyard of hundreds of combines that were forced to be taken back." Some were rebuilt, but most apparently remained unsold. Later in 1937, 30 new six-foot models were produced (15 T's and 15 S's) that were sold along with the newer 12-foot models E and F. Between 1929 and 1940, Gleaner had seven different models of combines on the market, with the 12-foot cut machine being the most popular. It was hoped that the small six-foot machine would eventually round out the line, but by 1942 it proved to be a very small part of the line. The Model S six-footer was discontinued in 1954.

Throughout the 1940s, Gleaner managed to hold its own, despite the fact there was a war going on. Like all other industries during this period, raw materials were in short supply, and production was cut to a certain extent. But an interesting event was about to occur in the Heartland of America with regard to combining, an event that would completely change the industry shortly after war's end. The Massey-Harris Company of Toronto, Canada,

At right is the Gleaner Model F in 1968. This particular machine, like the K, L and M, metamorphosed into the F2 and later the F3 until it was finally discontinued in 1987. It's interesting to note that even at this late date of combine innovations that the open air driver platforms were still being produced. This cab, on the other hand, is totally enclosed but affords the operator a tremendous view of the operating parts of his combine. This "floor to ceiling" visibility enabled the operator to spend more time in the cab. The addition of on-board electric monitoring devices also aided greatly in non-stop performance. *AGCO*

The little Gleaner E III was only around for a year in 1968. It was kind of a mid-sized machine offering cuts up to 13-feet. The E III had a cylinder width of 27 inches and a separator that measured 32 inches wide. The E III was small compared to all other Gleaner models and didn't seem to fit in the larger machine market, probably one reason for its quick departure from the scene. *AGCO.*

was about to score a marketing coup with the introduction of the self-propelled Model 21.

Massey-Harris had convinced the War Department to ease restrictions on raw materials for production of 500 self-propelled combines in 1943. In exchange, the 500 Model 21's would harvest the nation's wheat from South Texas all the way to the Canadian border. Reaping the country's wheat in this manner gave them the name the "Harvest Brigade," giving Massey-Harris over 52 percent of the US combine market by 1948. The self-propelled was here to stay as demand skyrocketed in the early 1950s, prompting Gleaner engineers Lee Oberholtz and Gene Allen to tour the wheat belt in the summer and fall of 1949. Their mission was to talk to farmers and dealers as to what exactly they wanted in a self-propelled combine. The result was the Gleaner Model A self-propelled.

Early in 1950, the Model A was designed, and four prototypes were built for experimental purposes. Gleaner's timing couldn't have be better as reduced manpower on the farm along with advanced engineering technologies created a huge market for self-propelled combines. In 1951, Gleaner produced 500 Model A and R self-propelled combines.

The Model A's Centerline design was touted in company literature as the best in the business with regard to balance, proportion, and operation. The centering of weight on the combine was, and still is, an important component to efficient operation in the field, as is a low center of gravity; Gleaner maintained both in the Model A. According to a news release dated October 23, 1950, equal weight distribution to both drive wheels was essential to good traction. Gleaner engineers claimed that the weight of the Model A Centerline was perfectly centered so that the load would not shift regardless of the amount of grain in the bin.

The center of gravity on the Model A was 41 inches above the ground and 18. 3 inches to the rear axle, with no parts close to the ground susceptible to damage. Another feature was Gleaner's "balanced steering." The Model A had no chains, sprockets, or cables in its steer-

Gleaner's response to the hillside market in the Pacific Northwest was the Model GH brought out in 1969. This machine is harvesting club wheat in the hills around Walla Walla, Washington. Though Gleaner would attempt to stay in the Hillside fray along with Deere and IH, they quickly dropped out of the race by 1972, the last year that their hillsides were produced. *AGCO*

Field scene of the 1971 Gleaner Model G. Gleaner claimed that "If you can till it, you can harvest it with a Gleaner GH combine." The company compared the GH's low center of gravity to the crawler tractor and its hill-hugging performance. The rate of leveling on any given degree of slope was adjusted automatically, and was able to counteract any sudden change. The grain bin also came equipped with an automatic load leveler to distribute the grain evenly for better balance. *AGCO*

ing mechanism. Balanced steering was accomplished by controlling the steering gear from a center point. The result was that the tilting of the wheels didn't affect the turn of the wheels. The very wide 68-inch tread of the tires not only made the combine turn easier, but also enabled it to ride smoother over rough terrain.

The Model A, like earlier Gleaner Combines, was also "fully jeweled." All moving parts with the exception of the reel shaft was mounted on either roll, ball, or taper bearings of the anti-friction design. Gleaner pioneered this feature very early. The feed on the Model A was direct to the cylinder with the "down-front" design. With the cylinder so far forward, the cut grain traveled over 13 feet before being discharged from the rear of the separator. By 1954, the line was further increased with the addition of three new self-propelled models; the Model T2 (two-row bean) seven-foot, the T3 (three-row bean) 10-foot, and the Model P 80.

By February of 1955, the corporate winds of change began to blow once again as Gleaner became the Independence Works of Allis-Chalmers. After the acquisition, both the Model T and P 80 combines were dropped from the line. The Model T never really performed well in small grains, but was up to the task in edible beans. The unsold inventory wound up in Michigan where they could be put to good use.

AC-Gleaner Hillside Combines

An area Allis-Chalmers was looking into was a hillside combine, a must if they wanted to enter the lucrative Northwest market. Engineers wasted no time and, by 1959, came up with the self-leveling 14-foot Model AH. The Model AH was only manufactured until 1962, and probably less than 200 machines ever saw the field. Company records don't address the brief appearance of the Model AH, but it was a significant model.

The AH had a massive frame and drive axle to handle the added strain of hillside harvesting. Powerful hydraulic rams actuated by a mercury switch automatically leveled the AH. Wide-track wheels and the signature Centerline design were standard on the hillside. The header, drive, and steering axles tilted either way to permit combining in either direction and leveled smoothly on slopes of up to 42 percent. The Model AH's powerplant was a 260-cubic-

The level-land 1970 Gleaner Model G. *AGCO*

inch six-cylinder manufactured by parent company Allis-Chalmers. The separator was 36 inches wide and 13 feet long. The AH also featured the "Sure-feed" system with the standard "down-front" cylinder, which was the reverse rasp-bar instead of the spiked tooth.

The Model CH replaced the AH in 1963, but didn't last too long before being dropped from the line in 1968. With a total separation area of 6,840 square inches, the CH was touted as the largest of its kind on the market in 1963. It was also being compared to the crawler tractor in the way that it "hugged" the hillside while harvesting. The power-plant was upgraded from the AH to a 262-cubic-inch six-cylinder valve-in-head Allis-Chalmers Power-Crater engine, while a rotary air screen was added to the radiator to prevent clogging from chaff. Header sizes were 16 to 18 feet with a 5-bat reel. The leveling system remained the same with only slight improvements. The "Multi-Rate" leveling system automatically adjusted to the degree of slope, insuring that the separator remained level. When a sharp degree of slope change was encountered, the leveling system moved quickly to counteract then slowed to a lower rate to finish the process, avoiding sharp jerks and bouncing in the separator.

Following the CH was the GH, a hillside model that only lasted three years (1969–72). This model was the first to offer the choice of three different engines: 105hp (standard), a turbocharged diesel at 109hp, or the 95hp LP gas model, both optional. By 1969, the Gleaner GH came with hydrostatic power steering, variable speed cylinder controls, an on-the-go tailings check system, and a pressurized cab, all in an effort to improve the performance of hillside combining. The usual Centerline design, swivel header, wide-track tires, and hydraulics continued on with numerous improvements. Still there were higher demands placed on the combine market, and those that wanted to remain in the business needed to make changes. In an effort to meet this demand, Gleaner went from the GH to the new model MH in 1972. There was actually a series of Ms, the MH2 (1977-82) and MH3 (1983-86), though after 1986 Gleaner had dropped out of the hillside market.

Return of the Corn Head

As mentioned earlier, Gleaner had actually developed a bona fide corn combine as early as 1930. The

Right side view of the L with corn head. *AGCO*

In 1973, Gleaner introduced the Model L. The L, like the F-series, was produced for a lengthy period and wasn't discontinued until the company went off in a totally different direction with the R-Series (rotary) combines in 1987. Pictured here is an early Model L set up with a four-row corn head. Again, notice the open-air driver's platform, most common in the humid regions where extreme dust was not as bad as in the semi-arid wheat fields of the West. *AGCO*

problems the machine incurred were not due to design flaws or poor performance in the field, but to the lack of grain dryers. The corn head used in association with the combine would not reappear until 1957, when 105 heads were built for the Model A. These particular corn heads were the two-row models with 22-inch snapping rolls. Obviously, improvements were made since the 1930 introduction. The 1961 models were produced with long, low flexible snouts; two gathering chains per row with slip-clutch protection in order to keep the corn moving in a steady stream; adjustable stripper plates for reduced shelling losses at the rolls; and grass shields under the rolls to reduce wrapping and plugging. Initial production of the corn heads resumed at the Independence Works but after 1959 was transferred to the La Porte plant in Indiana as most of the corn related production was carried on there.

By 1962 the use of the corn head was expanded to the models C and E. Advertised as the Model 2-A and 2-E, these machines carried the two-row heads while the Model 4-C had the four-row head. In addition to the features mentioned above, options such as the variable speed cylinder control was available on the Model E along with cob shields, Walker set-back plates (that reduced the tendency of cobs to back feed), and lapped filler bars used when shelling corn to keep the cobs out of the center of the cylinder. Wheel shields were also an option designed to keep lodged corn out of the path of the drive wheels.

One of the strongest sales arguments for the corn head was the fact that field shelling corn enabled the farmer to market his crop earlier when prices were at their highest level. Shelled corn required only half the space that eared corn did, so storage was another point to consider. The cobs were left in the field freeing up both bin and wagon space and increasing harvest time in the field. The average yield in 800 acres of corn using the four-row head could be as high as 140 bushels to the acre. The Gleaners proved themselves amid a wide audience, and at the 1964 National Corn Picking Contest five out of eight combines were the Models A and E. It

This is a three-quarter front view of the Model L with the conventional grain header. By this time the machine was equipped with the 24-foot header and could also be fixed up with the newer eight-row corn head if desired. The unloading tube is swiveled back along side the combine when not in use, although many operators will tend to load on-the-go depending on the experience of the truck driver. You haven't lived until you've seen some guy claim to know what he's doing, only to find that most of the grain from the bin is being loaded either on the ground or on the hood of the truck. *AGCO*

was noted that the Gleaners had the lowest ear corn loss, and none were deducted in points for excessive cracking or trash in the bin. One of these combines went on to become a national champion.

But improvements were ongoing, and by 1970, the new Low-Profile corn head was introduced by Gleaner. The Low-Profile heads were quite different from anything on the market at the time. These heads were much lower to the ground and were increased in length, enabling the snouts to travel at ground level to pick up even the most stubborn lodged crop. The snapping rolls were also set at a reduced angle for the same reason and lengthened to 30. 75 inches. Corn heads for the Model L in 1973 included the 4-38, 6-30, 6-38, and 8-30. The Model M was a bit smaller in capacity. Further improvements in 1977 brought out a line of adjustable heads with the K2, F2, M2, and L2.

The fully adjustable corn head was hawked in sales literature as tackling the most obnoxious of crops including downed corn, tangled stalks, and low hanging ears. The row units were individually mounted on a 5x5 inch tool bar and could be adjusted two inches either way from center. In other words, the four-row 30 inches could be adjusted to four-row 28 inches or the other way to four-row 32 inches. Once in the field, the new head would "skim between rows and under the lowest hanging ears" while rubber ear deflectors grabbed the bouncing ears and guided them into the gathering chains.

The 1973 Gleaner Model L in the field. From 1973 on, the L's power plant was either the 350-cubic-inch eight-cylinder gasoline engine or the six-cylinder turbocharged diesel rated at 130 horsepower.

By the time the N-Series combines were out in 1979, the corn head had increased to two-row capacity. Some new features included double spiral-fluted snapping roll extensions that aided in maximizing continuous crop flow; positive control at higher ground speeds; reversible snapping roll blades for longer life and center-line hook-up for changing heads. The K2 and F2 models went from two-row to six-row; the M2 and L2 from four- to six-row and the rotary N6 and N7 from four- to two-row capacity. By the mid-1980s, corn head production had returned to the main combine plant at Independence where the corn head made an easy transition from the N-Series to the R-Series machines.

Models K, F, L, and M

The years 1968-69 saw the introduction of the Model F and K into the Gleaner line. Standard on both F and K models was the Sure-Feed system with down-front cylinder, two stage separation, and the two-fan cleaning system. The K operated with a 27-inch rasp bar cylinder (reversible bars) and had header widths of 10, 12, 13, 14, and 15 feet. The K also came with three-row 30-inch and two-row 38-inch corn heads. The power plant consisted of a 250-cubic-inch six-cylinder gas engine. The Model F was basically the same as the K but with a larger separator capacity, a wider header, running from 13 to 20 feet, and three different engine options.

New for 1971 on both models was the one-man header hook-up. With the use of a header stand, one man could simply drive the combine to the header, attach the hooks, raise the thresher housing, and latch the lower wedge pins all in one safe and efficient operation. Gleaner prided itself when it came to safety. Often times when a tube (unloading auger) would bang up against a tree or other obstacle a lot of damage could occur, not only to the auger but to framing and other moving parts as well. To remedy this, Gleaner installed the spring-loaded unloader tube and self-aligning auger coupler to make it easy for one man to swing the tube into the unloading position. If by accident the tube was to hit an obstruction, the spring-loaded latch would release, causing the tube to swing harmlessly out of the way. According to company literature, this feature greatly reduced damage to the mechanism.

Still more innovations were on the AC-Gleaner horizon in 1972 with the introduction of the giant Model L combine. This gargantuan machine took a swath of 24 feet in one pass in small grains or up to eight rows of 30-inch corn. With a separator capacity of 53 inches, the L was the largest machine produced by Allis-Chalmers at the time, and also came with numerous new features. The weight of the model L came in at just over 13,000 pounds, an overall length of more than 27 feet, a height of 11 feet 7 inches, and a width of 25 1/2 feet. There were apparently three optional versions: a model with hydro-traction drive, a corn-soybean special, and another that was a combination of the two. The L was also the first model that utilized the dual-outlet transverse fan.

Like the Model L, the smaller version Model M incorporated much of the same features. Far from the early innovations of Holt's hinged headers and balance beams, Gleaner was now offering Electro-Hydraulic Controls for all facets of header and separator operations. With one push of a button, reel height could be achieved instantly for varying crops. The same functions could be used for reel speed, lifting or lowering, and stopping or starting without interfering with separation. The "floating" cutter bar was optional for cutting close to the ground in crops like soybeans, being carried on leaf springs and kept at a constant height regardless of irregularities in the field.

In 1977, the Rice/Soybean Model L and M with Hydro-Traction went into production, featuring single-lever control for forward and reverse speeds that provided more maneuverability and ground speed control in muddy conditions. These models had a 16- or 18-foot header that was chain-driven with slip clutch protection for the header conveyor auger. The Hydrostatic reel drive was

The machine above is the Gleaner N7 Rice/Soybean combine, first produced in 1979. This was Gleaner's "New Concept" combine that featured a true rotary threshing system that is still used exclusively by Gleaner. The N-Series was soon replaced by the R-Series in 1987. *AGCO*

The upgraded F2 in 1977 outfitted with tracks for rice harvesting. The idea of tracks isn't all that old. Some of the early Holt machines also had tracks for the muck that came along with harvesting in parts of California. Even Deere's famous Model 55 tried on a pair of these tracks at one time or another. What could be used in simple tillage operations could also be adapted for use on the combine in one form or another. *AGCO*

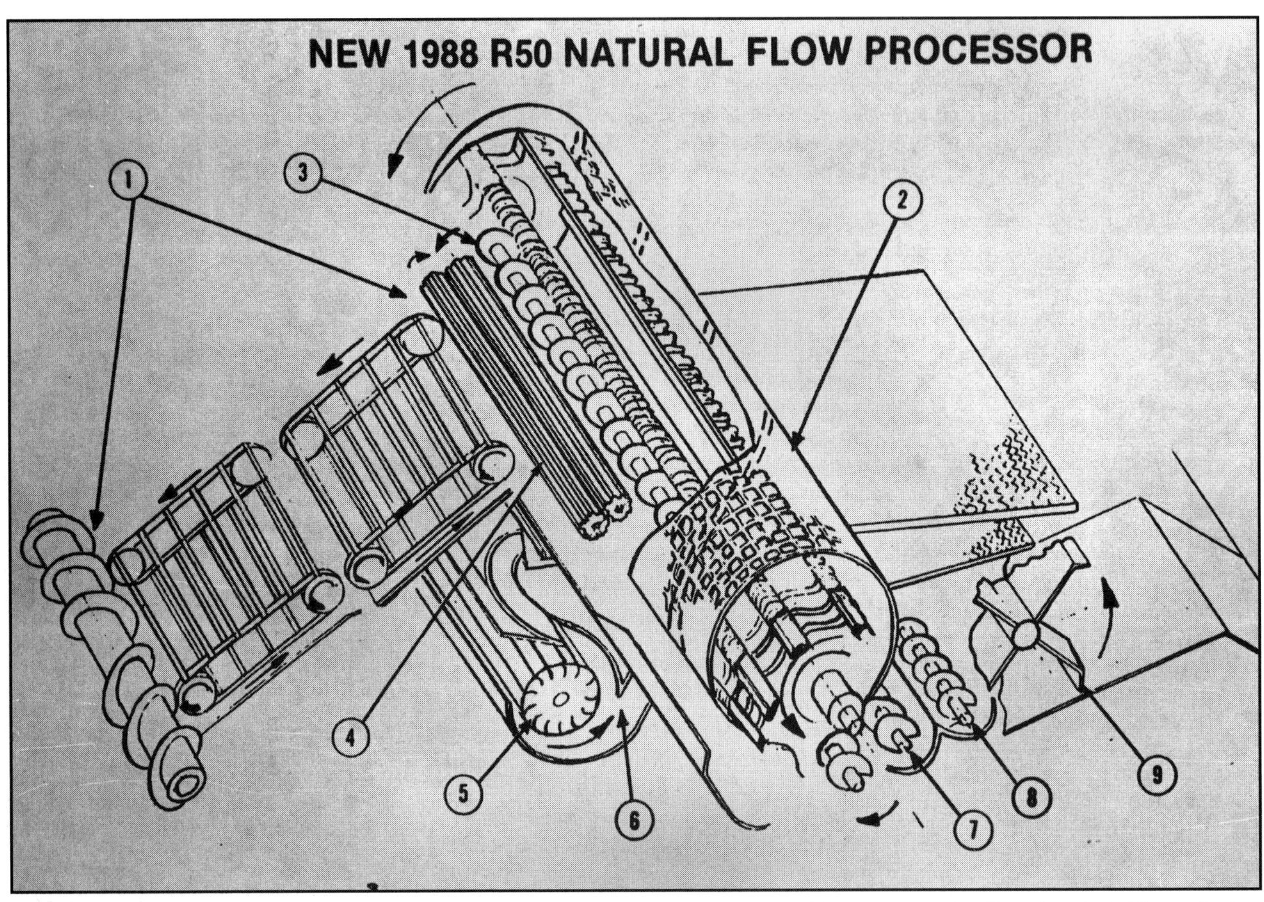

Above is a factory illustration of the "Natural-Flow" processor (threshing cylinder) featured on the R-50 in 1988. The cylinder is encased by 360 degrees of mesh, instead of the traditional 180 degree concave. The idea was that the grain would only have to go through the threshing process once. Beneath the cylinder are two accelerator rollers spinning in opposite directions, forcing the threshed grain downward at high speeds, defying gravity and insuring one-time threshing. You will also note that the straw walkers are entirely eliminated. *AGCO*

optional. The L and M were soon upgraded in 1978 as the L2 and M2 and included increased grain bin capacity, Hydro-traction drive motors with 25 percent more torque output, and Tattletale monitoring systems with lights over gauges for greater operator efficiency. The L2 and M2 were upgraded to the L3 and M3 from 1983 to 1987, the last year they were made.

The F2 and K2 models were also an upgrade from the F and K, offering similar features as the L and M. Floating cutter bars with wobble box drives were offered on all four combines. It seemed that no small detail was left out of the Gleaner machines for increased performance. Air flow was extremely important in the harvesting of small grains and could easily be adversely affected in hilly terrain. To remedy this, Gleaner introduced its Air-Flow Grain Saver that could be used by a level-land machine in hilly fields. The grain saver delivered a controlled blast of air to the downhill side of the shoe to spread grain more evenly across its width to insure optimal cleaning. In addition to improvements for harvesting, attention towards comfort was also taken care of with amenities like air-conditioning, heater, cigarette lighter, AM/FM stereo, and even an eight-track stereo tape player. And if this was not enough, in 1979 the company was about to abandon the conventional combine altogether with the introduction of its new rotary machines, the N Series combines.

The N and R Series Combines

The rotary concept was not all that new as Curt Baldwin had three patents awarded to him way back in the 1930s. As a matter of fact, this rotary idea of threshing grain goes back into the 1800s. Gleaner went as far as building a prototype model in 1967. Regardless, Gleaner engineering was on the verge of proving the idea with the introduction of 50 Model N6 combines for a pilot run in 1978. This would be the debut of the first totally new combine brought out by Gleaner since the introduction of the Model L in 1972.

The rotary design allowed for 360 degree threshing and separation with the cylinder mounted transversely. This was done for a variety of reasons. The N series was the first to mount the cylinder crossways and midway between the front and rear axles taking up less space, providing optimal weight distribution and eliminating the

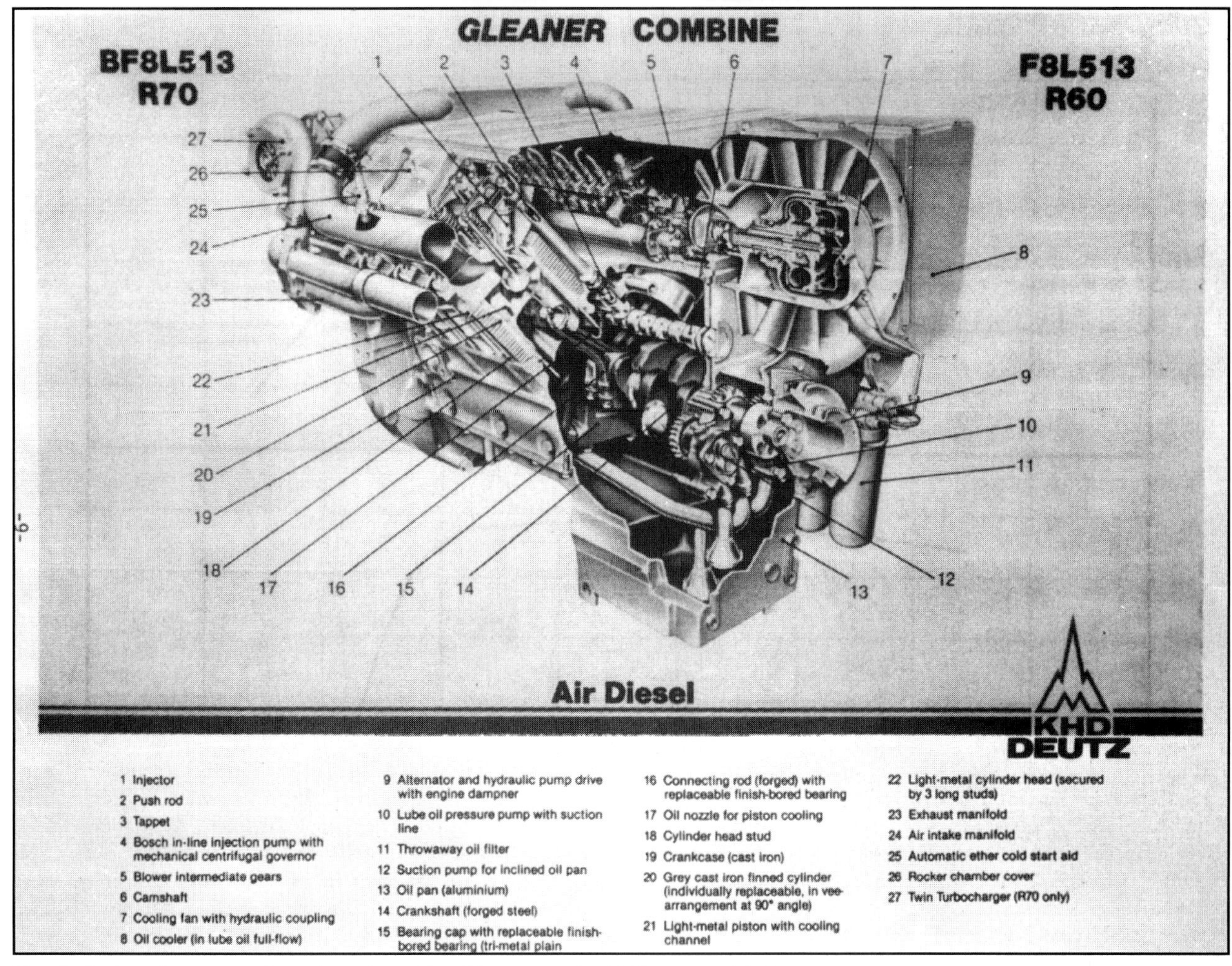

The R-Series air-cooled diesel introduced by Gleaner under KHD ownership in 1988.

need for a 90 degree gear box. It also allowed for a "Natural-Flow" feed, assuring less tangling of crop during the feeding process. The cylinder measured 90 inches and was mounted inside a cage with perforation a full 360 degrees around. This design allowed the grain to be separated at any spot on the cylinder/cage.

Sales literature pointed out that with conventional rotary cylinders, only the bottom half of the cylinder has open grates for grain to pass, half the separating capacity of the Gleaner design. They also claimed that with the 360 degree method, grain only had to pass through the process once instead of twice and greatly reduced grain damage in the long run. The Gleaner design was similar to the International Harvester Axial-Flow model, except that the cylinder was mounted sideways rather than longitudinally.

The Gleaner N Series machines used centrifugal force and high velocity air movement to improve separating and cleaning. It must be remembered that the difference between conventional and rotary designs is gravity; the former depends on it, and the latter defies it. The N Series used augers to displace chaff and grain from the cylinder/cage area downward to the accelerator rolls (patented in 1977) at a rate of four times faster than normal free-fall. The accelerator rolls consisted of fluted rubber that traveled at opposite directions, forcing the chaff and grain down into a very thin stream enhancing aerodynamic separation. This design also enhanced delivery to the cleaning shoe leaving the chaff to be sent to the rear of the machine. Paddles on the end of the cylinder shaft directed straw to an impeller that sent it to the rear for discharge (straw walkers were eliminated in the rotary design). Another advantage was that grain and chaff could be directed in an even layer across the full width of the shoe, eliminating shifting of the material to the down-hill side while combining on slopes. As a matter of fact, some of the company literature claimed that this exclusive design did away with the need for a side-hill model altogether.

Gleaner produced three N models (the N5, N6, and N7), the difference being in size. The largest of the models, the N7, boasted a grain bin capacity of 315 bushels, a grain head and floating cutter bar of up to 24 feet, rasp bar cylinder, and corn head sizes ranging from four to eight row capacity. The N7 also operated with a 270-horsepower six-cylinder in-line turbocharged and inter-

The New A-C RUMELY Spring Mounted Thresher

When Allis-Chalmers acquired Rumely in 1931, they also came into possession of a superb line of threshing machines like the spring-mounted machine above. With springs located on both the front and the rear of the machine, the company claimed that lost bolts through simple vibration would be a thing of the past. No "shaking to pieces on the road" was another benefit, mainly due to the option of using rubber overtires for transporting down the usually rough county roads. *Allis-Chalmers Yearbook, 1934*

In addition to threshing machines A-C profited for a time with the Rumely combines. Above is the A-C Rumely No. 2 Combine Harvester available in both 16- and 20-foot cuts. This machine featured a heavy duty four-cylinder engine and the all-steel balanced hinged header. All of the A-C Rumelys could be equipped to thresh everything from soybeans to clover and edible peas. *Allis-Chalmers Yearbook, 1934*

A three-quarter rear view of the A-C Rumely No. 3 Harvester, another prairie type, that was available in either 10- or 12-foot cuts. Though the Rumely proved to be a fine combine, A-C would phase all of the machines out by the late 1930s to make way for their own line of machines. Nevertheless, some of these old machines made their way out to the wheat belt of the Northwest and can still be found sitting idle around forgotten farmsteads. *Allis-Chalmers Yearbook, 1934*

Another A-C Rumely No. 3, this one a hillside model with the 10- or 12-foot cut. These particular machines were designed specifically for the Northwest farmer. The leveling device was power operated and could level on upgrades of 40 percent and on downgrades of 22 percent. *Allis-Chalmers Yearbook, 1934*

cooled diesel engine and a four-speed Hydro-Traction Drive transmission. The N6 was powered by an Allis-Chalmers 670 HI turbocharged and intercooled diesel rated at 220 horsepower. The N5 engine was a 190-horsepower Model 670 HI engine. These machines were a far cry from the tractor and auxiliary-powered Ford Model T power plant!

The machines had the largest fuel tank capacity in the industry at the time at 150 gallons, and an unloading tube that could kick out more than two bushels per second! In addition to the exclusive rotary design, the Ns also featured the clean grain elevator, concave door stone protection, exclusive transverse flow cleaning fan, two-stage high velocity air cleaning, 14-inch auger, sloped gather sheets, individually mounted row units (corn), and a push-button activated unloading tube that could unload the entire 315 bushel bulk tank of the N7 in about two minutes.

The N-Series combine was a success for Gleaner, but things were about to change once again. In 1985, the Allis-Chalmers Agricultural Business, including the Credit Corporation that owned Gleaner was sold to Klockner-Humboldt-Deutz of West Germany. Besides the discontinuation of the Model K in 1983, the N-series was dropped in 1987, and the M, L, and F in 1988. The R-series combine also made its debut in 1987 with the R5, R6, and R7. The R40 debuted in 1988, a zero added to its model number denoting the air-cooled diesel produced by Deutz. The new model also came with a new name as well as colors of blue, silver, and green, a deviation from the trademark silver-gray.

The R-series combines retained many of the features pioneered in the N-series machines, and in 1990 the "Silver Hawk" line was introduced. From a confidential company circular dated February 15, 1990, changes to the R40, R50, R60, and R70 model were detailed, with upgrades to the 60 and 70 machines. The most important changes had to do with the rotary process, switching from the P1 to the P3 Natural-Flow rotary processor. The P3 design enlarged the area of the concave arch from a 52 degree one-piece to a 105 degree two-piece concave; replaced the 49 flat bars with 15 channel bars, and converted the cage sweep from axial motion to radial motion. Later, the so-called "High Wire" concave and cage was introduced to provide a 25 percent increase in the open area of separation.

The company changed ownership again in 1990. In May, the Deutz-Allis management led a buy-out from Klockner-Humboldt-Deutz, forming the Allis-Gleaner Company (AGCO). The newly formed company also acquired the Hesston Corporation in a joint ownership venture with Case; acquired the White Tractor Division of

This larger hillside model No. 1 could be had with a 20-foot cut if desired. You will notice that this machine has been outfitted with the horse-powered drivers platform. Inasmuch as tractors became the power of choice by the mid-1930s, some areas of the Northwest were still obliged to use the horse. This particular model experienced limited success in hillside country. Notice the rack type power leveling system similar to the Harris of California. *Allis-Chalmers Yearbook, 1934*

Allied Products Corporation, with more than 600 dealerships; and a new line of tractors from SLH Italy to replace the tractor loss from Klockner-Humboldt-Deutz, all in 1991. Further acquisitions followed as the harvesting industry became more competitive. Where at one time the playing field was crowded, there were only three large producers of combines left: Gleaner, John Deere, and Case-IH, who continued manufacturing the Axial Flow combine developed by the International Harvester Company in the mid-1980s.

Indeed, much has changed since the introduction of the Holt and Harris machines of the Pacific Coast. But the combine had finally arrived in the Midwest, not only with Curt Baldwin's Standing Grain Thresher, but with other "old line" companies jumping into the arena as well. The mid-1920s was a proving ground for these "combination" machines, long distrusted in the humid regions. Numerous reports and field tests, however, were being conducted by state and federal agricultural agencies, and slowly the tide began to turn in favor of the combine. Combines were getting smaller, and acceptance was on the rise due to favorable studies done in the Great Plains region. With Harris as the lone combine manufacturer on the Pacific Coast, the combine industry would soon shift from west to east and eventually dominate the entire market.

AC-Rumely: Before The Gleaner Years

Another interesting acquisition by Allis-Chalmers was the Advance Rumely Company and their line of combines. Once the Midwest market for combines began to boom, small companies sprang up overnight to try to get a piece of the action. As in the Pacific Northwest, most of the smaller companies were squeezed out by the deeper pockets and broader base of the more established competition.

Such was the case with the Rumely Company when Allis-Chalmers purchased it in 1931. With the purchase, Allis-Chalmers inherited the Oil Pull tractor, a premium line of threshers, and three models of combines: the No. 1 and No. 2 prairie type, and the No. 3 hillside. The surviving models from the buy-out were two model threshers and the hillside combine. In 1936, they were all discontinued.

The No. 2 Allis-Chalmers Rumely combine harvester was still being advertised in the 1934 catalog. The prairie type was offered in the 16- and 20-foot cuts. A lot like the old Holts, the No. 2 featured an all-steel header that was hinged at the thresher, an extra large feeder house that was the same width as the cylinder, and double-action straw racks for even threshing. The No. 2 could be adjusted for combining soy beans, peas, and clover. It also featured a four-cylinder auxiliary engine that was economical in use of fuel and oil.

The No. 3 prairie type came with either the 10- or 12-foot cut and was very popular in the Corn Belt as well as in wheat. Sales literature claimed that the threshing unit in the No. 3 was "the greatest separating device ever built into a combine." It had a newly developed built-in grain recleaner with a tailings discharge into the feeder house; grain tight pans with endless grain drags; a 30-bushel grain bin that was center-mounted insuring proper weight distribution; and swather and pick-up attachments for windrowing. The No. 3 hillside was virtually the same as the prairie type with the exception of the leveling device. The hillside was produced mainly for the Pacific Northwest, and claimed the machine could be perfectly level at slopes up to 40 percent on the upgrade and 22 percent on the downhill side. The No. 3 was offered in 10- and 12-foot cuts. The No. 1 hillside offered the 12-, 16- and 20-foot cut and was level up to 60 percent. The leveling device on all the hillside models was power-driven, leveling being accomplished by the rack and pinion method common to the early Harris and Holt machines.

In addition to the combines, Allis-Chalmers continued for a time with the Rumely threshers. Advertised in the 1933–34 catalogs was the Rumely Spring-Mounted Thresher; the Rumely Steel thresher, and the newly acquired Birdsell clover and alfalfa huller. The spring-mounted machine was an improvement devised by Allis-Chalmers to avoid excessive vibration during operation. Both front and rear of the thresher was provided with springs, claiming "no more loose bolts. No shaking to pieces on the road." Rubber overtires were provided for transporting on roadways, with all rubber tires as an option. This particular machine was so sleek that it could be pulled by a car "hauled behind an automobile." The Spring-Mounted came with a 22-inch cylinder and 38-inch separator. The all-steel thresher was virtually the same, only with a larger thresher/separator unit.

Probably more than anything else, the Great Depression speeded up the discontinuation of the entire Rumely line. Competition was stronger than ever and the push for smaller machines was at hand. Allis-Chalmers took it upon themselves to produce their own combines for a time, offering up several small machines for the Corn Belt. One machine in particular was the Corn Belt Combine Harvester.

Advertised as a machine "for diversified farms," the little corn combine could be operated by any two-plow tractor equipped with power take-off. It had a five-foot cut and could harvest from two to 22 inches above the ground. The machine had a five-foot threshing cylinder which made it a straight-through feed. One of the best things about it is that it weighed only 2400 pounds. Though the Corn Belt Harvester wasn't in the line very long, its replacement, the All-Crop 60, would fare better and become the longest-produced combine in the line.

The All-Crop 60

Produced from 1935 to 1953, the All-Crop 60 literally took over the harvesting duties on the small diversified farm. In his book *Allis Chalmers*, historian Norm Swinford has gone so far to say that, "this unimpressive little machine challenged the autocracy of the binder-steam engine-threshers and relegated them to the museums."

It has already been noted how the combine had liberated the farmer from having to locate scarce labor at times of harvest. Not only was the farmer freed from having to hire a large crew to bring in the harvest, but the cook, usually the woman of the household, was liberated from having to feed the harvest crew. This was a dirty, monumental task. Tons of potatoes and other fresh vegetables had to be prepared, cook cars were typically filthy,

Still operated at the county fair as a stationary thresher, this old Rumely has seen better days. This prairie type machine resides in a weed patch just off I-90 in Eastern Washington.

Above is a rear view of the famous All-Crop 60 produced by Allis-Chalmers in 1934. Weighing around 2,800 pounds, the little machine cut a swath of only 5 1/2 feet. A-C had the harvester mounted on rubber tires to reduce draft. Note the sideways separator. Outside of the All-Crop 72, the 60 was the longest produced combine by A-C

help was hard to find during clean-up, and hours upon hours were spent preparing meals. Oddly enough, if you research the harvest long and hard, you will find this farm wife/combine connection as being very important to the decision of the "man-of-the-house" when considering the purchase of a combine.

Though the All-Crop is not unique when considering the above proposition, its impact on the Midwest was remarkable. The All-Crop 60 was a simple, efficient machine. The 60 featured a 66-inch width of cut and threshed with a 60-inch rubber bar cylinder. The separator was of the rack style, and unlike most other combines, it separator was smaller in width than its cylinder. This is due to the fact that the "Model 60's" separating unit sat cross-wise instead of in the standard longitudinal direction. The width of the separator was a mere 32 inches with a length of 117 inches. The All-Crop 60 could be used for harvesting even the most delicate of crops such as legumes and various grasses, largely because of its rubber-on-rubber cylinder/concave design. With one man operating the whole works he could cut anywhere from 10 to 25 acres per day. For diversified small farming the little orange All-Crop 60 and its successors proved valuable to the regions they served.

Chapter Five

John Deere's Combine

John Deere got into the harvester business around 1910 with their own version of the grain binder. Initially the grain binder was built for the Canadian market, and plans to erect a plant somewhere in the provinces was investigated. One early attempt to acquire a facility led to discussions with the Acme Company in 1908, but to no avail. The Deere people looked at the Frost & Wood plant at Smith Falls, Ontario, in 1909. Again Deere was out of luck, as Frost & Wood was just wrapping up a deal with the Cockshutt concern. Still, the leadership at Deere

The Deere Model 55H doing its thing in the Northwest in 1954. Produced from 1945–60, the 55H had a 30-inch cylinder and offered a header size of 14 feet. The Model 95H had already begun to replace the 55H in 1958. Bigger was better, and the 95 with its larger cylinder and header sizes soon became the choice for many hillside farmers. *Deere Archives*

This early Deere prototype combine was developed in 1925. Deere Harvester Works started to tinker around with experimental models in order to grab a piece of the combine market that was beginning to take hold in the Midwest. Gleaner and IH already had several models in the field by the mid to late twenties, so it was imperative that Deere act fast. The building in the background is the old Marseilles Works. Today part of that building houses the Deere Archives. *Deere Archives*

Well before Deere pursued the combine, the company produced a pretty good grain and rice binder. In this photo, taken in 1939, the Deere rice binder is being pulled by a John Deere Model D tractor. Because rice fields tended to be quite damp, and in some cases down right murky, the tractor wheels were outfitted with cleats in order to "plow" through the muck. One good thing about rice harvesting; no dust! *Deere Archives*

was intent upon finding some place to begin production of its grain binder north of the border.

Meanwhile, development continued back at Moline under the watchful eye of Harry J. Podlesak, a former McCormick employee. Other talent from companies such as Champion were brought into the harvester works around the same time period. With stiff competition from Massey-Harris and the many divisions of the International Harvester Company, Deere needed a machine that would prevail against any and all comers. Deere was extremely slow to jump into the harvester fray in the first place, considering that several companies were already putting combined harvesters in the field. If the grain binder was to succeed at all, it would have to be top of the line.

With that in mind, Deere put a half dozen prototypes in the field between 1909 and 1910. Satisfied with the field tests, approximately 500 binders were produced for the 1911 harvest season, not in Canada, but in East Moline. The company intended to move combine production to Canada until the spring of 1911, when word came that the Canadian venture had been shelved in favor of keeping the Harvester Works in East Moline. Deere seemed to be committed to create a bona fide harvesting line.

The Harvester Works was actually a rented plant, formerly occupied by the Root and Vandervoort Company, and 500 binders were constructed and later sold to the Canadian trade. Just prior to 1912, the harvester management was assigned to Joseph Dain (who would later lend his name to the All-Wheel Drive tractor in 1915), a job that he agreed to assume only temporarily. Under his rein, 2,000 binders were produced by early 1912, leading to the eventual purchase of the rented facilities. Shortly thereafter, management passed into the hands of W. R. Morgan, an extremely able individual who had been in

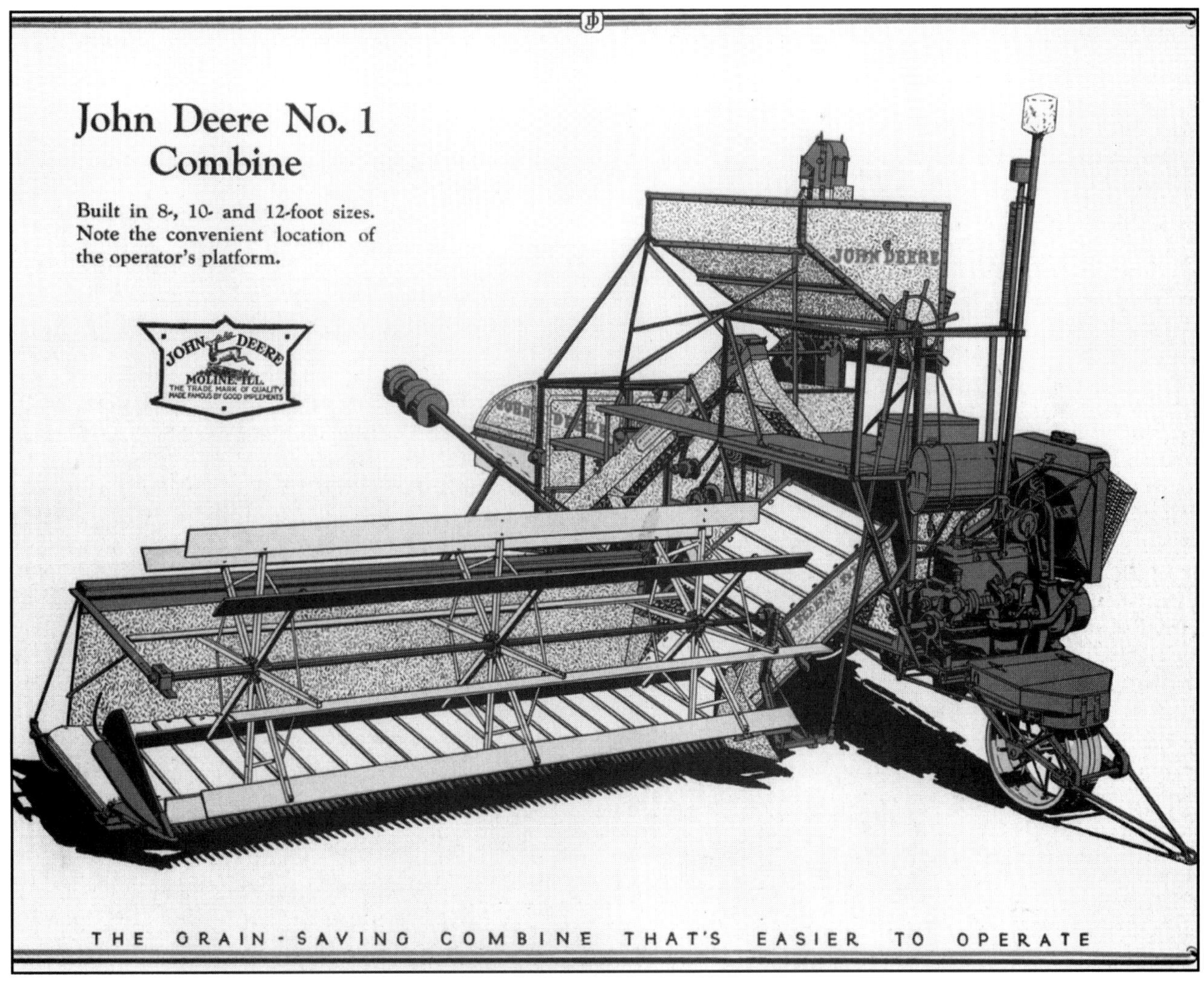

Out of the 1928 sales catalog comes one of Deere's first combines, the No. 1, produced in that same year. Oddly enough, the No. 1 was released after the No. 2 machine. The No. 1 operated with either an eight-, 10-, or 12-foot cut. It almost resembles the old Holt model 30. The No. 1 came with the standard 24x22-inch spike-tooth cylinder as well as a built-in grain recleaner. The No. 1 was produced from 1928–29. *Deere Archives*

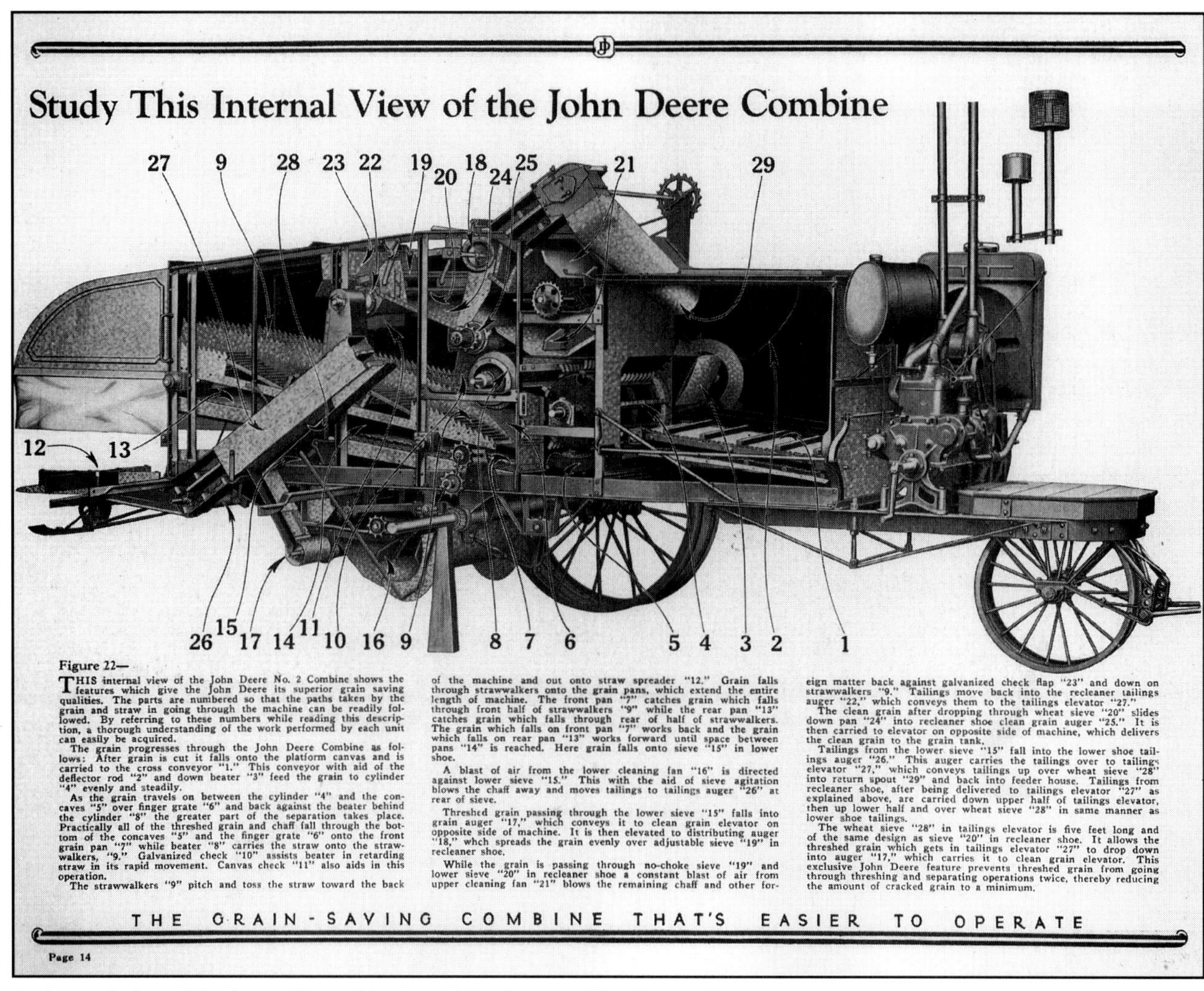

Study This Internal View of the John Deere Combine

Figure 22—

THIS internal view of the John Deere No. 2 Combine shows the features which give the John Deere its superior grain saving qualities. The parts are numbered so that the paths taken by the grain and straw in going through the machine can be readily followed. By referring to these numbers while reading this description, a thorough understanding of the work performed by each unit can easily be acquired.

The grain progresses through the John Deere Combine as follows: After grain is cut it falls onto the platform canvas and is carried to the cross conveyor "1." This conveyor with aid of the deflector rod "2" and down beater "3" feed the grain to cylinder "4" evenly and steadily.

As the grain travels on between the cylinder "4" and the concaves "5" over finger grate "6" and back against the beater behind the cylinder "8" the greater part of the separation takes place. Practically all of the threshed grain and chaff fall through the bottom of the concaves "5" and the finger grate "6" onto the front grain pan "7" while beater "8" carries the straw onto the strawwalkers, "9." Galvanized check "10" assists beater in retarding straw in its rapid movement. Canvas check "11" also aids in this operation.

The strawwalkers "9" pitch and toss the straw toward the back of the machine and out onto straw spreader "12." Grain falls through strawwalkers onto the grain pans, which extend the entire length of machine. The front pan "7" catches grain which falls through front half of strawwalkers "9" while the rear pan "13" catches grain which falls through rear of half of strawwalkers. The grain which falls on front pan "7" works back and the grain which falls on rear pan "13" works forward until space between pans "14" is reached. Here grain falls onto sieve "15" in lower shoe.

A blast of air from the lower cleaning fan "16" is directed against lower sieve "15." This with the aid of sieve agitation blows the chaff away and moves tailings to tailings auger "26" at rear of sieve.

Threshed grain passing through the lower sieve "15" falls into grain auger "17," which conveys it to clean grain elevator on opposite side of machine. It is then elevated to distributing auger "18," whch spreads the grain evenly over adjustable sieve "19" in recleaner shoe.

While the grain is passing through no-choke sieve "19" and lower sieve "20" in recleaner shoe a constant blast of air from upper cleaning fan "21" blows the remaining chaff and other foreign matter back against galvanized check flap "23" and down on strawwalkers "9." Tailings move back into the recleaner tailings auger "22," which conveys them to the tailings elevator "27."

The clean grain after dropping through wheat sieve "20" slides down pan "24" into recleaner shoe clean grain auger "25." It is then carried to elevator on opposite side of machine, which delivers the clean grain to the grain tank.

Tailings from the lower sieve "15" fall into the lower shoe tailings auger "26." This auger carries the tailings over to tailings elevator "27," which conveys tailings up over wheat sieve "28" into return spout "29" and back into feeder house. Tailings from recleaner shoe, after being delivered to tailings elevator "27" as explained above, are carried down upper half of tailings elevator, then up lower half and over wheat sieve "28" in same manner as lower shoe tailings.

The wheat sieve "28" in tailings elevator is five feet long and of the same design as sieve "20" in recleaner shoe. It allows the threshed grain which gets in tailings elevator "27" to drop down into auger "17," which carries it to clean grain elevator. This exclusive John Deere feature prevents threshed grain from going through threshing and separating operations twice, thereby reducing the amount of cracked grain to a minimum.

THE GRAIN-SAVING COMBINE THAT'S EASIER TO OPERATE

Page 14

An internal view of the larger Deere No. 2 combine in 1927. The No. 2 offered cut of either 12- or 16-feet. Note the straw walkers located at the rear of the separator, walkers similar to today's Deere combines. The optional straw spreader is also located at the end of the separator body. This particular factory cut gives a good look at the interior of the feeder house and spike-tooth cylinder. *Deere Archives*

the trenches with both Osborne & Company before and after they were absorbed by the International Harvester Company in 1902. Under his stead, the Harvester Works increased in size with the addition of buildings and a new foundry. In 1914, Deere's Harvester Works experienced an explosion in production due to crop demand brought on by World War I, and no less than 33,000 machines were produced that year. According to Quick and Buchele, 11,600 grain binders, 7,200 mowers, 6,500 rakes, and 2,500 of the new corn binder were produced by John Deere in 1914.

The John Deere "Light-Running" grain binder remained in the harvest line until 1953. Though the Deere binder was popular, it was not a leader in the industry, and the fact that the combined harvester was beginning to gain a following didn't help. The Deere machine was designed to be run by animal power, with a ground wheel driving the binder. The ground wheel machine was used with tractors until the power take-off was widely available. The binder came in the six-, seven-, and eight-foot cut in 1930, increasing to a 10-foot cut option in 1937.

After almost 15 years producing the binder, Deere had yet to develop a combine. This may have been because the harvester division didn't even show a profit until 1926. But the interest in combine development was there, and Charles Wiman would serve as a catalyst to get the ball rolling. Many in the Deere management were extremely conservative when it came to the combine. As noted in Chapter Three, the combine did not immediately take in the Midwest. Deere management, some of them anyway, shared those same sentiments and wanted to steer clear of development altogether. Still, the combine market was wide open, and field tests conducted as far back as 1924 in Stonington bolstered the company's decision to at least conduct some preproduction studies.

This is a rear view of the somewhat lighter version of the No. 2, the No. 3, from the Deere sales brochure of 1929. The lighter the machine the better. This was not only preferred because of a lighter draft, but also because of the need to haul one of these around with an all-purpose tractor. The photo illustrates the company's use of galvanized sheet steel. *Deere Archives*

Largely because of Wiman, appropriations were granted to develop a prototype in 1925. The next order of business would be whether to build a machine from scratch or purchase a proven combine. Wiman decided to take a look at an existing company, the Universal Company (Gleaner) of Kansas City. But a few of the board members became concerned, mainly because of the problems associated with leadership at Universal. As noted earlier, there were many problems between Curtis Baldwin and the rest of the management at the fledgling company, problems that Deere didn't want to get involved with. Besides, as far as initial reports on the Universal machine were concerned, it wasn't all that good of a combine anyway.

Regardless, a Universal machine was purchased along with a Massey-Harris pull-type. In addition, a prototype from the Deere engineers was also put together, and all three machines were sent to LaCrosse, Kansas, for test purposes. By the end of the test the Universal product in the eyes of Deere engineers proved to be unsatisfactory and was dropped from further consideration. On the other hand, both the Massey-Harris and Deere prototype performed quite well. Further tests were conducted the following year in 1926 with another addition to the har-

This is a three-quarter front view of the Deere No. 2 combine photographed in 1928. Note the decorative stenciling on the body of the combine, a classic styling that eludes manufacturers of today. The flat-belt from the main drive is running to the threshing cylinder that in turn powers the moving parts such as grain pans, straw walkers, etc. This model is equipped with grain spouts for unloading from the bulk tank. The No. 2 was manufactured from 1927–29. *Deere Archives*

Another view of the No. 3 in the field being pulled by the John Deere Model D tractor. Again, note the extension wheels and cleats affixed to the rear wheels of the tractor. Not only was the No. 3 lighter in actuality, it gives the same appearance in the photographs. This was no accident as competition began to accelerate in the combine market. Mind you, these early machines were unstyled, and to be quite frank, they all started to look like one another. When Deere enlisted the services of industrial stylist Henry Dreyfuss in the late 1930s, it wasn't only to put a better face on the A and B tractor, but on the combine as well. This bcomes more evident in the later photographs. *Deere Archives*

A look at the classy Deere No. 5 combine produced from 1929–34. This photo shows the sacking shelf and tray for "windrowing" sacks onto the field for later pick-up, located above the rear wheel. Also you will note the grader situated in the top-center. These machines were not just thrown together. Precise machining and engineering was a hallmark with the Deere Harvester people. The lines on this machine are in fact quite stunning and hearken back to a time when similar attention and detail was prevalent in the auto industry. *Deere Archives*

vesting line. The corn picker was developed as early as 1925, being tested in the Omaha area, and exceeded expectations in very wet conditions. The corn picker was a sure bet and was put into production in 1927 while combine production limped in at 40 machines for the season.

When Charles Stone put his opinion on the table things really began to move. According to Deere historian Wayne Broehl, Stone told the board that, "we must act promptly now and move faster in this development than is usually necessary in our business." Stone further stated that to go ahead with production at full-tilt in an "amateurish" manner could mean disaster. It was also his opinion that if the combine was pursued in a "half-hearted" way, they should not pursue it at all. With that said, Wiman proposed 500 combines be built for the 1928 season, followed by another 1,500 for the next harvest year along with a new building. The board approved the proposal.

The Harvester Works first offering in 1927 was the No. 2 combine, the No. 1 being added to the line the following year. The No. 2 was a medium machine, by Midwest standards anyway, featuring either a 12- or 16-foot cut and a 35-horsepower Hercules four-cylinder auxiliary engine (the 24-horsepower Lycoming was used on the No. 1). The cylinder measured 24 inches wide and 22 inches in diameter with a separator width of 40 inches. The smaller No. 1 offered an 8-, 10-, or 12-foot cut with the same cylinder. All cylinders at this time were the spiked-tooth design. The separators in both machines were straw walker type and also featured a built-in recleaning unit. Bulk grain tanks were featured on the No. 1 and 2 machines with a capacity of 65 and 40 bushels, respectively.

By 1929, however, both machines were discontinued and replaced. The No. 2 was a heavy machine and hard for the tractor to pull in soft soils and mud. The No. 5 was lighter and less expensive while the No. 3 catered to those who required a larger but lighter weight machine. By 1934, the No. 5 would be upgraded to the 5A. This machine was a bit smaller than the No. 5 as the separator width was decreased by 10 inches and the bulk grain tank held 15 fewer bushels of grain. The 5A was geared toward the small farms of the Midwest. The little combine could be pulled by a small general purpose tractor without much trouble at all.

Around the same time period, the No. 3 would be replaced by the No. 17 Tanker. The 17 featured a 16-foot cut and retained many of the features of the displaced No. 3. The pick-up attachment for windrowing and rubber tires were added in 1940. The No. 17 disappeared briefly during World War II, then was discontinued entirely in 1948.

Though Deere was doing fairly well with its larger combines, smaller machine were more popular in the 1930s. Deere needed to develop a smaller combine to stay competitive. The company's first attempt was the No. 6 with a six-foot cut. It was tested between 1936-38, and the results were far from glowing. Broehl quotes John Deere engineer Theo Brown as referring to the No. 6 "as a real lemon" when tested side by side with the Allis-Chalmers All-Crop, which was the industry standard in the late 1930s. John Deere put the No. 6 to rest in 1939. It's slightly larger stable mate, the No. 7, did quite a bit better. With its eight-foot cut the No. 7 also became the company's first one-man

The No. 5 would be upgraded to the 5A in 1934 and have a decent run until 1941. Above is the 5A being pulled by a John Deere GP tractor in the mid-1930s. The 5A came equipped with a 50-bushel grain tank and the grader as an option. The 12-foot cut and 24-inch cylinder was standard. Just about all Deere combines were outfitted with four-cylinder auxiliary engines to run the thresher/separator units. *Deere Archives*

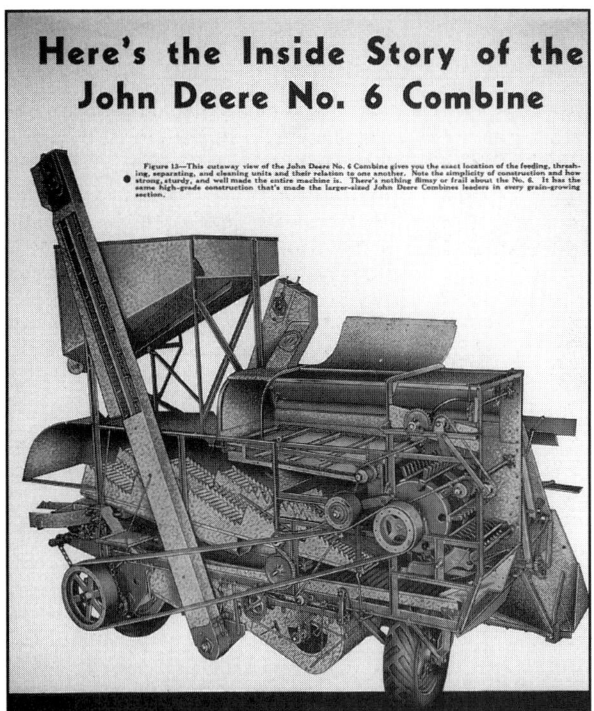

Here's the Inside Story of the
John Deere No. 6 Combine
Figure 13—This cutaway view of the John Deere No. 6 Combine gives you the exact location of the feeding, threshing, separating, and cleaning units and their relation to one another. Note the simplicity of construction and how strong, sturdy, and well made the entire machine is. There's nothing flimsy or frail about the No. 6. It has the same high-grade construction that's made the larger-sized John Deere Combines leaders in every grain-growing section.

No, this isn't the Allis-Chalmers All-Crop 60 but Deere's little No. 6 manufactured from 1936-39. The No. 6 retained the 24-inch threshing cylinder and cut a swath of 6-feet. Obviously unique to the All-Crop 60 as well as the No. 6 is the sideways position of the separator. A better draft was one of the reasons for this design, that and the fact that by the mid-to-late 1930s a boom for a small combine was at hand. Everybody and his brother was trying to get it right. The No. 6 could be operated via the auxiliary engine or PTO-driven. *Deere Archives*

Above is a pre-production Deere No. 9 combine photographed during field tests in 1938. The machine is being pulled by a styled John Deere Model A tractor. The No. 9 offered the 12-foot cut and in 1939 featured the auger feed header. The "9" operated with either a four-cylinder Hercules or PTO drive. The machine had a respectable run from 1939-46. *Deere Archives*

combine and was very similar to the 5A . The No. 7 was in the line until 1941 when war rationing spelled its demise along with several other models. Another small machine was the 12A, produced after the war from 1946 to 1952. A forerunner to the Model 30, the 12A featured a six- or seven-foot cut with a 60-inch cylinder (straight through feed). It was PTO-driven, though an auxiliary engine was also available for threshing and separating.

Though the 1930s ushered in a decade of small combine production, Deere would change the face of its harvester production with the 1935 acquisition of the hillside combine from Caterpillar Company. Long respected in the industry as probably doing more for combined harvesting than anyone else, Benjamin Holt's legacy was about to get a new paint job.

Deere Gets a Hillside

If Deere was lacking anything in its combine line, it was a hillside machine. Discussions of such a machine went on as early as 1926 when the newly formed Caterpillar Company had approached Deere with a deal. Caterpillar, formed between the old Holt and Best concerns, had wanted to rid themselves of their harvester line in order to concentrate on tractors and heavy equipment. During that same time, Deere was planning a hillside machine of their own when it was learned that Caterpillar was ready to sell. Deere put their own machine on hold to find out what the Caterpillar people were willing to do. Caterpillar's selling price was $1. 2 million, which was more than John Deere was willing to pay. Deere's plans for their own hillside combine remained on the table never to be acted upon.

In 1935, nearly 10 years later, the Caterpillar and Deere people were holding discussions about jointly selling each other's tractors from their respective dealerships throughout the country. Caterpillar tractors were a mainstay in California due to the immense size of acreage and soil conditions, but there was also a need for smaller tractors. By the same token, in joining with Deere, Caterpillar dealerships could serve both markets while extending their own product into a greater region served by Deere. For the Deere people, the deal would also give them access to Caterpillar's extensive network of dealerships abroad.

Right about the time joint-dealership sales material was being printed Caterpillar extended the glad hand, literally giving Deere the legendary Model 36 Hillside combine.

Apparently there was more to the tractor link, for Caterpillar anyway, that met the eye. The old Holt line could now be passed on to a reputable old-line firm while the folks at Caterpillar could concentrate on heavy equipment. What Deere got out of the deal was truly amazing. At the time of the deal, Caterpillar's Western Harvester Works were producing two level-land and one hillside model combine. The hillside version would revert to Deere, the level-land models would be phased out. Deere would be given a royalty free and have a non-ex-

At left is a rare photo of the 3 1/2-foot cut Deere No. 10 combine with the header on the right-hand side. The No. 10 was only produced for one year in 1939, as was the No. 11 with the five-foot and the No. 12 with the six-foot cut. All three of these small combines were essentially "straight-through" feed machines. Not pictured are the upgrade models 10A, 11A, and 12A with the right-hand cut switched to the left-hand side. Wartime restrictions forced the eventual demise of all but the 12A, a popular machine that stayed in production until 1952. *Deere Archives*

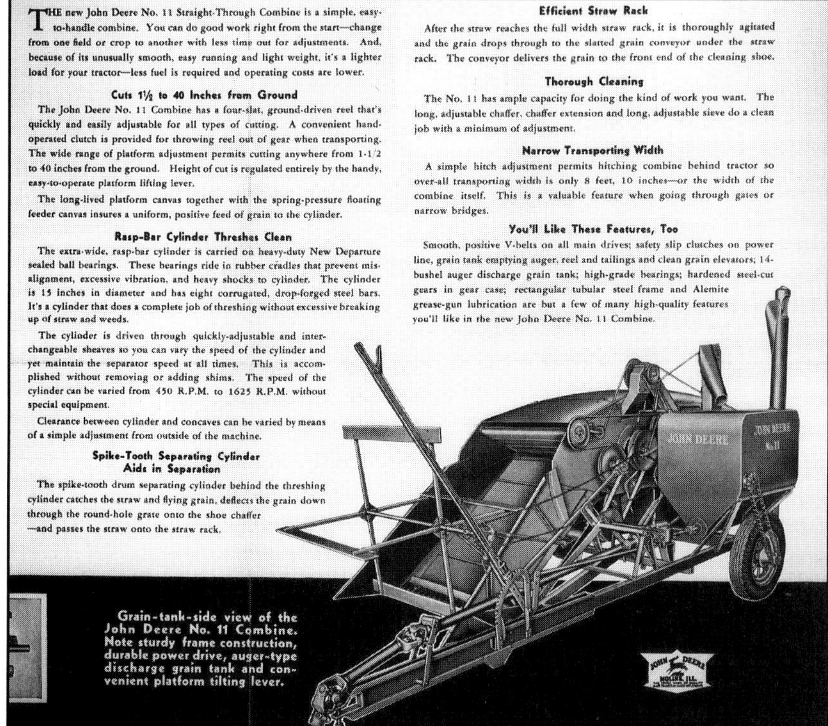

THE new John Deere No. 11 Straight-Through Combine is a simple, easy-to-handle combine. You can do good work right from the start—change from one field or crop to another with less time out for adjustments. And, because of its unusually smooth, easy running and light weight, it's a lighter load for your tractor—less fuel is required and operating costs are lower.

Cuts 1½ to 40 Inches from Ground

The John Deere No. 11 Combine has a four-slat, ground-driven reel that's quickly and easily adjustable for all types of cutting. A convenient hand-operated clutch is provided for throwing reel out of gear when transporting. The wide range of platform adjustment permits cutting anywhere from 1-1/2 to 40 inches from the ground. Height of cut is regulated entirely by the handy, easy-to-operate platform lifting lever.

The long-lived platform canvas together with the spring-pressure floating feeder canvas insures a uniform, positive feed of grain to the cylinder.

Rasp-Bar Cylinder Threshes Clean

The extra-wide, rasp-bar cylinder is carried on heavy-duty New Departure sealed ball bearings. These bearings ride in rubber cradles that prevent misalignment, excessive vibration, and heavy shocks to cylinder. The cylinder is 15 inches in diameter and has eight corrugated, drop-forged steel bars. It's a cylinder that does a complete job of threshing without excessive breaking up of straw and weeds.

The cylinder is driven through quickly-adjustable and interchangeable sheaves so you can vary the speed of the cylinder and yet maintain the separator speed at all times. This is accomplished without removing or adding shims. The speed of the cylinder can be varied from 450 R.P.M. to 1625 R.P.M. without special equipment.

Clearance between cylinder and concaves can be varied by means of a simple adjustment from outside of the machine.

Spike-Tooth Separating Cylinder Aids in Separation

The spike-tooth drum separating cylinder behind the threshing cylinder catches the straw and flying grain, deflects the grain down through the round-hole grate onto the shoe chaffer —and passes the straw onto the straw rack.

Efficient Straw Rack

After the straw reaches the full width straw rack, it is thoroughly agitated and the grain drops through to the slatted grain conveyor under the straw rack. The conveyor delivers the grain to the front end of the cleaning shoe.

Thorough Cleaning

The No. 11 has ample capacity for doing the kind of work you want. The long, adjustable chaffer, chaffer extension and long, adjustable sieve do a clean job with a minimum of adjustment.

Narrow Transporting Width

A simple hitch adjustment permits hitching combine behind tractor so over-all transporting width is only 8 feet, 10 inches—or the width of the combine itself. This is a valuable feature when going through gates or narrow bridges.

You'll Like These Features, Too

Smooth, positive V-belts on all main drives; safety slip clutches on power line, grain tank emptying auger, reel and tailings and clean grain elevators; 14-bushel auger discharge grain tank; high-grade bearings; hardened steel-cut gears in gear case; rectangular tubular steel frame and Alemite grease-gun lubrication are but a few of many high-quality features you'll like in the new John Deere No. 11 Combine.

Grain-tank-side view of the John Deere No. 11 Combine. Note sturdy frame construction, durable power drive, auger-type discharge grain tank and convenient platform tilting lever.

From a 1939 sales mailer comes the Deere Model No. 11 already described and similar to the No. 10. This little machine was also referred to as the tanker combine because of the bulk tank located on the right-hand side above the rear wheel. *Deere Archives*

clusive license to use all Caterpillar combine patents. And that's not all.

Deere would receive all patterns, blueprints, tools, specifications, and stock records; all parts common to the machines and all sales advertisements; all existing inventory to be given to Deere at cost, and all for a song. Caterpillar also offered the "Cat" auxiliary engines for the combine even though it wasn't even in the deal. Now Deere finally had what it needed; a hillside machine to round out the line and the ability to capture the lucrative Pacific Coast and Northwest markets. Indeed, even today the 36 and 36Bs can be found in the Big Bend region of eastern Washington, operating with the help of a Caterpillar tractor if only on a gratuitous 10 to 20 acres.

The sales literature that came out after the acquisition touted the 36 hillside as being "ruggedly built for the rugged west." Deere knew that if the machine was to continue to be popular in the hillside regions then improvements would have to be made. Not that over forty years of Holt expertise would be ignored, but minor changes would appear over the years. Deere offered three versions of the 36; the level-land, the medium hillside, and the extreme hillside.

JOHN DEERE No. 36 HILLSIDE COMBINE...
THESE FEATURES MAKE IT OUTSTANDING...

SIMPLICITY—Inexperienced operators can quickly learn to successfully operate John Deere No. 36 Combines. All adjustments and lubrication points are arranged for convenience, speed and safety of the operator.

HUSKY LEVELER—The leveler on the No. 36-B Hillside Combine is simple, positive and long-lived. It levels on grades up to 55% uphill and on 35% grades downhill.

HINGED HEADER SAVES THE GRAIN—Header follows the lay of the land independently of the separator, saving all the grain. It's easily controlled and drive gears are enclosed. Reel is easily adjusted and drapers are of highest quality.

THRESHING CYLINDER—All-steel, spike-tooth cylinder has big capacity for fast, clean threshing in all crops. Concaves can be quickly and easily raised or lowered for all threshing conditions.

SEPARATION—Uphill, downhill or on the level, the No. 36-B does a complete job of separating grain from straw. Positive agitation from cylinder to end of separator saves the grain.

CLEANING—Big-capacity separator shoe and cleaner, together with powerful cleaning fans, assure clean, weed-free grain in the tank or sacks.

POWERFUL MOTOR—Has plenty of power to maintain correct operating speed in heavy grain. Main drive to cylinder is a flat belt.

SAFETY SLIP CLUTCHES—Header drive, reel drive, feeder drive, straw carrier drives and augers are protected by snap-type safety slip clutches.

HIGH-GRADE BEARINGS—All friction points have high-grade bearings of the type best suited to individual requirements to reduce draft and lengthen life of the combine.

SPECIAL EQUIPMENT—A wide selection of special equipment to match your every need is available.

One of the two most famous John Deere combines ever produced is this advertisement photo of the legendary Deere No. 36 Hillside, acquired by Deere from the Caterpillar Company in 1935. The No. 36 would give Deere a tremendous leg-up in the hillside region of the Pacific Northwest. The 36 from the 1930s through the 1950s was as prolific as the Volkswagen was in the 1960s. The No. 36 shown here is the 1948 model. It wouldn't be discontinued until 1951.
Deere Archives

Straight out of the No. 36 operator's manual is an illustration of the Extreme's leveling device. Note the single rack to the left of the photo. When leveling up, the rack would track down, forcing the wheel's swing frame to raise the left-hand side of the of the combine. Initially developed by Holt, Deere would keep this method of operation pretty much the same for the life of the machine.

The 36 was built especially for the grain growers in California and the Pacific Northwest, but with its 20-foot swath, it was preferred for level-land use as well. The extreme hillside model came with a double swing frame allowing the separator to be level on grades up to 55 percent on the uphill and 35 percent on the downhill. The 16 1/2-foot header enabled the farmer to harvest from 45 to 60 acres per day and with longer hours in the field accomplishing even more. Just like the Holt version, the Deere retained the hinged-header. The I-beam that carried the header was hinged to the separator frame while the outer end was carried by the grain wheel. This allowed the header wheel to operate independently allowing the header to follow the uneven ground assuring a clean cutting swath. The header platform was balanced by weighted beams for easy raising and lowering depend-

The Deere No. 36 Extreme Hillside in action outside of Harrington, Washington. The header tender is at the wheel; the fellow sitting with his back to the photographer is handling the leveling duties. You can see his left hand on the power-leveling lever. The wheel is in its "swing" position, raising the left-hand side of the machine to level the separator. *Courtesy of Marciel Cronrath*

ing on the height of cut. T-beams were also put in place to insure strength.

The maneuverability of the hinged header made the header tenders job easier. From the wheel platform, he had a perfect view of the grain before the sickle reached the cut, enabling him to make adjustments for either tall or downed grain. On even ground the header wheel could be locked into place while the "tender" could attend to other duties on the machine. Sales literature claimed that the raising and lowering of the header was so easy that a "boy can operate it handily." The leveling device on the extreme featured both main wheels mounted in a swing frame that operated in unison to level the separator. The leveling was achieved by a power friction drive controlled by a lever on the operator's platform. An automatic locking device held the separator in the desired position when the control lever was in neutral. Where the extreme model achieved actual lifting or lowering by the rack and pinion, the medium hillside's motion was provided by a crank axle. The crank axle was mounted on the left-hand main wheel, being raised and lowered by a power-propelled screw. The medium machine also came with the 16 1/2- or 20-foot header.

All of the 36s came with a 30-inch ten-bar threshing cylinder and was supposedly balanced like the crankshaft of an automobile. Other features included heavy-duty undershot fans for separating and cleaning, enclosed header drive gears, safety clutches, and numerous accessories like windrow attachments, adjustable hitches, straw spreaders, and sacking attachments. The 36 also came with the standard Hercules model "JXC" six-cylinder auxiliary engine. The 36 would eventually receive a green and yellow paint job and be fitted with rubber tires for easier mobility. So popular was the 36 that it wasn't discontinued completely until 1951. The 36A extreme ran from 1927 to 1942 and the "B" from 1936 to 1942. The straight 36's ran from 1943 to 1951. Deere also came out with a smaller version of the 36 hillside, the Model 35, but was only manufactured for five years between 1937 and 1942. One of the reasons for the discontinuation of the five models in 1942 was World War II. Still, the Model 36 had a very long run between Holt and Deere and proved to be one of the industry's most popular models. Deere wasn't finished with combines. The replacement for the 36, the Model 55,

Out of the same manual is an illustration of the medium hillside leveling device, referred to as the crank axle or power-driven screw.

At left is the balanced beam hinged header originally pioneered by the Holt Manufacturing Company prior to the turn of the century. The weights at the end of the beam could be added or reduced depending on the height of cut desired.

Folded and a little weather-beaten is this cover from the operators manual for the Model 36. These old manuals are treasured by combine enthusiasts all over and can demand a high price when found. This particular manual comes from Rob Dewald, long-time farmer outside the Ritzville, Washington, area, who still drags out his 36B to harvest five to 10 acres a season.

Pictured above is the smaller version of the 36, the Model 35, being pulled by a Caterpillar D-4 in 1942. The 35 offered either the 12- or 14-foot platform. The auxiliary engine was a six-cylinder Hercules that ran at 1400 rpm. The smaller 35 could be leveled on grades up to 55 percent uphill and 35 percent downhill. *Courtesy of Harold Wegner*

would surpass all expectations and become the benchmark for all combines to follow.

The Model 55

Deere's first self-propelled combine was the Model 55, built as an experimental machine in 1944. During World War II, many companies had been experimenting with self-propelled combines, and the success of the Massey-Harris Model 21 alerted the industry to the machine's potential. Deere had experimented with a small self-propelled based on the model 12A, but it never made it out of the pre-production phase. All efforts at the time were on a larger machine with the 12-foot cut; this would eventually become the Model 55. Deere historians Macmillan and Jones describe the early 55 as being "originally based on the No. 9's threshing unit, with a sloping hood from the cylinder to the straw outlet." The machine was tested with both auger and canvas feed; both the sacking platform and bulk grain tank were also used. Placement of the engine was on the left-hand side of the combine, much like the International Harvester 123 and 125 models. The Model 55 was also tested with crawler tracks for rice harvesting.

The final design had the engine behind the bulk tank and the operator platform in a centralized position up front instead of off to the side of the machine. The Model 55 was introduced and was hailed as being ahead of its time. Sales literature had the operator "Upon the King's Throne" when sitting high atop the platform and

Left
The cover from a 1948 sales brochure on the Model 36 shows the direction in which the Deere company was taking with the newly acquired Caterpillar combine. The hillside market was and still is the second home of the 36.

Above is the medium Model 36 hillside being pulled by the ever-present crawler tractor in the Northwest. The straw coming out of the rear of the separator is being dispersed by a straw spreader. Note the sandbag for extra weight on the end of the balance beam. Also visible is the crank-axle leveler running through the middle of the triangular frame above the wheel. *Ritzville Library Archives*

A rear view of the Model 36 unloading on-the go. You might also notice that the height of the balance beam suggests a cut pretty close to the ground. If that visual doesn't convince you, take a look at the stubble in the foreground. *Ritzville Library Archives*

in total command of the harvest. From Prattville, Alabama, to Preeceville, Saskatchewan, it had appeared that it was "a great day when you take delivery of the No. 55."

One of the most innovative features of the 55 was its selective ground speed control that permitted combining at any speed from a crawl to transporting speeds of up to 10 1/2 miles per hour. This feature accurately adapted the speed of travel to the capacity of feeding, threshing, separating, and cleaning. It did so with the aid of a three-speed transmission that could be shifted without stopping. The ground speed was hydraulically controlled from the operator's platform using a pedal to change the size of drive for the desired speed. Indeed, it didn't take the pioneers of hydraulics long to make the self-propelled more efficient.

Like the people over at Gleaner, Deere also mounted the engine and grain tank dead center on top of the machine to increase proper weight distribution. As stated earlier, this concept provided greater floatation of the wheels in soft soils, made for easier steering, and generally held a swath, even with a full grain tank. This type of design also left the sides of the machine uncluttered for the servicing and lubrication of drive parts. The header platform as well came with what was called the Double-Ram hydraulic lift for raising and lowering the platform.

The feeder housing was similar to other manufacturers featuring the auger, beater, and feed conveyor that led to the cylinder for threshing. The cylinder itself was a rasp-bar type measuring 30x22 inches and had a separator width of 30 inches. Like the Model 36, the cylinder was also balanced similar to the automotive crankshaft to insure proper balance. The 55 had the ability to incorporate 25 different cylinder speeds with just four separate sprockets, with speeds ranging from 195 to 1195 rpm. This feature alone was a plus to anyone who farmed the Midwest with its diversity of crops. Easy access to the threshing grate also allowed adjusting for crop conditions from outside of the machine. As the cylinder drive was independent from all others, the grate could be adjusted without disturbing companion drives.

The separator was just under 11 feet in length and utilized the wing-type separating beater behind the threshing cylinder. The wing beater actually slowed down the grain and straw from flying around too much, then deflected it down onto the grain conveyor, passing the straw on to the straw walkers. Behind the beater was a canvas/metal curtain that prevented the grain and straw from being thrown too far back on the walkers. The 55 also came with a straw spreader at the rear of the separator housing.

The No. 10 two-row corn attachment could also be fitted to the 55. The corn attachment could pick, shell,

This is a right rear view of the 1948 Model 36B and Caterpillar tractor belonging to Mr. Dewald of Ritzville. This green and yellow tandem still operates the fields, mainly for fun, and the owner has even advertised in the local paper when it does.

and clean corn all in one operation, handle 20 acres a day, and even harvest corn with up to 30 percent moisture content without damage. Windrowing and pick-up attachments were also available to handle flax, beans, timothy, clover, and maize. James E. Kick of Agate, North Dakota, stated that the Model 55 was the only machine that would harvest his tangled Durum windrowed wheat. It didn't much matter whether it was straight combining or otherwise, the 55's popularity was unquestionable.

The only thing that was missing on the Model 55 was the ability to do hillsides. Deere remedied that problem in 1954. With the Model 36 gone in 1951, it seemed only right that a machine like the 55 should carry on and be a hit in the rolling hills of the Pacific Northwest. The 55H was virtually the same as the level-land model with the exception of the leveling device and a self-swiveling header platform that would pivot ahead of the feeder housing on uneven ground. One ad said that the 55H "clings to the hills like a mountain goat." Like the 36, the 55H was well received. The 55R and 55RC, both for rice harvesting, made their debut in 1946. The R models could also be fitted with tracks for harvesting the often muddy rice fields. As popular as the 55 was, the farmer and custom cutter still demanded a larger machine. By the late 1950s, Deere gave them what they wanted in the Model 95.

The Model 95

The model 95s, built in various forms from 1958 to 1969, were very similar to the 55 with a few improvements. With innovations like an increased cylinder width to 40 inches, a fast fan-speed adjustment, two-speed automatic leveling, and a much more powerful engine, Deere claimed that the 95 was the closest thing available to push-button harvesting. The fan-speed adjustment allowed the operator to vary the speed of the fan from 400 to 1,000 rpm from the driver's platform. This on-the-go feature enabled adjustment to varying crop conditions without stopping the combine. Another update from the 55 was the power plant. The Hercules "QXD" six-cylinder engine was replaced with high torque 303-cubic-inch gas or diesel engine that delivered 100hp at 2500rpm; 3.86x4.33 inch bore and stroke; wet-sleeve cylinder-wall design, with pressure lubrication.

With the improved independent two-speed automatic leveling feature (up to 42 percent) the 95 could begin a slow, gentle adjustment to gradual slopes, but also had a fast response to sudden steep increases of slope. The fully hydraulic system used a solenoid valve that bypassed 3. 7 gpm on slopes under five percent and nine gpm on the steeper slopes. There was also an override lever under the operator's seat that would deliver the higher rate of nine gpm for making emergency changes for slope correction. A second hydraulic system operated steering, reel height,

The Caterpillar combine, umbrella, and awning with the Ford grain truck in the early 1950s. It's hard to believe just how popular this duo was up until the self-propelled finally took hold by the 1960s. Sure there were self-propelled models before that time, but many were slow to make the change simply because the Caterpillar and the Model 36 were an institution. You know the old saying, "If it ain't broke don't fix it." *Ritzville Library Archives*

reel speed, and travel speed without clutching or changing gears.

It may be hard to believe, but some combine manufacturers were still using flat belts for separator drives on their combines. The 95 utilized not one, but two V-belts to power its separator. The Double-V-Belt drive was implemented mainly because of the high torque delivered from the engine. With this feature there was less belt slippage and reduced shock load when the separator was engaged. This design also eliminated belt scorching, drag, and squealing when the 95 was transported down the road with the separator disengaged.

There were actually two different threshing cylinders to be had on the 95; the eight-rasp bar type and the 10-bar spike-tooth. As mentioned before, the cylinder had been enlarged to 40 inches wide with a diameter of 22 inches. The double roller-chain drive could generate cylinder speeds of 195 to 1,190 rpm. Like the 55, cylinder-to-concave spacing was adjusted from the operator's cab. The separator and cleaners were also improved. In addition to options such as windrow and pick-up attachments, one could also get extra long unloading augers, straw spreaders, straw choppers, stone traps, and reel-end shields.

The Model 36 stopped for a pose with it's crew in 1952. A scene that is now frozen in time only to be viewed in black and white. In fact, when this photo was taken the Model 36 was already on its way out. The self-propelled was the harvester of the future, and Deere was wasting no time in developing its own model. With the pull-combine slowly being phased out, so to was a piece of harvesting history, only to be seen occasionally at the county fair or demonstrated by those who would still have the passion to re-create some of that history every season on a few acres of wheat. *Ritzville Library Archives*

The right side view of the Model 36B showing single-rack leveler and more belts and pulleys than you can shake a stick at!

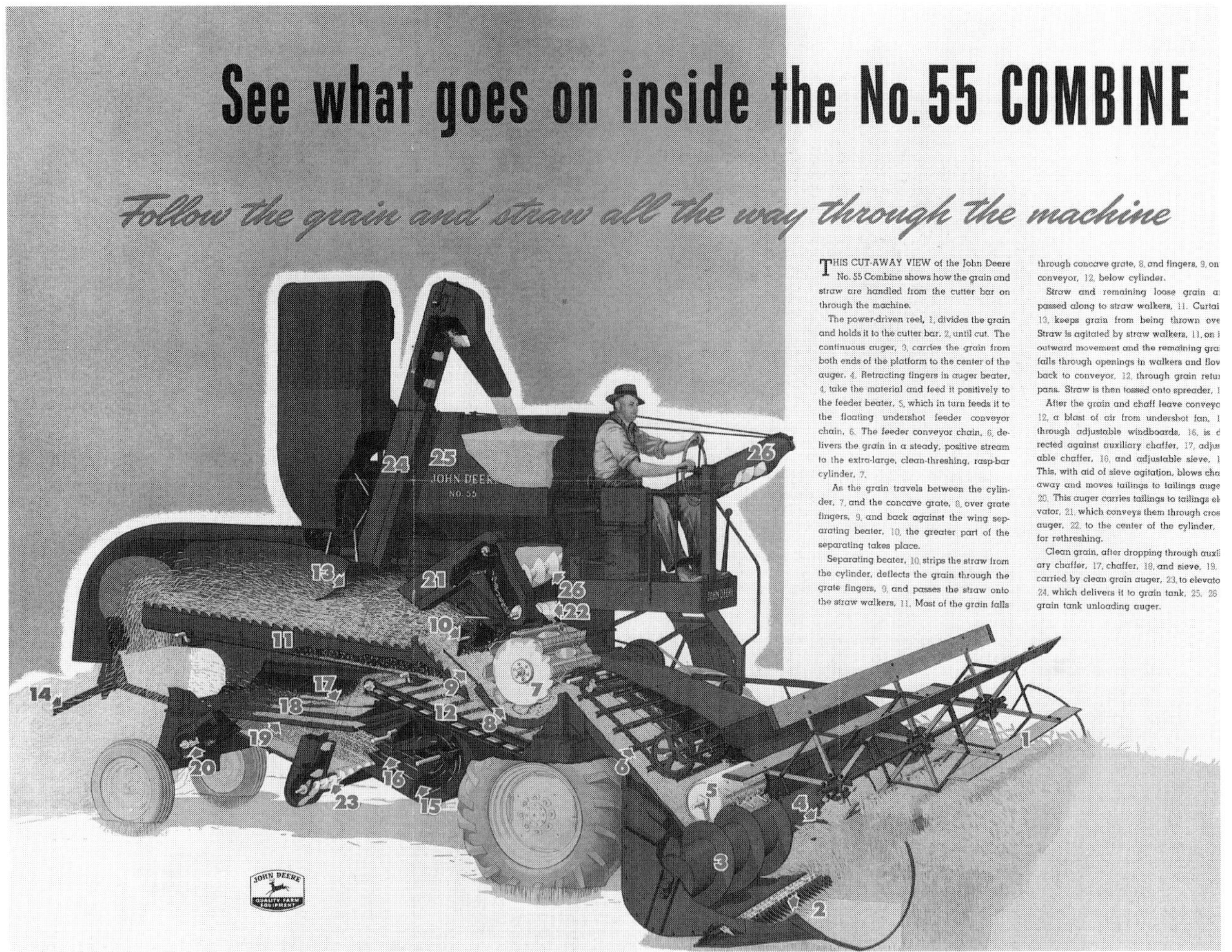

Deere would enter the self-propelled market with what would later become the most emulated combine ever, the famous Deere Model 55. This cut-a-way comes from the 1955 sales catalog and displays graphically the typical SP design and mode of operation. Experimentation on the 55 actually started back in the mid-1940s, with the model going though many changes before a final design was determined. All that tinkering paid off because the 55 became a major league machine in an industry that was going wild. *Deere Archives*

The 95 readily took its place among the finest combines made at the time. The 95H was especially important to Northwest farmers who required something just a bit larger than the 55. In fact, 95s are still being used in the Big Bend region of eastern Washington, with literally hundreds of others keeping the old Harris 30-38's company in dry ditches and coulees throughout the area.

The Model 30 Pull-Type

One other small machine built by Deere was the pull-type Model 30, unveiled in 1956. The 30 was primarily for the Midwest market, and with its seven-foot cut could easily be pulled by the Model 50 tractor. The cylinder measured 60 inches across making it a bona fide straight-feed machine for both windrowing and conventional combining. What was new for this particular model was its patented "Even-Flow Feed" system. Literature for the little Model 30 compared the action of the threshing unit to being "smooth and even as water over a dam." The "Even-Flow Feed" in cooperation with the auger-type platform enabled the cylinder to receive the grain in an even, smooth manner, lessening grain loss and reducing clogging at the point of threshing.

Acting in unison with the auger platform, the Model 30 was outfitted with retracting fingers that would reach out and comb the crop towards the feed conveyor. The feed conveyor itself utilized an undershot chain with saw tooth steel slats for better grain feed. The large straight-through feeding system also allowed for larger separating and cleaning units. Company literature claimed that the separating unit alone measured 30 square feet and the cleaning unit close to 16 square feet, reducing almost completely the possibility of crop overload. The Model 30 also utilized the Quick-Change Cylinder Speed Control, enabling the operator to change cylinder speeds with the use of a hand crank. This was extremely efficient for the diversity of crops common to the Heartland.

This is an early 55, the Model 55C in 1945. The three-quarter rear shot shows the original off-set operator platform design. The separator body is also very reminiscent of the No. 9. The engines on the early models were located on the left side of the machine, similar to several of the IH models. Note the flat-belt drive to the threshing unit. *Deere Archives*

A left-side view of the same Model 55C in 1945. In front of the threshing cylinder, down low, are flax rollers. By this time a few changes had already begun to appear, mainly the use of V-belts to drive the cylinder, straw spreader, and other drives. *Deere Archives*

The 30 was also equipped with snap-in inserts for various crop conditions. The inserts were designed to clip onto the grate in order to close up some of the open area, giving extra threshing action for harvesting crops like clover and flax. Inserts were easily installed from outside the machine. A wagon hitch was another feature that enabled the combine to tow a wagon alongside for unloading threshed grain. In general, the Model 30 was very similar to the Models 12A, 25, and Model 65. The 65 was especially popular in areas where windrowing was prevalent. The small combines enjoyed somewhat of a heyday from 1936 to roughly 1960, the self-propelled becoming the norm after that time. Production figures show that the 12A enjoyed the longest run for a small combine, a mere six years in the line. The industry on the whole found the smaller machines to be short-lived mainly because of the medium cut self-propelled efficiency even in areas where the small pull-type was thought to be the most economical to operate.

New Generation and Maximizer Combines

The 1960s became the era for further experimentation in combine development for the Deere harvester engineers. Success with the Model 55 and 95 wasn't quite good enough. They would now strive for perfection. Beginning in 1963, ground work for the combine of the future was already being laid. Agricultural historians Quick and Buchele describe the scene of Deere engineers congregating under a salt cedar tree in the Arizona desert, watching as the 1964 models were being tested. From the desert to the laboratory emerged a "full scale glass-sided separator embodying the threshing and separating mechanisms . . . with a full scale cleaning shoe test stand

Pictured above is the Deere Model 55R or rice model combine outfitted with tracks and a canvas platform. Note the engine placement at the lower left rear of the machine. Various designs were tested in the mid to late 1940s before the final product was unveiled in 1948. Actually the 55R was on oversized tires while the 55RC was mounted on tracks. The hillside model joined the 55 family in 1954 and finally the 55B with edible bean attachment came out a little later. *Deere Archives*

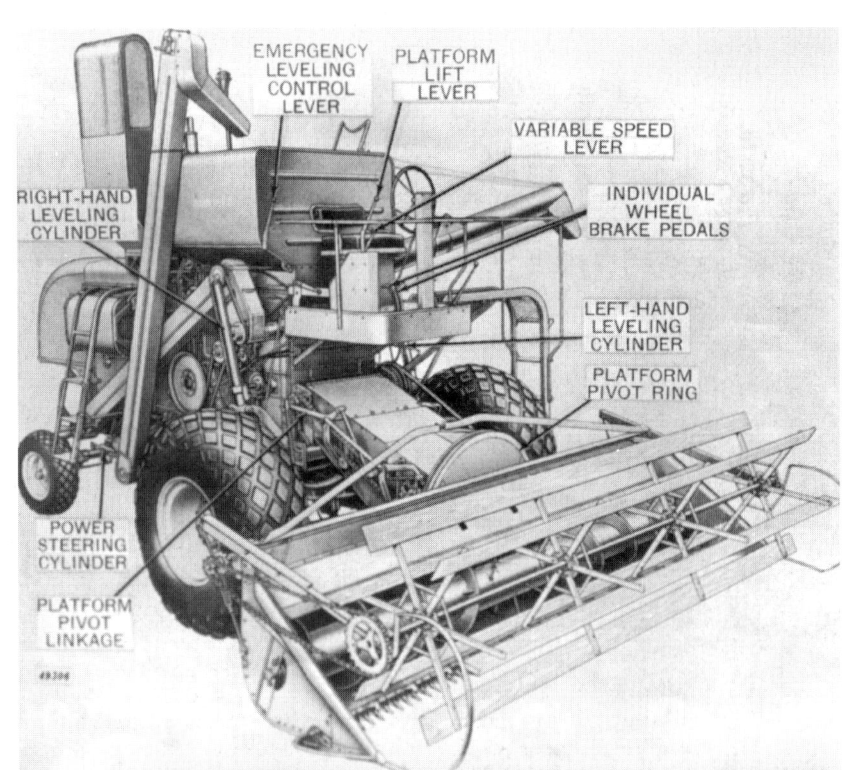

The final design as illustrated in a early operators manual has the engine placed directly behind the bulk tank and the drivers platform centered just above and behind the feeder housing. Similar to the Gleaner machines, Deere touted the 55's low center of gravity and proper weight distribution for better operation, control, and handling. Also note that the auger feed had replaced the canvass feed.

alongside." From there, a Model 95 combine was used to carry the experiment and a custom operator in North Dakota was snared to put the whole thing to use. Success!

Deere engineers wasted no time, and three groups of prototypes were tested from 1965 to 1967. Refinements were made, and in 1970 Deere's "New Generation" combines were introduced. The new line consisted of a PTO Model 6601 pull-type and four self-propelled models: the 3300, 4400, 6600, and the 7700. These new machines operated with a combination auger grain pan and augers situated underneath the walkers. The theory was that with the use of augers at both locations, grain would reach the entire width of the cleaning shoe enhancing the whole process. Other nuances included on-the-go controls, new engine cooling and radiator screen functions. One other Deere patented feature was the "Quik-Tatch" header-mounting system taken out in 1965. This allowed for any combination of headers to be quickly attached to the feeder housing, as the feeder was now mat-

The Deere Model 55H operating in the hills of the Pacific Northwest. Both the left and right-hand side of the machine utilized hydraulic cylinders for leveling. If you look closely you can also see the automotive tilt steering wheel styling that replaced the upright wheel with the final design. *Ritzville Library Archives*

This early Deere Model 55 is being operated with a canvas feeder and rear shelf for sacking grain. Behind the driver's head is a grader with sacks being filled directly below from spouts. The fellow sitting is the sack sewer. You'll also notice the ramp that runs from the shelf to the ground. This was set up to enable the sewer to let several sacks fall to the ground for later pick-up. This machine still operated with the engine at the lower rear and the upright steering wheel, a configuration that pre-dated the final product. *Deere Archives*

A conflagration of combines in flat country. This photo taken in the late 50s displays a few Model 55s and just a couple of Massey-Harris machines. Given the number of combines out at one time gives one the impression that this was a community effort to help another farmer in need. *Ritzville Library Archives*

Up close and personal is this unknown operator putting the level-land Deere Model 55 through the paces. *Ritzville Library Archives*

ed with the separator body. The West Coast hillside trade wasn't forgotten either as the 6602H made its debut in 1971, followed by the 6600 Side-Hill in 1975.

The next version of Deere combines was the "Maximizer." The series consisted of the 9400, the 9500, and the 9600, all three with new innovations for harvesting. John Deere entered the computer age with the new Maximizers and introduced the Combine Data Center. The pocket sized key-pad has 12 different crop settings and allows the operator to find out immediately how many bushels or acres he has harvested. It works something like this: total acreage harvested is calculated on the ground speed of the combine multiplied by the width of cut;

The narrow version of the 55 was this Deere Model 45 originally produced in 1954. The 45 offered an eight- or 10-foot cut with the smaller 26-inch cylinder. The photo above was taken in 1957. The 45 could also be fitted with a corn head. This photo gives the classic automotive steering wheel look, and the guy driving looks just as classy. *Deere Archives*

The little Deere Model 30 had only a four year run from 1956–60. The 30 was a "straight-feed" machine, operating with a 60-inch cylinder and seven-foot cut, and utilizing the auger/raddle feed. The machine being pulled is the small John Deere tractor, and could either be PTO-driven or powered by an auxiliary engine. Machines like the little Model 30 were used mainly on small diverse farms where the use of a self-propelled machine was not very economical. *John Deere Sales Brochure*

The Deere Model 30 windrowing in Illinois with the help from a styled Deere tractor. Actually the 30 is picking up a previously windrowed crop. Out of the picture is the Model 30's 25-bushel bulk tank located at the rear of the machine. *John Deere Sales Brochure*

There was a movement on in the late 1950s and early 1960s for larger machines. Above was Deere's answer to the big machine market with the introduction of the Model 95. The header on the 95 was available from 12 to 20 feet, and the enlarged separator handled four straw walkers instead of three that were standard on the 55. The photo shows the 1967 Deere Model 95 hillside combine from the sales brochure of the same year.

Deere increased the separator on the Model 95 to 40 inches wide as well as the cylinder that measured 40x22 inches. Later models of the 95 series used high-torque gas or diesel engines rated at 100 horsepower at 2,500 rpm. The auger feed was now standard on all Deere combines. You might ask yourself what the heck that large silver thing is above the operators head. Well, some old-timers referred to this "thing" as a "prairie air-conditioner." Actually it was an overhead fan designed to cool the driver somewhat on hot August days. Unfortunately, if you were harvesting barley, this contraption was a nightmare. One source explained to me that taking a shower in barley chaff wasn't his idea of keeping cool. The problem was that even on a calm day, anything floating above the fan in-take would more than likely end up down the back of the operator's shirt. *Ritzville Library Archives*

One last look at a Deere Model 95R rice combine in 1957. *Deere Archives*

bushels are calculated each time the operator unloads based on the volume of grain flowing through the unloading auger over a given period of time. All of this is based on the speed of the auger. The bushel counter can also be calibrated to increase accuracy in different crops. Remembering cylinder speed and concave settings from one year to the next was solved by the memory of the data center and could easily be stored with the use of key-pad buttons. Cylinder rpm, fan rpm, concave, chaffer, and pre-cleaner settings could all be stored for future reference, along with the 12 different crops.

Next came the improved feeder house. Deere engineers widened the feeder house to insure a uniform, thin crop mat when it entered the threshing area, an improvement that lessened grain damage and slug-feeding. The extra long feeder house of 78 inches also reduced the sharp angle of delivery, easing the impact of the grain hitting the rasp bars. Feeder house widths are 55 inches on the 9400 and 9500 and 66 inches on the 9600. The stone

The Deere No. 8 two-row cotton picker in 1957. *Deere Archives*

The Deere Model 95H operating the hillsides. A two-speed hydraulic leveling system enabled the 95 to attack the slopes two different ways; a slow speed for gradual inclines and a fast speed for steep slopes. The driver's compartment was also set up with a manual override switch for fast leveling ability in the event of an emergency. *Ritzville Library Archives*

This Deere Model 95 was captured while windrowing a crop on the Henderson farm in Rolla, North Dakota, 1957. Clearly shown is the fore-carriage lifting the previously cut crop onto the platform, where the auger feed then delivers it to the threshing cylinder. *Deere Archives*

trap door, a feature that removed rocks and other foreign objects is standard on all models. Deere also claimed that 90 percent of the crop was separated at the cylinder and concave, a claim they continue to make with the "Maximizers." In these particular models, the cylinder is 18 percent larger than the previous ones, and the threshing area has been increased by 40 percent. Rasp bars were increased from eight to ten and three different types were offered for varying crops.

The power plant for the 9000 series combines, especially the 9500 and 9600, were touted as being "the first true combine engines." The John Deere 7. 6 liter comes with the advanced Engine Control Unit (ECU), that is supposed to think like the combine works. The ECU feature was designed to automatically adjust programmed fuel delivery in the event of engine lugging. If the engine falls below a rated speed, the ECU meters the right amount of extra fuel to compensate for power loss. Sales literature gives the following example: the 9500 with the 235-horsepower engine hits a tough spot. As the rpm drops below the rated speed, the engine increases up to 16 more horsepower to compensate for the loss of power. In addition, the Power Boost feature increased an extra 25 horsepower for unloading on-the-go. All "Maximizers" offered the turbocharged air-to-air intercooled engines with horsepower ranging from 185 to 260.

Other features include new header controls and what is called the Contour Master lateral tilt system for combining on uneven terrain. This is actually an automatic self-leveling system that tilts both feeder house and header to follow sloped or rolling ground. The header is designed to tilt up to a maximum of four degrees. Two different sensors are used to achieve this process. The first type of sensor is used with both rigid headers and corn heads and consists of a non-contact sensor that uses ultrasound or "echoes." This is similar to the ultrasonic devices used in the medical field. The other type is for the flex header and is of the contact type, working in unison

From the "New Generation" line that was introduced in the 1970s comes this Deere 7700 Turbo with the 218 platform operating in Brawley, California, in 1976. *Deere Archives*

This Deere 6600 sidehill from a sales brochure in 1976 shows the combining of corn in the Midwest. Note the tilt of the header as the machine operates in this field. Pretty soon all combines would become stationary machines, meaning that the tilting or swivel header was adequate in most hillside situations instead of the fully operational leveling separator body. *Deere Archives*

with the skid shoes. When the shoes move up or down the sensor acts accordingly. This is without a doubt the Electronic Age.

The John Deere line of combines continue to improve and refine, for as one mechanic at the local dealership told me, "everything's going high-tech." There is word now that some kind of satellite link-up for performance purposes is in the works at Deere in order to stay ahead of the competition. According to the same source, Deere combines at this writing enjoy almost 64 percent of the market, the other 36 percent being split up between Gleaner (AGCO) and Case-IH. The field has gotten quite small and could get even smaller, but it would be hard to imagine John Deere without a combine.

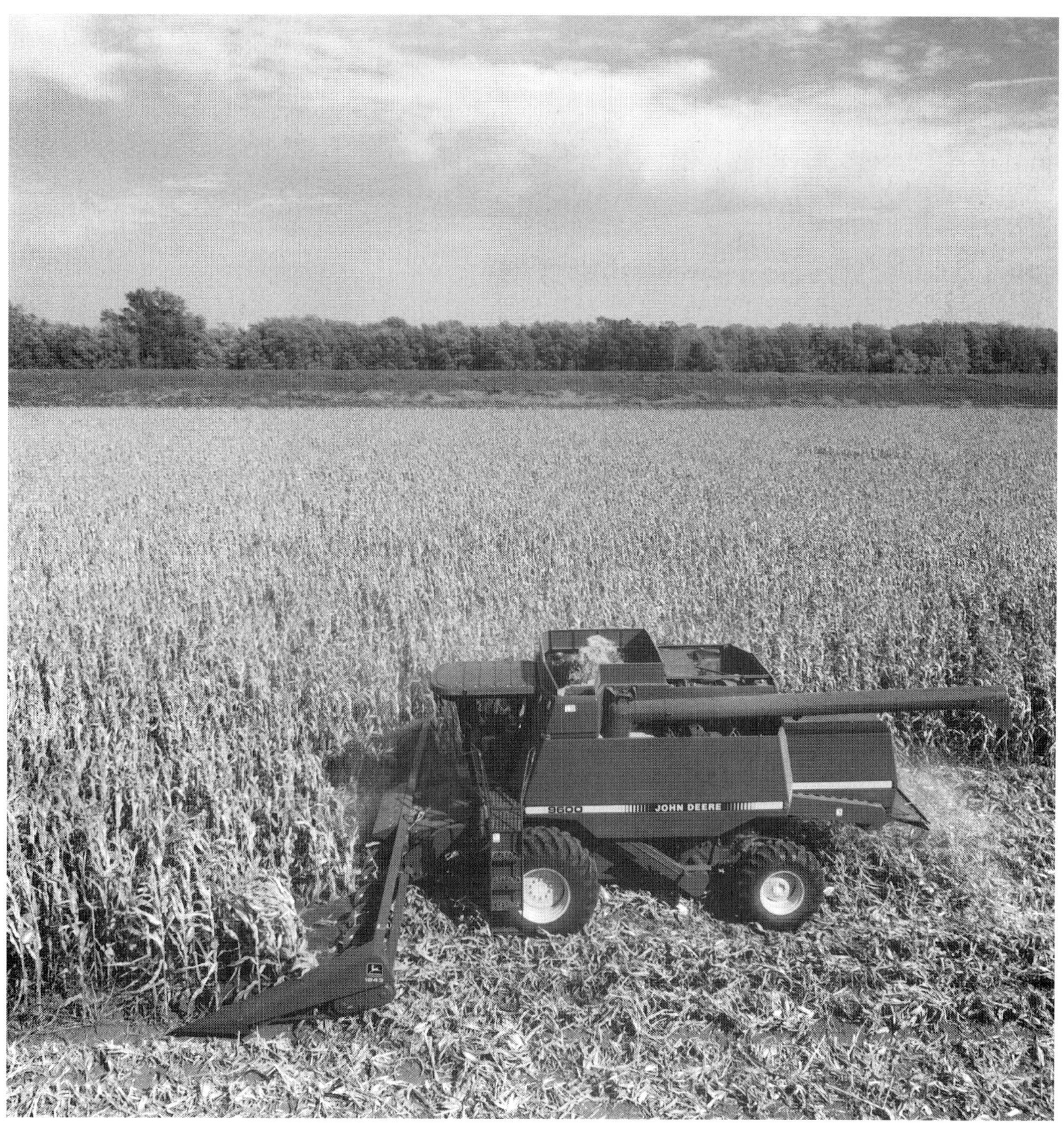

Above is the 1988 Deere 9600 "Maximizer" with the giant 1243 corn head. The 9600 is the largest of the trio of Maximizers, operating with a threshing cylinder of over 65 inches in width and utilizing five straw walkers that were 177 inches in length. The air-to-air intercooled six-cylinder turbocharged engine could generate up to 260 horsepower with the optional package. *Deere Archives*

The Deere Maximizer 9400 with conventional platform, cutting wheat in 1988. The smallest in the Maximizer line, the 9400 could also be set up with tracks for rice harvesting. *Deere Archives*

CHAPTER SIX

MASSEY-HARRIS

One other manufacturer that had an impact on the success of the combine in the humid regions was the Massey-Harris Company, Ltd., of Toronto, Canada. Though their influence would not be felt in the United States until the early 1940s, the company had a long history of harvester expertise involving the European continent and Australia with the introduction of the Stripper-Harvester in 1901.

The Massey-Harris story actually starts way back in 1891 when the two autonomous firms merged to form one of the largest farm harvester manufacturers in all of Canada. Both the A. Harris, Son and Company of Brantford, Ontario, and H. A. Massey of Toronto were pioneers of harvest implements dating back to the mid-19th century. Though the Massey concern was larger in most respects than the rival Harris, both by 1890 were making virtually identical products. Literally every facet of the two companies was the same, right down to "showrooms, warehouses, and agencies from one side of Canada to the other." Just about the only threat to the Massey Company

Above is the Massey-Harris Model 92SP produced from 1957-59; the similar Model 82SP lasted in the line until 1963. You can clearly see the extra-long feeder housing that contained the floating elevator. The 92 could be had with either the rasp bar or spike-tooth cylinder. By the late 1950s, much of the combine industry was producing similar machines, making it difficult to tell one machine from another. The Massey-Harris combine, however, was quite distinct. They continued the design of the offset driver's platform next to the feeder house and the low profile appearance of the machine in general, making it recognizable just about anywhere. The photo above shows just how sleek and low-riding the Massey-Harris really was. *Ritzville Library Archives*

Above is the 1903 Massey-Harris No. 2 Stripper-Harvester produced for the Australian wheat market. These five- and six-foot machines were built exclusively for Australia and was second only to Europe in total sales. This "combine" was first introduced to the land "down under" shortly after the turn of the century. While the binder maintained its dominance in the United States, the stripper-harvester enjoyed success in parts of Africa and South America as well as in Australia. Looking more like a bread box on wheels, the machine worked quite well and was highly efficient. Note the roller bar over the stripping comb for use in extremely tall crops. *Ontario Ag Museum*

Massey-Harris officially entered the combine market in 1910 with the No. 1 Reaper-Thresher, again with the Australians in mind. Pictured above is the Massey-Harris No. 2. These small machines could be operated by two men and harvest up to 25 acres per day. All of the early reaper-threshers cut a swath of 8 1/2 feet and were ground-driven, receiving motive power from horses. You might also notice the straw walker separator positioned sideways, much like the All-Crops and the little Deere No. 6 produced some 35 years later. *Ontario Ag Museum*

A right side view of the Massey-Harris No. 2 Reaper-Thresher in 1912. Note the trip-door on the side of the little bulk tank. This was used for off-loading. Looking oddly primitive, there's not much difference between the binder and this little machine, and one might wonder why American manufacturers didn't jump into the lucrative Australian trade as well. *Ontario Ag Museum*

was Harris' new development of the "open-end binder," a machine that would allow the farmer to harvest grain with any length of straw.

This development didn't mean much to grain growers in North America but was a welcomed innovation in numerous parts of Europe where straw was almost as important as the grain itself. The only real difference between the open-end and conventional binder was the windboard that was removed from the Harris machine. There appears to be some special mechanism having to do with the elevator, but that didn't stop English binder companies from reproducing the binder feature almost immediately.

Obviously there were other reasons for merger talks besides the binder issue. It simply made sense to cut production costs, as well as reduce retail prices of the machines themselves in the competitive market of the first half of the century. The amalgamation of the two firms was written in stone in 1891. Shortly after the merger, Massey-Harris would consume Patterson and Brothers Company, Ltd. of Woodstock and J. O. Wisner Son and Company of Brantford, two implement companies who had merged in order to bolster their own interests in light of the recent Massey-Harris "marriage" of convenience. With the eventual absorption of Patterson and Wisner, Massey-Harris became the biggest harvester and implement concern in Canada.

Though the company was doing a huge volume of business with its binder, they had yet to develop a combined harvester. That would change in 1900. Australian John V. McKay already perfected such a machine, however crude, in 1884, a machine that was very similar to Pliny's first century stripper. McKay took the machine one step further by adding a thresher/separator unit. Massey-Harris wasted no time in trying to tap into the lu-

Another model of the reaper-thresher series was this Massey-Harris No. 3. Oddly enough, the No. 3 was produced as early as 1910. Though similar to the No. 2, the No. 3 had larger slats on the reel and used a knife instead of the comb stripper in the front of the machine. This machine was designed especially for the Argentine trade. *Ontario Ag Museum*

Just about all the information on this Massey-Harris No. 7 combine is in Spanish, another indication of the targeted market for this particular machine. However, I can tell you that the No. 7 came with the 12-foot header, was auxiliary powered, and was very similar to the No. 9. These larger auxiliary powered machines could harvest up to 50 acres in a 12-hour day. Combines similar to the No. 7 also aided in breaking down barriers against the use of the combined harvester in not only the prairie provinces of Canada but also portions of the Midwest. The No. 7 was only produced in 1925 and 1926 and was replaced in 1927 by the Model 9A. *Ontario Ag Museum*

crative Australian market with the production of their own stripper/thresher in 1889. The machine operated with the standard stripper comb that severed the grain from the stalks. From there, the grain was sent to the threshing cylinder and closed concave for separation. The grain was then cleaned by a shaker mechanism and finally delivered to the grain bin for off-loading.

ESPIGADORA-TRILLADORA "MASSEY-HARRIS" N.° 7 CON MOTOR
PLATAFORMA DE 12 PIES, SACAPAJAS Y CERNIDOR ESPECIAL
MASSEY HARRIS
Corta y trilla perfectamente Trigo, Avena, Cebada, Lino, Alpiste, Alfalfa, Sorgo azucarado o cualquier otra semilla que esté en condiciones de trillar, en planta, montones o en parva
Espigadora - Trilladora N.° 7 con Motor MASSEY - HARRIS

Apparently, four test machines were sent to Australia in 1900, and the results were so promising that 350 stripper/threshers were produced for the following year. Not only did the little stripper/thresher succeed, it doubled Massy-Harris business in that region for some time. This was even in light of high tariffs imposed on the Canadian company. By 1909, Massey-Harris enjoyed 35 percent of the Australian market and even began to tap into New Zealand and the South Sea Islands. Still, if Massey-Harris was to move forward and break into the American market, they would have to develop a full fledged combined harvester just as Holt had done almost 25 years earlier.

arris No. 9 Reaper-Thresher
d threshes successfully Wheat, Oats, Barley, Flax,
imilar grains in one operation at much lower cost
harvest work to be done with the minimum of help.
MASSEY HARRIS

Above is the Massey-Harris No. 9A reaper-thresher produced in 1927. The 9A had the standard 12-foot cut and operated with a threshing cylinder that was 33 inches wide. Regular equipment included the bulk tank, fore carriage, and straw spreader. If you really wanted to go all out you could special order the eight- or 10-horse hitch; straw carrier dump, bagger attachment, and the platform that goes along with it. *Ontario Ag Museum*

This is the cousin to the 9A, the Massey-Harris No. 9B. This was actually just a larger version of the 9A and was manufactured a year later in 1928. The one thing that really stands out in this picture is the bulk tank. If you didn't know this was a combine, you'd swear it was a concrete batch plant! *Ontario Ag Museum*

A view from the top. Another angle of the Massey-Harris No. 9 from a factory illustration. The 9A power plant was the four-cylinder Buda with a 3 3/4 bore and 5 1/8 stroke. The 9B featured the four-cylinder Red Seal Continental with 4 1/4 bore and 4 1/2 stroke. The No. 9s also came with pick-up attachments for windrow harvesting. *Ontario Ag Museum*

All dressed up is this Massey-Harris No. 15 manufactured from 1937–50. The No. 15 was made in the eight-foot cut only and operated by PTO drive. The bulk tank capacity was 25-bushels, and the rubber tires were standard. This particular machine weighed some 3,000 pounds less than its predecessor. Note the long drive shaft to the separator drive. A V-belt was used to power the threshing cylinder while all other drives were chain-driven. *Ontario Ag Museum*

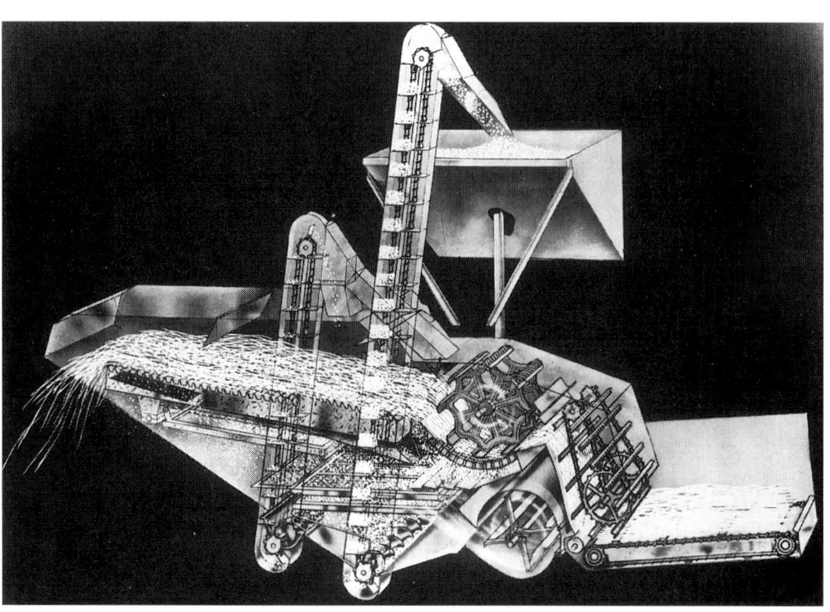

The photo at right is a factory cutaway of the Massey-Harris No. 15. Although not visible, the separator is the four-straw walker type, an innovation that predated even the Deere machines. Massey-Harris utilized a corrugated bar cylinder to rub the grain out instead of the popular spike-tooth cylinder. This change was probably due to the fact that different cylinders were needed for different crops, an innovation that began to appear industry-wide in order to meet the needs of diversified crop farmers east of the Rocky Mountains. Note the "floating" elevator in the feeder housing. With chain-operated slats, Massey-Harris claimed that the grain could be delivered to the threshing cylinder in a smooth manner, not clogging with excess grain and straw. *Ontario Ag Museum*

The task fell on J. Charlton and M. H. East, two able Massey-Harris engineers who had been working for the company in Australia. After three years of tinkering with this and that and finally mastering the main components of the early combine that was so prolific in California, the Massey-Harris Reaper-Thresher No. 1 was introduced in 1910. Offered at the outset with a nine-foot cut, the little No. 1 could harvest up to 25 acres per day with only two men operating the whole thing. This ground-driven machine pulled by horses was developed specifically for the grain market "down under."

Altogether there were seven models in the Reaper-Thresher series manufactured from 1910-26, all of which were exported to Australia, Argentina, and North Africa. The first Reaper-Thresher to come with an auxiliary engine was the No. 5 in 1922, followed by the No. 6 and No. 7 in 1925. These machines could either be drawn by horses or tractor. The No. 5 was introduced to the Argentine trade and was such a success that by 1923, 1,500 machines had been purchased and put into the fields. The No. 6 and No. 7 were also popular in Argentina. Oddly enough, the only information available on the No. 7 was in Spanish. While these machines performed quite well in the foreign trade, the situation at home was different. Much like the humid regions of the lower 48 states, combining was not practiced in the Canadian provinces for reasons already noted in the previous chapters. In order to break down the barriers that stood in the way of commercial success in both the United States and at home, tests would have to be conducted. Massey-Harris wasted no time.

The Massey-Harris No. 17 was a medium size machine developed at the time as the No. 15. The No. 17 had a header cut of 10 feet and was either PTO- or auxiliary engine-powered. This combine was the ticket for the one-man harvester or custom cutter, so the sales literature claimed. At any rate, the 17 was a step up from the 15. *Ontario Ag Museum*

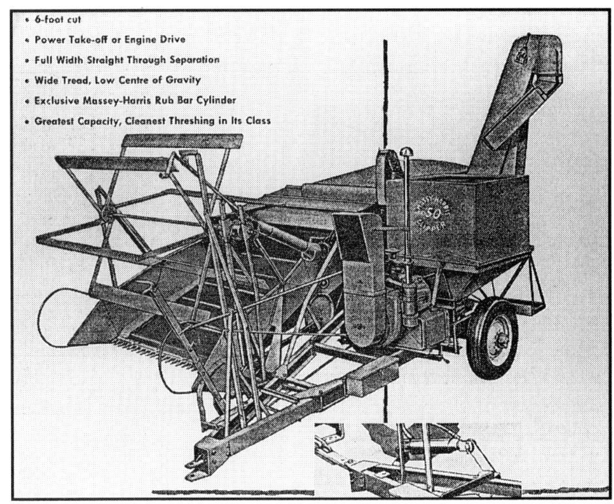

Probably one of the most popular Massey-Harris pull-type combines of all time was this No. 50 "Clipper," manufactured from 1938–58. Interestingly enough, the Clipper was produced almost exclusively in the United States. With a 60-inch threshing cylinder and six-foot cut, the little "60" was classed as a straight-through feed sharing the market with the All-Crop 60 and the Deere No. 6. The Massey-Harris No. 50 Clipper was powered by PTO drive or auxiliary drive and offered a wide range of cylinder speeds for even the toughest crop condition. The Clipper could also be fitted with an optional hydraulic table lift to adjust the cutting height by a simple hand lever. Although the bulk tank doesn't look very big it could hold 25 bushels, which wasn't too shabby for a machine of this size. *Ontario Ag Museum*

The Western United States wasn't a problem. The No. 5 had been introduced in that region during World War I and within a short time the company had to establish a warehouse at Hutchinson, Kansas, to satisfy the demand. Getting the machine accepted on the plains of Canada, however, took a little bit more work. Determined to convince the powers that be that a combined harvester could be used in that region, Massey-Harris in 1922 loaned one of their machines to the Dominion Experimental Farm at Swift Current, Saskatchewan, to prove the point. Initially impressed by the results of the first harvest, the Dominion government purchased the machine and loaned it to farmers for test purposes throughout Saskatchewan and Alberta. This event is credited for the inevitable adaptation and use of the combine in western Canada.

Even more important to the United States market was the use of the Reaper-Thresher at Stonington and Bloomington in 1924. In fact, one report states that the Massey-Harris machine operating at Stonington on the Garwood Brothers farm was the first to do so east of the Mississippi! It was no secret that most harvest and implement companies in the eastern United States were wary of getting into the combine business for obvious reasons. But to their surprise, and probably a certain amount of embarrassment, the little machine from Toronto proved that soybeans, one of the most obstinate crops to harvest, could indeed be handled by the combined harvester. Tests would continue through-out the late 1920s in the

Another view of this "Clipper 50" comes from the 1951 *Yearbook of Implement and Tractor*. In this cutaway photo you can clearly see the Rub-Bar threshing cylinder operating with straw racks as opposed to the conventional straw walkers. It was thought that the racks gave the grain more room to distribute itself more evenly through the cleaning process. Note that the straw racks are sitting sideways in the separator compartment.

humid regions and eventually force those companies that had the capital to build a combine.

For Massey-Harris, work continued back at Toronto to increase the line. Though the No. 5 experienced great success, with models even being shipped to Mexico, the push was on for a larger machine. In 1927 came the No. 9A with a 12-foot cut followed by the 9B in 1928 with a 15-foot cut. Nineteen twenty-eight was also the year that Massey-Harris acquired the old J. I. Case Plow Company in Racine, Wisconsin, to house their new American subsidiary, with plants not only in Racine, but in Batavia, New York, as well. But even with 11 machines in the line by 1928, it would be nine years until other models would emerge. In 1937, the No. 15 and No. 17 were introduced. The No. 15 was a small pull-type, offering the 31-horsepower Hercules or PTO-drive. This was also the first Massey-Harris that came with rubber tires. The No. 17 offered the same options of power and features with a 10- or 12-foot cut. These models were made exclusively in the United States and enjoyed moderate sales until their demise in 1950. But the company was still trying to find a winner, a line leader, and something that would be a direct challenge to the popular machines that United States manufacturers were pumping out in the late 1930s. Something like the All-Crop!

Developing the United States market was a priority within the Massey-Harris hierarchy in the late 1930s, and to do that would entail jumping right on top of the competition. Though the large combine was always a sure thing in anyone's line, the small machine was the rule of the day in post-Depression America. During this time period, the Gleaner "Six" and the Deere No. 6 were both proven small combines. None, however, was as devastatingly popular as the Allis-Chalmers All-Crop 60. At just about this same time, the engineering department at Racine was beginning development on a small combine of their own to meet the challenge in the American market. Enter the Massey-Harris "Clipper" combine.

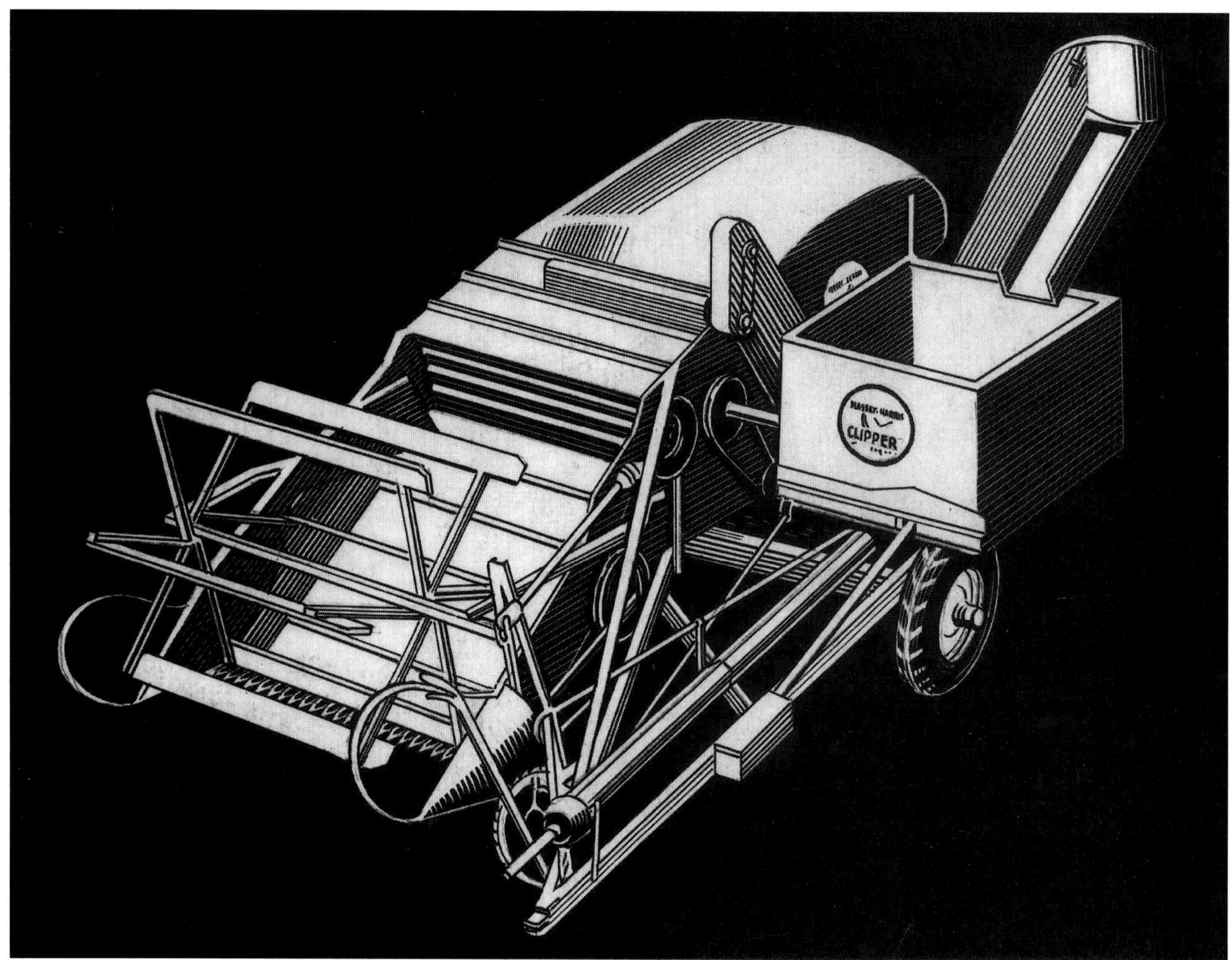

Above is an interesting production illustration of the Massey-Harris No. 50 Clipper. You've got to admit this machine doesn't really look like much, especially in comparison to the larger combines west of the Rockies. Still, when you take into consideration the type of farming done in the humid regions, these little machines performed quite well. All it took was an all-purpose tractor and one man. With the effects of the Depression still lingering, machines like the No. 50 were a bargain at almost any price. *Ontario Ag Museum*

The little Clipper enjoyed a pretty good run up until 1960. By that time the small to medium sized self-propelled machine had for the most part taken over the industry. This is a field scene of the Clipper operating in the upper Midwest. The little six-footer is being pulled by a general purpose Massey-Harris tractor. Note the elevator and spout where cleaned grain came to be deposited in the bulk tank. *Ontario Ag Museum*

Yet another field scene of the Massey-Harris No. 50 Clipper in the 1950s, this time being pulled by a mid-sized Massey-Harris tractor. *Ontario Ag Museum*

Based on the design of E. C. Everett and later marketed under the Massey-Harris name, the "Clipper" was a six-foot scoop type machine with a five-foot cut and threshing cylinder. The straight feed machine in a two-year period became a smashing success in the American market and finally enabled Massey-Harris to become a full-time player in United States combine production. Given the size and simplicity of the "Clipper," it actually had an extremely long run, being produced from 1938–58 and almost exclusively built in the United States. Massey-Harris was also contemplating the production of a self-propelled combine around the same time period, a move to further their position in American agriculture. To do that they would call on the services of long time visionary Tom Carroll.

Carroll was originally hired by a Massey-Harris Argentine distributor in 1911 to help introduce the companies early reaper-thresher models. In fact, the first machines were so unsuited for crop conditions in that region that Carroll actually helped to redesign the machine to assure its success. By 1917, he had joined the Massey-Harris staff in Toronto and in 1936 was already beginning work on a self-propelled prototype. The first machine was the massive No. 20. Massive mainly due to its extreme weight and cost to produce it . The No. 20 was built in 1937 and tested in Argentina. Though the machine performed admirably in the field, a smaller, less expensive model was desired. The redesign came out in 1942 as the versatile Massey-Harris Model 21. The 21 was reported to be the world's first practical self-propelled combine, capable of doing the work of 300 laborers in one day! Tom Carroll didn't just develop a good self-propelled combine. In the words of the ASAE in 1958, Carroll had "in-

This sales brochure photo is of the Clipper self-propelled combine, the obvious successor to the little 50 pull-type. Initially introduced in 1946, the machine in this picture shows the combine set-up for conventional grain harvesting. However, Massey-Harris also produced this same model as the Peanut clipper. It was designed to pick-up and separate the vines from the peanuts. Instead of an auger feed it had a long endless canvass that delivered the nuts and vines to the threshing cylinder. The Clipper SP was only slightly bigger than the pull-type Clipper and had a cut of seven feet. Initially, the little Clipper self-propelled utilized the four-cylinder industrial engine produced by Massey-Harris. *Ontario Ag Museum*

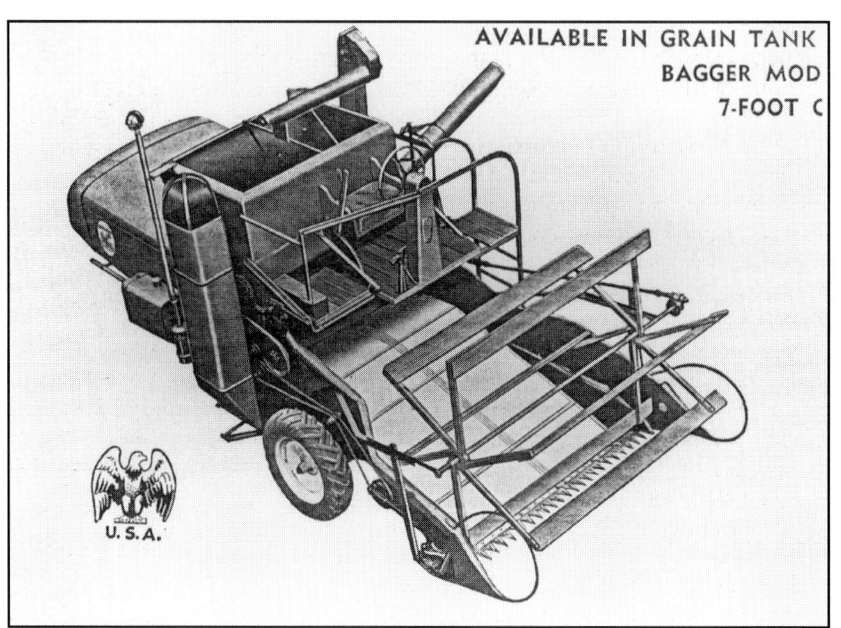

Above is the Massey-Harris Model 21A manufactured from 1941–49. This particular machine was responsible for bringing the benefits of the self-propelled machine to the forefront during a time of worldwide upheaval. Pictured above is a jubilant crew and some Massey-Harris personnel who probably took part in the famous "Harvest Brigade" in 1944, where 500 21A's harvested American grain from South Texas to the Canadian provinces for the war effort. In that harvest season alone the 500 machines harvested over 1,000,000 acres of grain and dumped nearly 25 million bushels into various granaries all over the place. More importantly the "Brigade" operation created a tremendous market for the self-propelled combine at war's end. By 1947, Massey-Harris, who owned less than 3 percent of the United States' combine market, would find itself sitting at the table enjoying over 52 percent of a very lucrative pie. *F. Hal Higgins Collection*

troduced a new era in farm mechanization." What was to happen next with the No. 21 was truly amazing and probably one of the greatest marketing coups in mechanized farm history.

The 21 went into production shortly after America's involvement in World War II. With rationing imminent and implement production frozen, Massey-Harris was the only company that was in a position to produce a self-propelled of any quality. To continue production, MH would have to convince the Combined War Production Board that the one-man self-propelled machines could harvest more bushels of grain for a given investment of steel "than any other machine or combination of machines in existence." The task fell on the shoulders of Joe Tucker, Vice-President and Sales Manager of Massey-Harris USA.

The plan went something like this: Tucker called for the production of 500 Model 21 combines over and above the quotas set for 1944. The machines would then be sold to custom cutters, who would harvest upwards of 2,000 acres per machine under Massey-Harris supervision. The company figured that the 500 No. 21s could be expected to harvest nearly 1,000,000 acres and bring in at

A field scene of the Massey-Harris No. 21A in the Northwest. The letter "A" after the model number meant that the machine now used the auger feed exclusively, in fact all self-propelled combines made by Massey-Harris after that time featured the auger instead of the canvass feed. The 21 was available in both 12- or 14-foot cuts and operated with the Chrysler T125 engine. In addition to the Peanut Special mentioned above, you could also get the 21A in the Rice Special as well. A record 10,279 units were produced at the Massey-Harris factory at Racine, Wisconsin, in 1949, making it one of the top selling self-propelled combines at that time. *Ritzville Library Archives*

Massey-Harris "Super 26SP"

Massey-Harris Co., Racine, Wis.

Following the extremely popular Model 21 was the Massey-Harris Super 26SP, which was manufactured from 1948–52. The 26 was very similar to the 21; the biggest difference between the two models was the squared bulk tank on the 26SP; a round one was used on the Model 21. This factory cutaway shows the mid-range positioning of the threshing cylinder and the down-front location of the "floating elevator" right behind the auger. Like the 21, the Super 26 offered a 12-foot cut and could be ordered with tracks for rice harvesting. *Implement and Tractor, 1951*

Massey-Harris "Super 27SP"

Massey-Harris Co., Racine, Wis.

This advertisement photo of the Massey-Harris Super 27SP from the *Implement and Tractor Yearbook* of 1951 depicts one of the last popular models put out by Massey-Harris from 1948–52. The old 21, 26, and 27 models litter boneyards all over wheat country much like the Deeres, Holts, and Harris models of yesterday. Noticeably absent are Massey-Harris combines produced before and after these three famous models. The Massey-Harris SP success in the United States would be short-lived. When World War II was over, the rest of the industry would catch up. Though Massey-Harris continued to produce a quality machine, the dominance they once enjoyed was gone.

The Massey-Harris Model 27 pictured above was produced a year after the 26. This larger machine was available in the 12-, 14-, or 16-foot cuts and operated with the bigger 250-cubic-inch industrial-type engine with directional cooling and pressure lubrication. The engines were located under the feeder housing area, one of the reasons for the elevated radiator screen on the opposite side of the machine. *Ritzville Library Archives*

least 15,000,000 bushels of grain for the war effort. They also figured on side-lining anywhere from 600 to 1,200 tractors and nearly as many conventional combines in the process, saving a half million gallons of fuel and roughly the same amount in lost bushels of grain that tractor-combines lost just opening up a field. Though it took some doing, Massey-Harris had won over all opposition and in March of 1944 the "Massey-Harris Harvest Brigade" was born, as 30 flat cars loaded with the first shipment of self-propelled combines left Toronto bound for Corpus Christi, Texas, to begin the harvest. In all, 1,000,000 square miles of grain would fall under the sickle of the little red 21s.

Starting the harvest in April, the first wave of the No. 21s began north of Corpus Christi cutting flax, then moving on to tackle wheat, oats, and Texas maize. In May, another load of flatcars left Toronto for a rendezvous in the Central Plains along with other operators with their grain trucks in Enid and Altus, Oklahoma. By June nearly all 500 combines were working together like a hoard of locust, cutting their way through Kansas, Colorado, Nebraska, Iowa, Illinois, and north to the Canadian border.

Sharing the field with this Massey-Harris Model 21 is a McCormick-Deering No. 8 and an early pull-type combine bringing up the rear. If you look closely at the driver's platform on the Massey-Harris combine at the right , you will notice a large wheel. With this wheel the driver could manually raise or lower the cutter bar and platform for the desired height of cut. *Ritzville Library Archives*

The Far West came under the combine knife as well with another branch of the "Brigade" operating in the Imperial Valley of California and parts of Arizona. In fact, when it was all said and done, Wilford Phelps of Chandler, Arizona, took the top prize cutting over 3,438 acres. Nearly 5,000 American farmers had their crops harvested by the "Brigade" including crops like onions, lettuce, beets, alfalfa, and carrots. The final tally on small grains was a whopping 25,000,000 bushels!

The Model 21 showed everyone in striking fashion that the self-propelled combine had arrived. Like the machine tests at Stonington and the later success of the Clipper pull machine, the Massey-Harris self-propelled combine ushered in a wave of innovation that would sweep the industry. Not only that, but for the first time in the company's history, Massey-Harris, by 1947 would control 54 percent of the United States combine market. It wasn't until the war was almost over that manufacturers like John Deere started testing their own self-propelled models. The pre-production phase of all companies, however, jumped into high gear at war's end, and by 1950 just about everyone had a self-propelled in its line.

Indeed, the No. 21 was a hard act to follow, but that didn't detour Massey-Harris from coming up with another winner. The new model "Super 26" was unveiled in 1948 and became an immediate success. In all, four models were offered: the USA Standard, the California, California Flax, and the Rice Special. Each machine was available in either the 10- or 12-foot cut, a tad smaller than its predecessor the No. 21. The larger "Super 27" that came out in 1949 was virtually the same but with a larger cut of 16-feet and a four-inch increase in the separator. All three models were very popular and are today found in boneyards wherever small grains are harvested. Massey-Harris' heyday was from 1946-56, after that period fewer models could be found in wheat country.

With just about everyone in the self-propelled field in the 1950s, Massey-Harris would find itself lagging behind the competition. From 1946 to 1952, Massey-Harris produced over 80,000 model 21s, 26s and 27s combined; from 1960 on, all models put together totaled just under 40,000 machines, though many were produced under the imprint of Massey-Ferguson after 1958. Though the company would experience a brief increase in combine sales in the mid-1960s, by 1967 they had barely managed to hold to 17 percent of the market. Still, the Massey-Harris company continued to build popular machines; two were the Model 82 and 92.

Under the new Massey-Ferguson imprint; one last gasp attempt at a pull-type combine was this little Model 35, produced for one year in 1960. By the early 1960s, the pull models industry wide would be over shadowed by the self-propelled machines, although IH continued to manufacture a pull machine all the way up to 1971. The Massey-Ferguson Model 35 was reminiscent of the Clipper 50 with its six- and eight-foot cuts and PTO drive, manufactured almost exclusively for the small farmer. Even in its last year of production, the Model 35 was already being converted to a self-propelled machine. *Ontario Ag Museum*

Another angle of the Massey-Ferguson Model 35 hooked up to the small general purpose tractor in 1960. Unlike the Clipper, the 35 featured this unloading auger for faster grain delivery to a waiting truck. *Ontario Ag Museum*

This is an example of the Massey-Ferguson Model 35SP, which was a converted pull-type Model 35. The 35SP was produced by Massey-Ferguson from 1958–63. Touted as being "engineered for the small family farm," the 35SP featured the unusually small seven foot-three inch cut being powered by the four-cylinder 42-horsepower Continental engine. The 35 offered the rasp bar cylinder with a variable speed drive and an assortment of sprockets for diverse crop use. *Ontario Ag Museum*

The 82 and 92 were similar machines, both produced at the tail end of the 1950s and were very similar to the Model 90 produced from 1953-56. These newer models were referred to as "Harvest Streamliners" because of their sleek, low-ride appearance. One thing about the machines is that you can spot them a mile away. Red in color like all Massey-Harris combines, the models 82 and 92 were representative of the styling going on throughout industrial manufacturing at the time. Henry Dreyfuss was only one of many to bring fashion and appeal to agricultural equipment . The Massey-Harris combine represents styling at its best.

The Model 92 was an extremely popular machine. In its three-year run, over 14,000 models were produced. To put the numbers into a better perspective and show just how far combining had come, it took Holt over 43 years to produce 14,111 machines, and that included Housers and Bests. True, Massey-Harris had a larger marketplace than Holt, but they were also beginning to decline due to the competitive climate within the combine industry.

The Model 92 was the larger of the two models, offering a choice of 12-, 14-, or 16-foot cut. The cylinder was the rasp-bar type but could also be outfitted with the spike-tooth; the platform featured the hydraulic auger feed table. It's sibling, the Model 82, was virtually the same machine but with a smaller cut. Both combines offered the six-cylinder Chrysler Industrial gasoline engine with the closed gear transmission that had three gear ratios forward and one reverse. Massey-Harris also touted the center-line design along with John Deere and Gleaner, even though the off-set driver's platform went unchanged.

As with numerous companies in the implement industry, the 1950s witnessed more than a few mergers and consolidations. Massey-Harris was one of them. As early as 1953, talks between Massey-Harris and the tractor giant Harry Ferguson, Ltd., were in full gear, with both sides standing to gain quite a bit of prestige. Massey-Harris would benefit from Ferguson's tractor expertise while Ferguson would have an open door through the combine makers world-wide harvester market. Still, the problem of how much who was worth and the usual nit-picking of who would control what caused a great deal of consternation. Believe it or not, the whole thing came down to a toss of a coin.

It all happened when Ferguson and Massey-Harris executives were on their way to a machinery exhibition in August of 1953. Graeme Quick and Wesley Buchele explain that on the way to the demonstration, "Harry Ferguson ordered the driver to stop, got out, and produced a silver half-crown. They agreed to toss over the matter." Heads he called, but tails it was. "Massey-Harris won, and the 'million-dollar coin' was subsequently mounted and set in silver," later given to Ferguson for his good sportsmanship. Now known as Massey-Harris-Ferguson, the new company was an immense force world-wide. Though the usual problems arose, business went on even in light of a huge market slump and the departure of Harris. The shortened name Massey-Ferguson plowed ahead and introduced its first self-propelled combine under the new logo in 1958.

The little Model 35 was produced with the small farmer in mind. Less than eight feet wide and eight feet high, the little 35 was able to go through standard farm gates and even travel along the highway with no problem. Early sales literature made a point that the machine fits in any storage shed and in the owner's pocket book as well. The Model 35 had a cutting width of a little over seven feet and offered another Massey-Harris (Ferguson) first, featuring a "unibody" construction. By molding the frame and body together reduced excess weight and gave the machine great economic appeal. The engine was the 42-horsepower, four-cylinder Continental located behind the grain bin.

The Model 35 was produced from 1958 to 1964. Unfortunately the number of units manufactured over the six year period wasn't very impressive; 1,361 a year or 113 per month was about it. As a matter of fact, the 35 was the last machine produced by the company with the small seven-foot cut; all other machines would offer 10-foot or greater, and it seems that the 14-foot machine was the average up through the 1970s. Beyond the 35 came such machines as the 410, the 300, and the 751, all offered with either gas or diesel engines and all built for the mid to large size market that pervaded the industry from the late 1960s on.

Though the innovations of Massey-Harris/Massey-Ferguson seemed always to be on the cutting-edge of combine development, they would never again enjoy the success of the post-war models 21, 26 and 27, a success that catapulted them into the American market. Today the Massey-Ferguson combine is no longer. Like the International Harvester Company in the 1980s, mergers, takeovers, and later down-sizing took its toll on more than a few companies, agricultural or otherwise. The market today is represented by three major companies: John Deere, Case, who produces the IH, and Gleaner. Even with these three organizations, Deere holds a commanding 64 percent of the market. Quite possibly, however, without the existence of early combine companies on the scene, Deere's task would have been a great deal harder to complete. For instance, without Deere's acquisition of the Holt/Caterpillar Model 36 in 1935, how long would it have taken them to develop their own Hillside machine? And how far behind would the Midwest be in combining if it had not been for the success of the Massey-Harris at Stonington, Illinois?

Like Obed Hussey and Cyrus McCormick, the Shippees, Holts, Baldwins, and Deeres of the harvesting world would, out of necessity, build on the ideas of others to accelerate the progress of mechanized harvesting. First in the grain fields of California, then the Pacific Northwest, and finally in the Heartland and beyond, the combine would for all time displace all other forms of harvesting. "Power farming" would enter our vocabulary, with virtually every facet of the farm being connected in some way to the machine. The horse-drawn era is over; binders and threshers amuse the curious at the county fair, and it's up to the steam and gas clubs nation-wide to show the ways of the farm of years gone by. While we still have these folks around, we can enjoy firsthand stories of the harvest and of the machines that got it all done. Like the other companies mentioned in this book, Massey-Harris had a large role in the progress of power farming, and like their counterparts, helped enormously in getting the job done.

One final view of the small Massey-Ferguson Model 35. From the early stripper-harvester of 1903 to the larger 24-foot cut machines of the 1970s and beyond, the Massey-Harris/Massey-Ferguson product line could be found from Australia to Argentina and from Racine to Washington state in one form or another. Though only three major combine manufacturers exist today, the Masseys were among the few early producers of farm machinery that greatly influenced mechanized farming. *Ontario Ag Museum*

Sources

In addition to the sources listed below, pertinent archival material, newspapers, periodicals, company memos, and government documents were used to complete this project. I should also add that the oral tradition was utilized whenever possible in an attempt to "humanize" the machines that were so important to the livelihood of the American farmer.

Ardrey, Robert L. *American Agricultural Implements: A review of invention and development in the agricultural implement industry of the United States.* Parts I&II. 1894, reprinted 1972, Arno Press, New York.

Broehl, Wayne G. Jr. *John Deere's Company: A History of Deere & Company and its Times.* Doubleday and Company, New York, 1984.

Caterpillar Company. *The Caterpillar Story.* Peoria, Illinois, 1984, 1990.

Clymer, Floyd. *Album of Historical Steam Traction Engines and Threshing Equipment.* Stemgas Publishing, Lancaster, Pa., n. d.

Cronon, William. *Nature's Metropolis: Chicago and the Great West.* W. W. Norton&Company, New York and London, 1991.

Deaton, James L. "The Adoption and Diffusion of the Combined Harvester-Thresher in the United States." North Carolina State University at Raleigh, 1978, Univ. Microfilms Int., Ann Arbor, Michigan.

Denison, Merrill. *Harvest Triumphet: The Story of Massey-Harris.* Dodd, Mead & Company, New York, 1948.

Greeno, Follet L. ed. *Obed Hussey.* New York, 1912.

Isern, Thomas D. *Bull Threshers and Bindlestiffs; Harvesting and Threshing on the North American Plains.* University Press of Kansas, Lawrence, 1990.

Keith, Thomas B. *The Horse Interlude.* University Press of Idaho, Moscow, 1976.

Leffingwell, Randy. *The American Farm Tractor.* Motorbooks International, Osceola, Wisconsin, 1991.

Liebman, Ellen. *California Farmland; A History of Large Agricultural Landholdings.* Rowman & Allanheld, New Jersey, 1983.

McCormick, Cyrus. *The Century of the Reaper.* Houghton-Mifflin Company, Boston and New York, 1931.

Macmillan, D. & Jones, R. *John Deere: Tractors and Equipment.* 2 vols., American Society of Agricultural Engineers, St. Joseph, Michigan,1988.

Marsh, Barbara. *A Corporate Tragedy: The Agony of International Harvester Company.* Doubleday & Com., Garden City, New York, 1985.

Quick, G. & Buchele, W. *The Grain Harvesters.* American Society of Agricultural Engineers, St. Joseph, Michigan, 1978.

Rogin, Leo. *The Introduction of Farm Machinery.* University of California Press, Berkeley, California, 1931.

Swinford, Norm. *Allis-Chalmers: Farm Equipment 1914-1985.* ASAE, St. Joseph, Michigan, 1994.

Walter, Donald, ed. *Lincoln County: A Lasting Legacy.* Lincoln County Centennial Committee, Davenport, Washington, 1988.

Webb, Walter Prescott. *The Great Plains.* University of Nebraska Press, Lincoln & London, 1931.

Wendell, C. H. *150 Years of International Harvester.* Crestline Publishing, Florida, 1981.

Wik, Reynold M. *Benjamin Holt & Caterpiller: Tracks & Combines.* American Society of Agricultural Engineers, St. Joseph, Michigan, 1984.

U. S. Department of Agriculture. *Yearbook for the Department of Agriculture.* 1895-1940. Washington DC.

INDEX